9
9
8
-
9
9

STAR GUIDE™

1998-99

STAR GUIDE™

Published by:

Ann Arbor, Michigan 48107

1998-1999 STAR GUIDE™
Published by Axiom Information Resources
Ann Arbor, Michigan 48107 USA

Copyright ©1998 Axiom Information Resources

Published by:
Axiom Information Resources
P.O. Box 8015
Ann Arbor, MI 48107

Printed in USA
ISBN # 0-943213-28-2
ISSN # 1060-9997

Cover Design by: Concialdi Design

SPECIAL SALES
The 1998-1999 STAR GUIDE™ is
available at special quantity discounts
for bulk purchases. For information write:

Axiom Information Resources
P.O. Box 8015-TW
Ann Arbor, MI 48107

Contents

Introduction... 1

Section 1   **Movie and TV Stars** 3
              Major Stars of the Movies and Television
              from the 30's through the 80's

Section 2   **Famous Musicians and Recording Stars**............. 73
              Stars from Classical,
              Gospel, Pop, Rap, Rock,
              Soul, and Jazz Music

Section 3   **Sports Stars** 107
              Celebrities from Major
              Sports, Announcers, Coaches,
              Commentators, Managers, Olympians,
              Team Owners and Executives

Section 4   **Politicians and Royalty** 137
              Congressional Leaders,
              State and Local Politicians,
              Supreme Court Justices,
              White House Executives,
              World Leaders and Royal Families

Section 5   **Other Famous People** 159
              Artists, Astronauts, Authors, Cartoonists,
              Columnists, Famous Businessmen,
              Philanthropists, Religious
              Figures and Other Celebrated People

              Index.. 185

Order Blanks and Customer Response Form (See Back Page)

INTRODUCTION

The aim of Star Guide™ 1998-1999 is to provide a complete list that acknowledges today's stars in all fields of human accomplishment along with their most accurate, up-to-date address. The universe of stars—a universe as diverse as Oprah Winfrey, Candice Bergen, Jerry Seinfeld, Zubin Mehta, Tom Hanks, Roseanne as well as Rupaul—is completely indexed, and alphabetically arranged under five convenient categories: Movie and TV, Music, Sports, Politics, and Other Famous People.

Star Guide™ 1998-1999 is a valuable communications tool that allows you and the stars to enjoy the human contact which is not possible through a star's performance or activity. With the Star Guide™, your favorite star can receive your praise, reassurance, criticism or offer of help. In return, stars often provide thanks, encouragement, recommendations, photos, autographs or other tokens of appreciation.

More than just a tool for the ordinary fan, the Star Guide™ is an invaluable resource tool for the reference librarian, collector, fund-raiser, trivia buff or anyone with any reason to contact a person of prominence.

Every reasonable effort has been made to ensure accurate addresses at press time, but stars obviously may move or change the circumstance by which they receive mail. Therefore, we cannot accept responsibility for inaccurate addresses. If there's a star you think should be listed but isn't write to us, and we'll try to include them in the next edition. Please remember, when writing to Axiom Information Resources, as well as when writing your favorite star, it is always best to enclose a self-addressed, stamped envelope. Please send your comments to Axiom Information Resources, P.O. Box 8015, Ann Arbor, MI 48107.

Star Guide's 1998-1999 Stars of the Year:

Movie.......... John Travolta
Television.... Oprah Winfrey
Music.......... Boyz II Men
Sports.......... Tiger Woods
Politics....... Bill Clinton
Others......... Diana, Princess of Wales

(Please send us your star's of the year to the address above)

Movies/TV

A _____ A

Dihanne Abbott
460 West Avenue #46
Los Angeles, CA 90065

Ian Abercrombie
1040 N. Gardner
Los Angeles, CA 90046

F. Murray Abraham
40 Fifth Avenue #2C
New York, NY 10011

Victoria Abril
11 rue Chanez
F-75016, Paris, France

Ray Abruzzo
20334 Pacific Coast Hwy.
Malibu, CA 90265

Leslie Ackerman
4439 Worster Avenue
Studio City, CA 91604

Jay Acovone
3811 Multiview Drive
Los Angeles, CA 90068

Brooke Adams
248 S. Van Ness Avenue
Los Angeles, CA 90004

Cindy Adams
1050 Fifth Avenue
New York, NY 10028

Mason Adams
900 - 5th Avenue
New York, NY 10021

Maud Adams
2791 Ellison Drive
Beverly Hills, CA 90210

Isabelle Adjani
10 Avenue George V
F-75008, Paris, FRANCE

John Agar
639 N. Hollywood Way
Burbank, CA 91505

Jenny Agutter
6882 Camrose Drive
Los Angeles, CA 90068

Danny Aiello
4 Thornhill Drive
Ramsey, NJ 07446

Anouk Aimee
201 rue du Faubourg Street
Honore, F-75008 Paris FRANCE

Eddie Albert
719 Amalfi Drive
Pacific Palisades, CA 90272

Edward Albert
27320 Winding Way
Malibu, CA 90265

Dolores Albin
23388 Mulholland Drive
Woodland Hills, CA 91364

Alan Alda
641 Lexington Avenue #1400
New York, NY 10022

Frank Aletter
5430 Corbin Avenue
Tarzana, CA 91356

Denise Alexander
345 N. Maple Drive #361
Beverly Hills, CA 90210

Jason Alexander
6230-A Wilshire Blvd. #103
Los Angeles, CA 90048

Kristian Alfonso
P.O. Box 557
Brockton, MA 02403

Tatyana Ali
4924 Balboa Blvd. #377
Encino, CA 91316

Jed Allan
P.O. Box 5302
Blue Jay, CA 92317

Chad Allen
6489 Cavalleri Road #204
Malibu, CA 90265

Elizabeth Allen
P.O. Box 243
Lake Peekskill, NY 10537

Jonelle Allen
8730 Sunset Blvd. #480
Los Angeles, CA 90069

Sean Barbara Allen
1622 Sierra Bonita Avenue
Los Angeles, CA 90046

Steve Allen
15201-B Burbank Blvd.
Van Nuys, CA 91411

Tim Allen
1122 S. Robertson Blvd. #15
Los Angeles, CA 90035

Woody Allen
930 Fifth Avenue
New York, NY 10018

Kirstie Alley
4526 Wilshire Blvd.
Los Angeles, CA 90010

Christopher Allport
121 N. San Vincente Blvd.
Beverly Hills, CA 90211

June Allyson
1651 Foothill Road
Ojai, CA 93020

Maria Conchita Alonso
P.O. Box 537
Beverly Hills, CA 90213

Carol Alt
2823 Hedweg Drive
Yorktown Heights, NY 10598

Jeff Altman
5065 Calvin Avenue
Tarzana, CA 91356

Trini Alvarado
233 Park Avenue So. 10th Flr.
New York, NY 10003

Madchen Amick
8942 Wilshire Blvd.
Beverly Hills, CA 90211

Suzy Amis
8942 Wilshire Blvd.
Beverly Hills, CA 90211

Ana-Alicia
1148 4th Street #206
Santa Monica, CA 90403

Barbara Anderson
P.O. Box 10118
Santa Fe, NM 87504

Gillian Anderson
110-555 Brooks Bank Avenue, #10
No. Vancouver B.C. V7J 3S5
CANADA

Loni Anderson
3355 Clerendon Road
Beverly Hills, CA 90210

Melissa Sue Anderson
1558 Will Geer Road
Topanga, CA 90290

Michael J. Anderson
3838 Vinton Avenue #302
Culver City, CA 90232

Melody Anderson
1640 S. Sepulveda Blvd. #218
Los Angeles, CA 90025

Pamela Anderson-Lee
9255 Sunset Blvd. #920
Los Angeles, CA 90069

Richard Anderson
10120 Cielo Drive
Beverely Hills, CA 90210

Richard Dean Anderson
8942 Wilshire Blvd.
Los Angeles, CA 90067

Bibi Andersson
Tykovagen 28
Lidingo 18161 SWEDEN

Ursula Andress
Via F. Siaci 38
I-00197 Rome ITALY

Anthony Andrews
Unit 5/3-4, The Chambers
Chelsea Harbour
London SW10 OFX ENGLAND

Tige Andrews
4914 Encino Terrace
Encino, CA 91316

Vanessa Angels
9000 Sunset Blvd. #1200
Los Angeles, CA 90069

Michael Ansara
4624 Park Mirasol
Calabasas, CA 91302

Susan Anspach
473 16th Street
Santa Monica, CA 90402

Lysette Anthony
7920 Sunset Blvd. #400
Los Angeles, CA 90069

Susan Anton
16830 Ventura Blvd. #300
Encino, CA 91436

Gabrielle Anwar
5 Denmark Street
London WC2H 8LP ENGLAND

Christina Applegate
9055 Hollywood Hills Road
Los Angeles, CA 90046

Carmen Argenziano
753 Kemp Street
Burbank, CA 91505

Adam Arkin
2372 Veteran Avenue
Los Angeles, CA 90064

Curtis Armstrong
3867 Shannon Road
Los Angeles, CA 90027

Desi Arnaz, Jr.
P.O. Box 2230
Pine, AZ 85544

Lucie Arnaz
RR #3, Flintlock Ridge Road
Katonah, NY 10536

James Arness
P.O. Box 49599
Los Angeles, CA 90049

Tom Arnold
P.O. Box 15458
Beverly Hills, CA 90209

Patricia Arquette
8033 Sunset Blvd. #52
Los Angeles, CA 90046

Rosanna Arquette
7704 Woodrow Wilson Drive
Los Angeles, CA 90046

Beatrice Arthur
2000 Old Ranch Road
Los Angeles, CA 90049

Jane Asher
Coventry Street
London W1 ENGLAND

Elizabeth Ashley
1223 N. Ogden Drive
Los Angeles, CA 90046

Jennifer Ashley
11130 Huston Street #6
Hollywood, CA 91601

Edward Asner
P.O. Box 7407
Studio City, CA 91604

Armand Assante
367 Windsor Highway
New Windsor, NY 12553

John Astin
P.O. Box 49698
Los Angeles, CA 90049

Sean Astin
5438 Norwich Avenue
Van Nuys, CA 91411

Christopher Atkins
6934 Bevis Avenue
Van Nuys, CA 91405

Rene Auberjonois
8428-C Melrose Place
Los Angeles, CA 90069

Nadja Auermann
Via San Vittore 40
I-20123 Milan ITALY

Claudine Auger
151 El Camino Drive
Beverly Hills, CA 90212

Karen Austin
3356 Rowena Avenue
Los Angeles, CA 90027

Dan Aykroyd
1180 S. Beverly Blvd. #618
Los Angeles, CA 90035

Hank Azaria
6435 Bryn Mawr Drive
Los Angeles, CA 90068

Candice Azzara
1155 N. La Cienega Blvd. #307
Los Angeles, CA 90069

B _____ B

Lauren Bacall
1 W. 72nd Street #43
New York, NY 10023

Barbara Bain
1501 Skylark Lane
W. Hollywood, CA 90069

Scott Baio
4333 Forman Avenue
Toluca Lake, CA 91602

Scott Bairstow
9200 Sunset Blvd #710
Los Angeles, CA 90069

Joe Don Baker
23339 Hatteras
Woodland Hills, CA 91364

Tyler Baker
4731 Laurel Canyon Blvd. #5
North Hollywood, CA 91607

Brenda Bakke
21838 Encina Road
Topanga, CA 90290

Alec Baldwin
132 S. Rodeo Drive #300
Beverly Hills, CA 90212

William Baldwin
955 S. Carrillo Drive #200
Los Angeles, CA 90048

Paula Barbieri
P.O. Box 20483
Panama City, FL 32411

Brigitte Bardot
F-83990 La Madrigue
St. Tropez, FRANCE

Bob Barker
1851 Outpost Drive
Los Angeles, CA 90068

Ellen Barkin
9830 Wilshire Blvd.
Beverly Hills, CA 90212

Priscilla Barnes
8428-C Melrose Place
W. Hollywood, CA 90069

Majel Barrett
P.O. Box 691370
W. Hollywood, CA 90069

Drew Barrymore
11288 Ventura Blvd. #159
Studio City, CA 91604

Kim Basinger
4833 Don Juan Place
Woodland Hills, CA 91367

Angela Bassett
9911 W. Pico Blvd. PH #1
Los Angeles, CA 90035

Amelia Batchelor
14811 Mulholland Drive
Los Angeles, CA 90024

Jason Bateman
2628 - 2nd Street
Santa Monica, CA 90405

Justine Bateman
11288 Ventura Blvd. #190
Studio City, CA 91604

Alan Bates
122 Hamilton Terrace
London NW8 9UT ENGLAND

Kathy Bates
121 No. San Vicente Blvd.
Beverly Hills, CA 90211

Steven Bauer
8033 Sunset Blvd., #102
Los Angeles, CA 90046

Michael Beach
10100 Santa Monica Blvd., #2500
Los Angeles, CA 90067

Jennifer Beals
14755 Ventura Blvd. #710
Sherman Oaks, CA 91403

Allyce Beasley
147 N. Windsor Blvd.
Los Angeles, CA 90004

Ned Beatty
2706 N. Beachwood Drive
Los Angeles, CA 90028

9

Warren Beatty
13671 Mulholland Drive
Beverly Hills, CA 90210

Kimberly Beck
28775 Sea Ranch Way
Malibu, CA 90265

Shari Belafonte-Harper
3546 Longridge Avenue
Sherman Oaks, CA 91423

Kathleen Beller
11288 Ventura Blvd., #304
Studio City, CA 91604

Jean-Paul Belmondo
9 rue des St. Peres
F-75006 Paris FRANCE

James Belushi
8033 Sunset Blvd. #88
Los Angeles, CA 90046

Dirk Benedict
15315 Magnolia Blvd. #429
Sherman Oaks, CA 91403

Annette Bening
13671 Mulholland Drive
Beverly Hills, CA 90210

Richard Benjamin
719 N. Foothill Road
Beverly Hills, CA 90210

Daniel Benzali
10635 Santa Monica Blvd #130
Los Angeles, CA 90025

Tom Berenger
P.O. Box 1842
Beaufort, SC 29910

Candice Bergen
955 S. Carrillo Drive #200
Los Angeles, CA 90048

Peter Bergman
4799 White Oak Avenue
Encino, CA 91316

Sandahl Bergman
9903 Santa Monica Blvd. #274
Beverly Hills, CA 90212

Milton Berle
10750 Wilshire Blvd. #1003
Los Angeles, CA 90024

Corbin Bernsen
3500 West Olive #920
Burbank, CA 91505

Halle Berry
1122 S. Robertson Blvd #15
Los Angeles, CA 90035

Ken Berry
4704 Cahuenga Blvd.
N. Hollywood, CA 91602

Valerie Bertinelli
9255 Sunset Blvd. #1010
W. Hollywood, CA 90069

Mayim Bialik
8942 Wilshire Blvd.
Beverly Hills, CA 90211

Michael Biehn
11220 Valley Spring Lane
No. Hollywood, CA 91602

Barbara Billingsley
P.O. Box 1320
Santa Monica, CA 90403

Traci Bingham
5433 Beethoven Street
Los Angeles, CA 90066

Thora Birch
9560 Wilshire Blvd., #500
Beverly Hills, CA 90212

David Birney
20 Ocean Park Blvd. #11
Santa Monica, CA 90405

Joey Bishop
534 Via Lido Nord
Newport Beach, CA 92660

Jacqueline Bisset
1815 Benedict Canyon Drive
Beverly Hills, CA 90210

Yannick Bisson
55A Sumuch Street
Toronto Ontario
M5A 3J6 CANADA

Honor Blackman
11 Southwick Mews
London W2 1JG ENGLAND

Linda Blair
8033 Sunset Blvd. #204
Los Angeles, CA 90046

Robert Blake
11604 Dilling Street
N. Hollywood, CA 91608

Susan Blakely
421 N. Rodeo Drive, #15-111
Beverly Hills, CA 90210

Lindsay Bloom
P.O. Box 412
Weldon, CA 93263

Michael Boatman
1571 S. Kiowa Crest Drive
Diamond Bar, CA 91765

Heidi Bohay
48 Main Street
S. Bound Brook, NJ 08880

Lisa Bonet
1551 Will Geer Road
Topanga, CA 90290

Ernest Borgnine
3055 Lake Glen Drive
Beverly Hills, CA 90210

Tom Bosley
2822 Royston Place
Beverly Hills, CA 90210

Barry Bostwick
P.O.Box 5617
Beverly Hills, CA 90210

Bruce Boxleitner
24500 John Colter Road
Hidden Hills, CA 91302

Lara Flynn Boyle
12190 1/2 Ventura Blvd., #304
Studio City, CA 91604

Ed Bradley
285 Central Park West
New York, NY 10024

Kenneth Branagh
Studios Road
Shepperton, Middlesex
TW17 0QD ENGLAND

Marlon Brando
13828 Weddington
Van Nuys, CA 91401

Eileen Brennan
974 Mission Terrace
Camarillo, CA 91310

David Brenner
42 Downing Street
New York, NY 10014

Beau Bridges
5525 N. Jed Smith Road
Hidden Hills, CA 91302

Jeff Bridges
985 Hot Springs Road
Montecito, CA 93108

Lloyd Bridges
21540 Pacific Coast Highway
Malibu, CA 90265

Wilford Brimley
415 N. Camden Drive, #121
Beverly Hills, CA 90210

David Brinkley
111 E. Melrose Street
Chevy Chase, MD 20815

Morgan Brittany
3434 Cornell Road
Agoura Hills, CA 91301

Matthew Broderick
1775 Broadway #701
New York, NY 10019

Tom Brokaw
941 Park Avenue #14C
New York, NY 10025

James Brolin
P.O. Box 56927
Sherman Oaks, CA 91413

Charles Bronson
P.O. Box 2644
Malibu, CA 90265

Albert Brooks
1880 Century Park E. #900
Los Angeles, CA 90067

Mel Brooks
2301 La Mesa Drive
Santa Monica, CA 90405

Pierce Brosnan
23715 W. Malibu Road
Malibu, CA 90265

Rebecca Broussard
9911 W. Pico Blvd., PH #A
Los Angeles, CA 90035

Blair Brown
434 W. 20th Street #3
New York, NY 10011

Georg Stanford Brown
2565 Greenvalley Road
Los Angeles, CA 90046

Roscoe Lee Browne
3531 Wonderview Drive
Los Angeles, CA 90068

Genevieve Bujold
27258 Pacific Coast Hwy.
Malibu, CA 90265

Sandra Bullock
291 S. La Cienega Blvd. #616
Beverly Hills, CA 90211

Richard Burgi
2423 3/4 Cheremoya Avenue
Los Angeles, CA 90068

Carol Burnett
P.O. Box 1298
S. Pasadena, CA 91031

Ellen Burstyn
P.O. Box 217
Palisades, NY 10964

Gary Busey
18424 Coastline Drive
Malibu, CA 90265

Timothy Busfield
39-100 Z-Line Road
Clarksburg, CA 95613

Brett Butler
9100 Wilshire Blvd. #401E
Beverly Hills, CA 90212

Yancy Butler
6154 Glen Tower
Los Angeles, CA 90068

C   C

James Caan
644 Amalfi Drive
Pacific Palisades, CA 90272

Sid Caesar
1910 Loma Vista Drive
Beverly Hills, CA 90210

Nicholas Cage
8033 Sunset Blvd. #52
Los Angeles, CA 90046

Dean Cain
11718 Barrington Court #513
Los Angeles, CA 90049

Michael Caine
Rectory Farm House
North Stoke
Oxfordshire ENGLAND

Kirk Cameron
P.O. Box 8665
Calabasas, CA 91372

Colleen Camp
2050 Fairburn Avenue
Los Angeles, CA 90025

Bill Campbell
8942 Wilshire Blvd.
Beverly Hills, CA 90211

Neve Campbell
2401 Cliffe Street #102-3
Courtenay, BC 49N 2L5 CANADA

Tisha Campbell
5750 Wilshire Blvd., #640
Los Angeles, CA 90036

Dyan Cannon
8033 Sunset Blvd. #254
Los Angeles, CA 90046

Kate Capshaw
P.O. Box 869
Pacific Palisades, CA 90272

George Carlin
101 W. 57th Street #6H
New York, NY 10019

Art Carney
RR 20, Box 911
Westbrook, CT 06498

David Carradine
628C S. San Fernando Blvd.
Burbank, CA 91502

Keith Carradine
P.O. Box 460
Placerville, CO 81430

Robert Carradine
355 S. Grand Avenue #4150
Los Angeles, CA 90071

Tia Carrer
8228 Sunset Blvd. #300
Los Angeles, CA 90046

Jim Carrey
P.O.Box 57593
Sherman Oaks, CA 91403

Diahann Carroll
9255 Doheny Road
Los Angeles, CA 90069

Johnny Carson
6962 Wildlife Road
Malibu, CA 90265

Dixie Carter
10635 Santa Monica Blvd. #130
Los Angeles, CA 90025

Helena Bonham Carter
7 W Heath Avenue
London NW11 7S ENGLAND

Lynda Carter
9200 Harrington Drive
Potomac, MD 20854

Nell Carter
8484 Wilshire Blvd. #500
Beverly Hills, CA 90211

Gabrielle Carteris
1925 Century Park East #2320
Los Angeles, CA 90067

Angela Cartwright
10112 Riverside Drive
Toluca Lake, CA 91602

Veronica Cartwright
12754 Sarah Street
Studio City, CA 91604

David Caruso
270 N. Canon Drive #1058
Beverly Hills, CA 90210

Joanna Cassidy
230 S. Irving Blvd.
Los Angeles, CA 90004

Patrick Cassidy
10433 Wilshire Blvd. #605
Los Angeles, CA 90024

Gabrielle Cateris
12953 Greenleaf Street
Studio City, CA 91604

Phoebe Cates
1636-3rd. Avenue #309
New York, NY 10128

Maxwell Caufield
4770-B 9th Street
Carpinteria, CA 93013

Dick Cavett
109 E. 79th Street, #2C
New York, NY 10021

Christopher Cazenove
9300 Wilshire Blvd., #555
Beverly Hills, CA 90212

George Chakiris
7266 Clinton Street
Los Angeles, CA 90036

Richard Chamberlain
3711 Round Top Drive
Honolulu, HI 96822

Marilyn Chambers
4528 W. Charleston Blvd. #836
Las Vegas, NV 89102

Marge Champion
484 West 43rd Street
New York, NY 10036

Jacki Chan
10940 Wilshire Blvd. #1220
Los Angeles, CA 90024

Carol Channing
9301 Flicker Way
Los Angeles, CA 90069

Stockard Channing
10390 Santa Monica Blvd., #300
Los Angeles, CA 90025

Rosalind Chao
10100 Santa Monica Blvd. #2500
Los Angeles, CA 90067

Cyd Charisse
10724 Wilshire Blvd. #1406
Los Angeles, CA 90024

Chevy Chase
P.O.Box 257
Bedford, NY 10506

Don Cheadle
2454 Glendon Avenue
Venice, CA 90291

Robert Clohessy
9000 Sunset Blvd. #1200
Los Angeles, CA 90069

Anna Chlumsky
70 West Hubbard #200
Chicago, IL 60610

Glenn Close
1776 Broadway #800
New York, NY 10019

Rae Dawn Chong
4526 Wilshire Blvd.
Los Angeles, CA 90010

James Coburn
1607 Schuyler Road
Beverly Hills, CA 90210

Julie Christie
23 Linden Gardens
London, W2 4HD, ENGLAND

Michael Cole
6332 Costello Avenue
Van Nuys, CA 91401

William Christopher
P.O. Box 50698
Pasadena, CA 91105

Dabney Coleman
360 N. Kenter Avenue
Los Angeles, CA 90049

Connie Chung
1 W. 72nd Street
New York, NY 10023

Gary Coleman
4710 Don Miguel Drive
Los Angeles, CA 90008

Thomas Haden Church
8969 Sunset Blvd.
Los Angeles, CA 90069

Lisa Coleman
3105 Ledgewood
Los Angeles, CA 9068

Andrew (Dice) Clay
836 N. La Cienega Blvd., #202
Los Angeles, CA 90069

Gary Collins
2751 Hutton Place
Beverly Hills, CA 90210

Jill Clayburgh
P.O. Box 18
Lakeville, CT 06039

Joan Collins
9255 Doheny Road
Los Angeles, CA 90069

John Cleese
82 Ladbroke Road
London, W11 3NU, ENGLAND

Jeffrey Combs
13601 Ventura Blvd. #349
Sherman Oaks, CA 91423

Jeff Conaway
3162 Durand Drive
Los Angeles, CA 90068

Sean Connery
9830 Wilshire Blvd.
Beverly Hills, CA 90212

Carol Connors
1709 Ferrari Drive
Beverly Hills, CA 90210

Mike Connors
4810 Louise Avenue
Encino, CA 91316

Robert Conrad
11300 W. Olympic Blvd. #610
Los Angeles, CA 90064

Shane Conrad
21355 Pacific Coast Hwy.
Malibu, CA 90265

Michael Constantine
513 W. 54th Street
New York, NY 10019

Gary Conway
2035 Mandeville Canyon Road
Los Angeles, CA 90049

Kevin Conway
1999 Avenue of the Stars #2850
Los Angeles, CA 90067

Tim Conway
P.O. Box 17047
Encino, CA 91416

Jackie Cooper
9621 Royalton
Beverly Hills, CA 90210

Teri Copley
4334 Matilija Avenue #217
Sherman Oaks, CA 91423

Ellen Corby
9026 Harratt Street
Los Angeles, CA 90069

Don Cornelius
12685 Mulholland Drive
Beverly Hills, CA 90210

Bud Cort
955 S. Carrillo Drive, #300
Los Angeles, CA 90048

Bill Cosby
P.O. Box 4049
Santa Monica, CA 90411

Kevin Costner
2806 Nichols Canyon
Los Angeles, CA 90046

Katie Couric
320 Centural Park W. #19B
New York, NY 10025

Peter Coyote
9 Rose Avenue
Mill Valley, CA 94941

Yvonne Craig
P.O. Box 827
Pacific Palisades, CA 90272

Richard Crenna
3951 Valley Meadow Road
Encino, CA 91316

Hume Cronyn
63-23 Carlton Street
Rego Park, NY 11374

Cathy Lee Crosby
1223 Wilshire Blvd. #404
Santa Monica, CA 90403

Tom Cruise
14775 Ventura Blvd. #1-710
Sherman Oaks, CA 91403

Billy Crystal
9830 Wilshire Blvd.
Beverly Hills, CA 90212

Macaulay Culkin
124 West 60th Street
New York, NY 10023

Robert Culp
8306 Wilshire Blvd. #438
Beverly Hills, CA 90211

Mark Curry
12540 Kling Street
N. Hollywood, CA 91604

Tim Curry
9560 Wilshire Blvd. #516
Beverly Hills, CA 90212

Jane Curtin
P.O. Box 1070
Sharon, CT 06069

Valerie Curtin
15622 Meadowgate Road
Encino, CA 91316

Jamie Lee Curtis
P.O. Box 2358
Running Springs, CA 92382

Tony Curtis
11831 Folkstone Lane
Los Angeles, CA 90077

Lise Cutter
4526 Wilshire Blvd.
Beverly Hills, CA 90010

D   D

Maryam D'Abo
8391 Beverly Blvd. #200
Los Angeles, CA 90048

Olivia d'Abo
1122 S. Robertson Blvd. #15
Los Angeles, CA 90035

Willem Dafoe
33 Wooster Street #200
New York, NY 10013

Timothy Dalton
21 Golden Square #315
London, W1R 3PA, ENGLAND

Tyne Daly 6437 Drexel Los Angeles, CA 90048	**Pam Dawber** 2236-A Encinitas Blvd. Encinitas, CA 92024
Beverly D'Angelo 8033 Sunset Blvd. #247 Los Angeles, CA 90046	**Doris Day** P.O. Box 223163 Carmel, CA 93922
Patti D'Arbanville 444 E. 66th Street #6-11 New York, NY 10021	**Sandra Dee** 880 Hilldale Avenue #15 Los Angeles, CA 90069
Rodney Dangerfield 530 East 76th Street New York, NY 10021	**Ellen DeGeneres** 9830 Wilshire Blvd Beverly Hills, CA 90212
Jeff Daniels 137 Park Street Chelsea, MI 48118	**Olivia DeHavilland** Boite Postale 156-16 Paris Cedar 16-75764 FRANCE
Ted Danson 165 Copper Cliff Lane Sedona, AZ 86336	**Dana Delany** 2522 Beverly Avenue Santa Monica, CA 90405
Tony Danza 10202 W. Washington Blvd. #DLEANBL Culver City, CA 90232	**Michael DeLorenzo** 8271 Melrose Avenue, #110 Los Angeles, CA 90046
Robert Davi 6568 Beachview Drive #209 Rancho Palos Verdes, CA 90274	**Rebecca DeMornay** 760 N. La Cienega Blvd. #200 Los Angeles, CA 90069
Clifton Davis 141 Janine Drive La Habra Heights, CA 90631	**Patrick Dempsey** 2644 N. Beachwood Drive Los Angeles, CA 90068
Ossie Davis & Ruby Dee 44 Cortland Avenue New Rochelle, NY 10801	**Catherine Deneuve** 76 Rue Bonaparte F-75006 Paris FRANCE

Lydie Denier
5350 Sepulveda Blvd. #9
Sherman Oaks, CA 91411

Robert DeNiro
375 Greenwich Street
New York, NY 10013

Brian Dennehy
121 N. San Vicente Blvd.
Beverly Hills, CA 90211

Bob Denver
General Delivery
Princeton, W. VA 24740

Johnny Depp
500 Sepulveda Blvd. #500
Los Angeles, CA 90049

Bo Derek
3625 Roblar
Santa Ynez, CA 93460

Bruce Dern
23430 Malibu Colony Road
Malibu, CA 90265

Laura Dern
2401 Main Street
Santa Monica, CA 90405

William Devane
8942 Wilshire Blvd.
Beverly Hills, CA 90211

Loretta Devine
5816 Ernest Avenue
Los Angeles, CA 90034

Danny DeVito
P.O. Box 491246
Los Angeles, CA 90049

Joyce DeWitt
1250-6th Street #403
Santa Monica, CA 90401

Susan Dey
10390 Santa Monica Blvd. #300
Los Angeles, CA 90025

Angie Dickinson
9580 Lime Orchard Road
Beverly Hills, CA 90210

Phyliss Diller
163 S. Rockingham Road
Los Angeles, CA 90049

Matt Dillon
40 West 57th Street
New York, NY 10019

Donna Dixon
8955 Norma Place
Los Angeles, CA 90069

Kevin Dobson
P.O. Box 5617
Beverly Hills, CA 90210

Peter Dobson
1351 N. Crescent Heights #318
Los Angeles, CA 90046

Shannen Doherty
1033 Gayley Avenue #208
Los Angeles, CA 90024

Star Guide 1998-1999 TV/Movies

Elinor Donahue
4525 Lemp Avenue
N. Hollywood, CA 91602

Phil Donahue
420 E. 54th Street #22F
New York, NY 10022

Troy Donahue
1022 Euclid Avenue #1
Santa Monica, CA 90403

Sam Donaldson
1717 DeSales N.W.
Washington, DC 20036

James Doohan
P.O. Box 2800
Redmond, WA 98073

Stephen Dorff
2252 Verde Oak Drive
Los Angeles, CA 90068

Kirk Douglas
805 N. Rexford Drive
Beverly Hills, CA 90210

Michael Douglas
P.O. Box 49954
Los Angeles, CA 90049

Mike Douglas
1876 Chartley Road
Gates Mill, OH 44040

Leslie-Ann Down
10100 Santa Monica Blvd. #2490
Los Angeles, CA 90067

Robert Downey, Jr.
P.O. Box 6205
Malibu, CA 90264

Hugh Downs
157 Columbus Avenue
New York, NY 10023

Billy Drago
9000 Sunset Blvd. #1200
Los Angeles, CA 90069

Richard Dreyfuss
14820 Valley Vista Blvd.
Sherman Oaks, CA 91403

James Drury
P.O. Box 899
Cyprus, TX 77429

Julia Duffy
9255 Sunset Blvd. #1010
Los Angeles, CA 90069

Patrick Duffy
P.O. Box "D"
Tarzana, CA 91356

Olympia Dukakis
222 Upper Mountain Road
Montclair, NJ 07043

Patty Duke
5110 E. Dodd Road
Hayden, ID 83835

David Dukes
255 S. Lorraine Blvd.
Los Angeles, CA 90004

21

Faye Dunaway
P.O. Box 15778
Beverly Hills, CA 90209

Charles Durning
10590 Wilshire Blvd. #506
Los Angeles, CA 90024

Marj Dusay
1964 Westwood Blvd., #400
Los Angeles, CA 90025

Charles Dutton
12312 Viewcrest Road
Studio City, CA 91604

Robert Duvall
P.O. Box 520
The Plains, VA 22171

Shelly Duvall
9595 Wilshire Blvd. #505
Beverly Hills, CA 90212

E   E

Clint Eastwood
P.O. Box 4366
Carmel, CA 93921

Buddy Ebsen
P.O. Box 2069
Palos Verdes Peninsula, CA 90274

Barbara Eden
9816 Denbigh
Beverly Hills, CA 90210

Richard Edlund
13335 Maxella Avenue
Marina del Rey, CA 90292

Anthony Edwards
15260 Ventura Blvd. #1420
Sherman Oaks, CA 91403

Samantha Eggar
12304 Santa Monica Blvd. #104
Los Angeles, CA 90025

Nicole Eggert
20591 Queens Park
Huntington Beach, CA 92646

Jill Eikenberry
197 Oakdale Avenue
Mill Valley, CA 94941

Erika Eleniak
2029 Century Park E. #300
Los Angeles, CA 90067

Gordon Elliott
555 West 57th Street
New York, NY 10019

Sam Elliott
33050 Pacific Coast Hwy.
Malibu, CA 90265

Robert Englund
1616 Santa Cruz Street
Laguna Beach, CA 93651

Bill Engvall
8380 Melrose Avenue #310
Los Angeles, CA 90069

Emilio Estevez
P.O. Box 4041
Malibu, CA 90264

Erik Estrada
3768 Eureka Drive
Studio City, CA 91604

Dale Evans (Rogers)
19838 Tomahawk Road
Apple Valley, CA 92307

Linda Evans
6714 Villa Madera Drive S.W.
Tacoma, WA 98499

Greg Evigan
10433 Wilshire Blvd. #210
Los Angeles, CA 90024

F   **F**

Shelley Fabares
P.O. Box 6010 MSC 826
Sherman Oaks, CA 91413

Jeff Fahey
8942 Wilshire Blvd.
Beverly Hills, CA 90211

Bruce Fairbairn
9744 Wilshire Blvd. #308
Beverly Hills, CA 90212

Morgan Fairchild
2424 Bowmont Drive
Beverly Hills, CA 90210

Peter Falk
100 Universal City Plaza #507 1-B
Universal City, CA 91608

Deborah Farentino
9460 Wilshire Blvd. #700
Beverly Hills, CA 90210

Linda Farentino
10683 Santa Monica Blvd.
Los Angeles, CA 90025

Dennis Farina
203 S. Willard
New Buffalo, MI 49117

Chris Farley
9150 Wilshire Blvd., #350
Beverly Hills, CA 90212

Shannon Farnon
12743 Milbank Street
Studio City, CA 91604

Richard Farnsworth
Diamond D Ranch #123
Lincoln, NM 88338

Felicia Farr
141 S. El Camino Drive #201
Beverly Hills, CA 90212

Jamie Farr
53 Ranchero
Bell Canyon, CA 91307

Mike Farrell
MSC 826, Box 6010
Sherman Oaks, CA 91413

Shea Farrell
1930 Century Park W. #403
Los Angeles, CA 90067

Terry Farrell
1680 N. Vine Street #517
Hollywood, CA 90028

Mia Farrow
124 Henry Sanford Road
Bridgewater, CT 06752

Farrah Fawcett
3130 Antelo Road
Los Angeles, CA 90077

Alice Faye
49400 JFK Trail
Palm Desert, CA 92260

Alan Feinstein
9229 Sunset Blvd. #311
Los Angeles, CA 90069

Corey Feldman
1101 1/2 Victoria Avenue
Venice, CA 90291

Barbara Feldon
14 East 74th Street
New York, NY 10021

Norman Fell
4240 Promenade Way #232
Marina del Rey, CA 90292

Edith Fellows
2016 1/2 N. Vista Del Mar
Los Angeles, CA 90068

George Fenneman
11500 San Vicente Blvd. #304
Los Angeles, CA 90049

Conchata Ferrell
1347 N. Sewart Street
Los Angeles, CA 90028

Lou Ferrigno
621 - 17th Street
Santa Monica, CA 90402

Chelsea Field
P.O. Box 5617
Beverly Hills, CA 90210

Sally Field
P.O. Box 492417
Los Angeles, CA 90049

Kim Fields
4216 West Franklin
Burbank, CA 91505

Fyvush Finkle
8730 Sunset Blvd. #480
Los Angeles, CA 90069

Linda Fiorentino
9830 Wilshire Blvd.
Beverly Hills, CA 90212

Laurence Fishburne
5200 Lankershim Blvd. #260
N. Hollywood, CA 91601

Carrie Fisher
1700 Coldwater Canyon
Beverly Hills, CA 90210

Frances Fisher
8730 Sunset Blvd., #490
Los Angeles, CA 90069

Joely Fisher
9911 W. Pico Blvd. #PH I
Los Angeles, CA 90035

Fionnula Flanagan
13438 Java Drive
Beverly Hills, CA 90210

Susan Flannery
789 Riven Rock Road
Santa Barbara, CA 93108

Rhonda Fleming
2129 Century Woods Way
Los Angeles, CA 90067

Louise Fletcher
1520 Camden Avenue #105
Los Angeles, CA 90025

Nina Foch
P.O. Box 1884
Beverly Hills, CA 90213

Megan Follows
121 N. San Vicente Blvd.
Beverly Hills, CA 90211

Bridget Fonda
9560 Wilshire Blvd.#516
Beverly Hills, CA 90212

Jane Fonda
1050 Techwood Drive N.W.
Atlanta, GA 30318

Peter Fonda
RR #38, Box 2024
Livingston, MT 59047

Joan Fontaine
P.O. Box 222600
Carmel, CA 93922

Faith Ford
7920 Sunset Blvd. #350
Los Angeles, CA 90046

Glenn Ford
911 Oxford Way
Beverly Hills, CA 90210

Harrison Ford
3555 N. Moose Road
Jackson, WY 83001

Frederic Forrest
10100 Santa Monica Blvd. #2590
Los Angeles, CA 90067

Brian Forster
16172 Flamstead Drive
Hacienda Heights, CA 91745

Robert Forster
1115 Pine Street
Santa Monica, CA 90405

John Forsythe
3849 Roblar Avenue
Santa Ynez, CA 93460

William Forsythe
3171 Coldwater Canyon
Studio City, CA 91604

Fabian Forte
1800 N. Argyle Avenue, #201
Los Angeles, CA 90028

Jodie Foster
10900 Wilshire Blvd., #511
Los Angeles, CA 90024

Meg Foster
10100 Santa Monica Blvd. #2500
Los Angeles, CA 90067

Michael J. Fox
100 Universal City Plaza, #74
Universal City, CA 91608

Robert Foxworth
29235 S. Lakeshore Drive
Agoura, CA 91301

Jonathan Frakes
9135 Hazen Drive
Beverly Hills, CA 90210

Tony Franciosa
567 Tigertail Road
Los Angeles, CA 90049

Anne Francis
P.O. Box 5417
Santa Barbara, CA 93103

Genie Francis
9135 Hazen Drive
Beverly Hills, CA 90210

Joanna Frank
1274 Capri Drive
Pacific Palisades, CA 90272

Bonnie Franklin
10635 Santa Monica Blvd. #310
Los Angeles, CA 90025

Mary Frann
10100 Santa Monica Blvd. #2490
Los Angeles, CA 90067

Dennis Franz
11805 Bellagio Road
Los Angeles, CA 90049

Brendan Fraser
2210 Wilshire Blvd., #513
Santa Monica, CA 90403

Mona Freeman
608 N. Alpine Drive
Beverly Hills, CA 90210

Morgan Freeman
2472 Broadway, #227
New York, NY 10025

Phyllis Frelich
8485-E Melrose Place
Los Angeles, CA 90069

Susan French
110 E. 9th Street #C-1005
Los Angeles, CA 90079

Matt Frewer
6670 Wildlife Road
Malibu, CA 90265

Sir David Frost
130 West 57th Street
New York, NY 10019

Soleil Moon Frye
2713 N. Keystone
Burbank, CA 91504

Annette Funicello
16102 Sandy Lane
Encino, CA 91316

Edward Furlong
9830 Wilshire Blvd.
Beverly Hills, CA 90211

Stephen Furst
3900 Huntercrest Court
Moorpark, CA 93021

G   G

Princess Zsa Zsa Gabor
1001 Bel Air Road
Los Angeles, CA 90077

Courtney Gains
3300 Dabney Avenue
Altadena, CA 91001

Zack Galligan
924 Westwood Blvd. #900
Los Angeles, CA 90024

Teresa Ganzel
9300 Wilshire Blvd. #410
Beverly Hills, CA 90212

Andy Garcia
4323 Forman Avenue
Toluca Lake, CA 91602

James Garner
33 Oakmont Drive
Los Angeles, CA 90049

Janeane Garofalo
9560 Wilshire Blvd., #500
Beverly Hills, CA 90212

Teri Garr
9150 Wilshire Blvd. #350
Beverly Hills, CA 90212

Rebecca Gayheart
853-7th Avenue #9A
New York, NY 10019

Sarah Michelle Gellar
11350 Ventura Blvd. #206
Studio City, CA 91604

Lynda Day George
10310 Riverside Drive #104
Toluca Lake, CA 91602

Susan George
520 Washington Blvd. #187
Marina del Rey, CA 90292

Richard Gere
9696 Culver Blvd. #203
Culver Cith, CA 90232

Gina Gershon
120 W. 45 th Street #3601
New York, NY 10036

Estelle Getty
10960 Wilshire Blvd. #2050
Los Angeles, CA 90024

Leeza Gibbons
1760 Courtney Avenue
Los Angeles, CA 90046

Marla Gibbs
3500 W. Manchester Blvd. #267
Inglewood, CA 90305

Charles Gibson
1965 Broadway #500
New York, NY 10023

Mel Gibson
4000 Warner Blvd. #P3-17
Burbank, CA 91522

Melissa Gilbert
P.O. Box 57593
Sherman Oaks, CA 91413

Sara Gilbert
16254 High Valley Drive
Encino, CA 91436

Erica Gimpel
10100 Santa Monica Blvd., #2500
Los Angeles, CA 90067

Robin Givens
1999 Avenue of the Starts #2850
Los Angeles, CA 90067

Paul Michael Glaser
317 Georgina Avenue
Santa Monica, CA 90402

Sharon Gless
P.O. Box 48005
Los Angeles, CA 90048

Danny Glover
41 Sutter Street #1648
San Francisco, CA 94104

Tracey Gold
4619 Goodland Avenue
Studio City, CA 91604

Whoopi Goldberg
5555 Melrose Avenue #114
Los Angeles, CA 90038

Jeff Goldblum
2401 Main Street
Santa Monica, CA 90405

Ricky Paul Goldin
9320 Wilshire Blvd. #300
Beverly Hills, CA 90212

Valeria Golino
8033 Sunset Blvd. #419
Los Angeles, CA 90046

Michael Goorjian
9000 Sunset Blvd., #1200
Los Angeles, CA 90069

Mark Paul Gosselaar
27512 Wellsley Way
Valencia , CA 91354

Louis Gossett, Jr.
8306 Wilshire Blvd. #438
Beverly Hills, CA 90211

Elliott Gould
21250 Califa #201
Woodland Hills, CA 91367

Kelsey Grammer
3266 Cornell Road
Agoura Hills, CA 91301

Hugh Grant
76 Oxford Street
London W1N 0AX ENGLAND

Peter Graves
9777 Wilshire Blvd. #815
Beverly Hills, CA 90212

Erin Gray
10921 Alta View
Studio City, CA 91604

Linda Gray
P.O. Box 5064
Sherman Oaks, CA 91403

Kathryn Grayson
2009 La Mesa Drive
Santa Monica, CA 90402

Brian Austin Green
7217 La Presa Drive
Los Angeles, CA 90068

Michele Greene
2281 Holly Drive
Los Angeles, CA 90068

Jennifer Grey
500 S. Sepulveda Blvd. #500
Los Angeles, CA 90049

Richard Grieco
2934 1/2 N Beverly Glen Circle
Suite #252
Los Angeles, CA 90077

Andy Griffith
P.O. Box 1968
Manteo, NC 27954

Melanie Griffith
201 S. Rockingham Avenue
Los Angeles, CA 90049

Thomas Ian Griffith
5444 Agnes Avenue
N. Hollywood, CA 91607

Sam Groom
10000 Santa Monica Blvd., #305
Los Angeles, CA 90067

Robert Guillaume
11963 Crest Place
Beverly Hills, CA 90210

Bryant Gumbel
30 Rockefeller Plaza #1508
New York, NY 10020

Janet Gunn
9229 Sunset Blvd. #710
Los Angeles, CA 90069

Steve Guttenberg
15237 Sunset Blvd. #48
Pacific Palisades, CA 90272

Jasmine Guy
21243 Ventura Blvd. #101
Woodland Hills, CA 91364

H   H

Shelly Hack
1208 Georgina
Santa Monica, CA 90402

Mark Hamill
P.O. Box 124
Malibu, CA 90265

Gene Hackman
118 S. Beverly Drive #1201
Beverly Hills, CA 90212

George Hamilton
9255 Doheny Drive, #2302
Los Angeles, CA 90069

Larry Hagman
9950 Sulpher Mountain Road
Ojai, CA 93023

Linda Hamilton
8955 Norman Place
W. Hollywood, CA 90069

Corey Haim
316 N. Alfred Street
Los Angeles, CA 90046

Tom Hanks
23414 Malibu Colony Drive
Malibu, CA 90265

Khrystyne Haje
P.O. Box 8750
Universal City, CA 91608

Daryl Hannah
626 Santa Monica Blvd. #370
Santa Monica, CA 90401

Anthony Michael Hall
2103 Ridgemont Drive
Los Angeles, CA 90046

Kadeem Hardison
19743 Valleyview Drive
Topanga, CA 90290

Arsenio Hall
9560 Wilshire Blvd., #516
Beverly Hills, CA 90212

Dorian Harewood
810 Prospect Blvd.
Pasadena, CA 91103

Veronica Hamel
129 North Woodburn
Los Angeles, CA 90049

Mariska Hargitay
924 Westwood Blvd. #900
Los Angeles, CA 90024

Mark Harmon
2236 Encinitas Blvd. #A
Encinitas, CA 92024

Tess Harper
8484 Wilshire Blvd. #500
Beverly Hills, CA 90211

Valerie Harper
14 East 4th Street
New York, NY 10012

Woody Harrelson
2387 Kimridge Road
Beverly Hills, CA 90210

Mel Harris
6300 Wilshire Blvd. #2110
Los Angeles, CA 90048

Neil Patrick Harris
11350 Ventura Blvd. #206
Studio City, CA 91604

Richard Harris
76 Oxford Street
London, W1N 0AX, ENGLAND

Jenilee Harrison
15315 Magnolia Blvd., #429
Sherman Oaks, CA 91403

Kathryn Harrold
9255 Sunset Blvd. #901
Los Angeles, CA 90069

Mary Hart
150 S. El Camino Drive #303
Beverly Hills, CA 90212

Melissa Joan Hart
10 Universal City Plaza, 32nd Floor
Universal City, CA 91608

Mariette Hartley
10110 Empyrean Way #304
Los Angeles, CA 90067

Lisa Hartman
15301 Ventura Blvd. #345
Sherman Oaks, CA 91403

David Hasselhoff
5180 Louise Avenue
Encino, CA 91316

Teri Hatcher
10100 Santa Monica Blvd. #410
Los Angeles, CA 90067

Rutger Hauer
32 Sea Colony Drive
Santa Monica, CA 90405

Wings Hauser
9450 Chivers Avenue
Sun Valley, CA 91352

Ethan Hawke
1775 Broadway #701
New York, NY 10019

Goldie Hawn
500 S. Buena Vista #1D6
Burbank, CA 91505

John Heard
23215 Mariposa de Oro
Malibu, CA 90265

David Heavener
6442 Coldwater Canyon, #211
N. Hollywood, CA 91606

Jessica Hecht
280 S. Beverly Drive, #400
Beverly Hills, CA 90212

Katherine Helmond
9701 Wilshire Blvd. #700
Beverly Hills, CA 90212

Mariel Hemingway
P.O. Box 2249
Ketchum, ID 83340

Sherman Hemsley
15043 Valley Heart Drive
Sherman Oaks, CA 91403

Marilu Henner
2101 Castilian
Los Angeles, CA 90068

Pamela Hensley
9526 Dalegrove Drive
Beverly Hills, CA 90210

Pee Wee Herman
P.O. Box 29373
Los Angeles, CA 90029

Howard Hesseman
7146 La Presa
Los Angeles, CA 90068

Charlton Heston
2859 Coldwater Canyon
Beverly Hills, CA 90210

Christopher Hewitt
1422 N. Sweetzer #110
Los Angeles, CA 90069

Dwayne Hickman
P.O. Box 3352
Santa Monica, CA 90403

Catherine Hicks
15422 Brownwood Place
Los Angeles, CA 90077

Gregory Hines
377 W. 11th Street, PH#4
New York, NY 10014

Judd Hirsch
888-7th Avenue #602
New York, NY 10017

Dustin Hoffman
1926 Broadway #305
New York, NY 10023

Paul Hogan
8446 1/2 Melrose Avenue
Los Angeles, CA 90069

Hal Holbrook
9000 Sunset Blvd. #1200
Los Angeles, CA 90069

Polly Holliday
888 - 7th Avenue #2500
New York, NY 10106

Lauren Holly
13601 Ventura Blvd. #99
Sherman Oaks, CA 91423

Robert Hooks
145 N. Valley Street
Burbank, CA 91505

Bob Hope
10346 Moorpark
N. Hollywood, CA 91602

Sir Anthony Hopkins
7 High Park Road
Kew, Surrey,
Richmond, TW9 3BL, ENGLAND

Lee Horsley
15054 E. Dartmouth
Aurora, CO 80014

Arliss Howard
20220 Inland Avenue
Malibu, CA 90265

Ken Howard
11718 Barrington Court #300
Los Angeles, CA 90049

Ron Howard
1925 Century Park E. #2300
Los Angeles, CA 90067

Season Hubley
121 N. San Vicente Blvd.
Beverly Hills, CA 90211

Whip Hubley
9000 Sunset Blvd. #1200
Los Angeles, CA 90069

Finola Hughes
270 N. Canon Drive, #1064
Beverly Hills, CA 90210

Miko Hughes
924 Westwood Blvd. #900
Los Angeles, CA 90024

Renee Humphrey
9000 Sunset Blvd. #1200
Los Angeles, CA 90069

Helen Hunt
9171 Wilshire Blvd. #406
Beverly Hills, CA 90210

Linda Hunt
233 Park Avenue S., 10th floor
New York, NY 10017

Marsha Hunt
13131 Magnolia Blvd.
Sherman Oaks, CA 91423

Holly Hunter
19528 Ventura Blvd. #343
Tarzana, CA 91356

Tab Hunter
223 N. Guadalupe Street, #292
Santa Fe, NM 87501

William Hurt
370 Lexington Avenue #808
New York, NY 10017

Anjelica Huston
57 Windward Avenue
Venice, CA 90291

Will Hutchins
3461 Waverly Drive #108
Los Angeles, CA 90027

Betty Hutton
Harrison Avenue
Newport, RI 02840

Lauren Hutton
382 Lafayette Street #6
New York, NY 10003

I   I

Jeremy Irons
200 Fulham Road
London, SW10 9PN, ENGLAND

Chris Isaak
1655-38th Avenue
San Fransisco, CA 94122

Michael Ironside
3500 West Olive #1400
Burbank, CA 91505

Judith Ivey
15760 Ventura Blvd. #1730
Encino, CA 91436

Amy Irving
7920 Sunset Blvd. #400
Los Angeles, CA 90046

James Ivory
250 W. 57th Street #1913-A
New York, NY 10019

J   J

Jackee
8649 Metz Place
Los Angeles, CA 90069

Mary Ann Jackson
1242 Alessandro Drive
Newbury Park, CA 91320

Anne Jackson
90 Riverside Drive
New York, NY 10024

Melody Jackson
6269 Selma Avenue #15
Los Angeles, CA 90028

Glenda Jackson
59 Frith Street
London, W1, ENGLAND

Paul Jackson, Jr.
40 West 57th Street
New York, NY 10019

Kate Jackson
P.O. Box 57593
Sherman Oaks, CA 91403

Samuel L. Jackson
5128 Encino Avenue
Encino, CA 91316

Sherry Jackson
4933 Encino Avenue
Encino, CA 91316

Stoney Jackson
1602 N. Fuller Avenue #102
Los Angeles, CA 90046

Victoria Jackson
14631 Balgowan Road #2-5
Hialeah, FL 33016

Lou Jacobi
240 Central Park South
New York, NY 10019

Lawrence-Hilton Jacobs
3804 Evan #2
Los Angeles, CA 90027

Billy Jacoby
P.O. Box 46324
Los Angeles, CA 90046

Henry Jaglom
609 E. Channel Road
Santa Monica, CA 90402

John James
P.O. Box #9
Cambridge, NY 12816

Conrad Janis
1434 N. Genesee Avenue
Los Angeles, CA 90069

Famke Janssen
9560 Wilshire Blvd., #500
Beverly Hills, CA 90212

Lois January
225 N. Crescent Drive #103
Beverly Hills, CA 90210

Claude Jarman, Jr.
11 Dos Encinas
Orinda, CA 94563

Graham Jarvis
15351 Via de las Olas
Pacific Palisades, CA 90272

Sybil Jason
P.O. Box 40024
Studio City, CA 91604

Gloria Jean
6625 Variel Avenue
Canoga Park, CA 91303

Marianne Jean-Baptiste
233 Park Avenue So., 10th Floor
New York, NY 10017

Anne Jeffreys
121 S. Bentley Avenue
Los Angeles, CA 90049

Peter Jennings
47 West 66th Street
New York, NY 10023

Salome Jens
9400 Readcrest Drive
Beverly Hills, CA 90210

Ann Jillian
4241 Woodcliff Road
Sherman Oaks, CA 91403

Glynis Johns 121 N. San Vicente Blvd. Beverly Hills, CA 90211	**Angelina Jolie** 13340 Galewood Drive Sherman Oaks, CA 91423
Anne-Marie Johnson 3500 W. Olive Avenue #1400 Burbank, CA 91505	**Dean Jones** 500 N. Buena Vista Burbank, CA 91521
Arte Johnson 2725 Bottlebrush Drive Los Angeles, CA 90024	**Dub Jones** 223 Glendale Rusten, LA 71270
Don Johnson P.O. Box 6909 Burbank, CA 91510	**Grace Jones** 89 Fifth Avenue, 7th Floor New York, NY 10003
Kristen Johnson 8712 Sunset Plaza Terrace Los Angeles, CA 90069	**James Earl Jones** P.O. Box 610 Pawling, NY 12564
Laura Johnson 1917 Weepah Way Los Angeles, CA 90046	**Janet Jones** 9100 Wilshire Blvd. #1000W Beverly Hills, CA 90212
Lynn-Holly Johnson 405 W. Riverside Drive #200 Burbank, CA 91506	**Jennifer Jones-Simon** P.O. Box 50067 Pasadena, CA 91115
Michelle Johnson 1350 Pine Street #3 Boulder, CO 80302	**Jenny Jones** 454 N. Columbus Drive Chicago, IL 60611
Rafer Johnson 501 Colorado Avenue #200 Santa Monica, CA 90401	**Marcia Mae Jones** 4541 Hazeltine Avenue #4 Sherman Oaks, CA 91423
Russell Johnson P.O. Box 3135 La Jolla, CA 92038	**Sam J. Jones** 10000 Santa Monica Blvd. #305 Los Angeles, CA 90067

Shirley Jones
701 N. Oakhurst Drive
Beverly Hills, CA 90210

Tommy Lee Jones
P.O. Box 966
San Saba, TX 76877

James Carroll Jordan
8333 Lookout Mountain Avenue
Los Angeles, CA 90046

William Jordan
10806 Lindbrook Avenue #4
Los Angeles, CA 90024

Jackie Joseph
111 N. Valley
Burbank, CA 91505

Louis Jourdan
1139 Maybrook
Beverly Hills, CA 90210

Milla Jovovich
151 El Camino Drive
Beverly Hills, CA 90212

Gordon Jump
1631 Hillcrest Avenue
Glendale, CA 91202

K   K

David Kagen
6457 Firmament Avenue
Van Nuys, CA 91406

Madeline Kahn
975 Park Avenue #9A
New York, NY 10028

Helena Kallianotes
12830 Mulholland Drive
Beverly Hills, CA 90210

Steven Kampmann
801 Alma Real
Pacific Palisades, CA 90272

Steve Kanaly
828 Foothill Lane
Ojai, CA 93023

Sean Kanan
1999 Avenue of the Stars #2850
Los Angeles, CA 90067

Carol Kane
1416 N. Havenhurst Drive #1C
Los Angeles, CA 90046

Gabriel Kaplan
9551 Hidden Valley Road
Beverly Hills, CA 90210

Marvin Kaplan
7600 Claybeck Avenue
Burbank, CA 91505

Mitzi Kapture
4705 Ruffin Road
San Diego, CA 92123

William Katt
26608 Sunflower Court
Calabasas, CA 91302

Julie Kavner
25154 Malibu Road #2
Malibu, CA 90265

Lainie Kazan
9903 Santa Monica Blvd. #283
Beverly Hills, CA 90212

James Keach
P.O. Box 548
Agoura, CA 91376

Stacy Keach, Jr.
27525 Winding Way
Malibu, CA 90265

Stacy Keach, Sr.
8749 Sunset Blvd.
Los Angeles, CA 90069

Jean Kean
28128 W. Pacific Coast Hwy.
Malibu, CA 90265

Staci Keanan
8730 Sunset Blvd. #220W
Los Angeles, CA 90069

Diane Keaton
2010 La Brea Terrace
Los Angeles, CA 90046

Michael Keaton
11901 Santa Monica Blvd. #547
Los Angeles, CA 90025

Don Keefer
4146 Allott Avenue
Sherman Oaks, CA 91423

Howard Keel
394 Red River Road
Palm Desert, CA 92211

Bob Keeshan
40 West 57th Street #1600
New York, NY 10019

David Keith
449 S. Beverly Drive, #212
Beverly Hills, CA 90212

Penelope Keith
66 Berkeley House
Hay Hill
London, SW3, ENGLAND

Martha Keller
5 rue St. Dominique
75007 Paris, FRANCE

Sally Kellerman
7944 Woodrow Wilson Drive
Los Angeles, CA 90046

Sheila Kelley
10540 Cushdon Avenue
Los Angeles, CA 90064

Moira Kelly
106 S. Orange Drive
Los Angeles, CA 90036

Roz Kelly
5614 Lemp Avenue
N. Hollywood, CA 91601

George Kennedy
4116 Oak Place Drive
Thousand Oaks, CA 91362

Jayne Kennedy-Overton
230 Sunridge Street
Playa del Rey, CA 90293

Mimi Kennedy
9000 Sunset Blvd. #1200
Los Angeles, CA 90069

Patsy Kensit
14 Lambton Place
Nottinghill
London W11 ENGLAND

Ken Kercheval
P.O. Box 325
Goshen, KY 40026

Joanna Kerns
P.O. Box 49216
Los Angeles, CA 90049

Sandra Kerns
620 Resolano Drive
Pacific Palisades, CA 90272

Deborah Kerr
Los Monteros
E-29600 Marbella
Malaga, SPAIN

Linda Kerridge
9812 West Olympic Blvd.
Beverly Hills, CA 90212

Brian Kerwin
304 West 81st Street #2
New York, NY 10024

Evelyn Keys
999 N. Doheny Drive #509
Los Angeles, CA 90069

Mark Keyloun
3500 West Olive #1400
Burbank, CA 91505

Margot Kidder
220 Pine Creek Road
Livingston, MT 59047

Nichole Kidman
335 N. Maple Drive, #135
Beverly Hills, CA 90210

Val Kilmer
P.O. Box 362
Tesuque, NM 87574

Lincoln Kilpatrick
1710 Garth Avenue
Los Angeles, CA 90035

Richard Kind
1345 N. Hayworth Avenue #3112
Los Angeles, CA 90046

Roslyn Kind
8871 Burton Way #303
Los Angeles, CA 90048

Andrea King
1225 Sunset Plaza Drive #3
Los Angeles, CA 90069

Larry King
10801 Lockwood Drive, #230
Silver Springs, MD 20901

Perry King
3647 Wrightwood Drive
Studio City, CA 91604

Ben Kingsley
New Penworth, Stratford Upon Avon
Warwickshire, OV3 7QX, ENGLAND

Kathleen Kinmont
5261 Cleon Avenue
North Hollywood, CA 91601

Greg Kinnear
3000 W. Alameda Avenue, #2908
Burbank, CA 91523

Nastassja Kinski
1000 Bel Air Place
Los Angeles, CA 90077

Phyllis Kirk
321M S. Beverly Drive
Beverly Hills, CA 90212

Sally Kirkland
151 El Camino Drive
Beverly Hills, CA 90212

Terry Kiser
9911 W. Pico Blvd., #1060
Los Angeles, CA 90035

Tawny Kitaen
650 Town Center Drive #1000
Costa Mesa, CA 92626

Werner Klemperer
44 W. 62nd Street, 10th Floor
New York, NY 10023

Kevin Kline
1636-3rd Avenue #309
New York, NY 10128

Richard Kline
14322 Mulholland Drive
Los Angeles, CA 90077

Patrica Klous
18095 Karen Drive
Encino, CA 91316

Jack Klugman
22548 Pacific Coast Hwy.
Malibu, CA 90265

Christopher Knight
111 N. Sepulveda Blvd. #360
Manhattan Beach, CA 90266

Michael E. Knight
10100 Santa Monica Blvd. #2500
Los Angeles, CA 90067

Shirley Knight
1548 N. Orange Grove Avenue
Los Angeles, CA 90046

Don Knotts
1854 S. Beverly Glen #402
Los Angeles, CA 90025

Walter Koenig
P.O. Box 4395
N. Hollywood, CA 91607

Ted Koppel
11810 Glenn Mill Road
Potomac, MD 20854

Maria Korda
304 N. Screenland Drive
Burbank, CA 91505

Harvey Korman
1136 Stradella Road
Los Angeles, CA 90077

Yaphet Kotto
10100 Santa Monica Blvd., #2490
Los Angeles, CA 90067

Martin Kove
19155 Rostia Street
Tarzana, CA 91356

Harley Jane Kozak
2329 Stanley Hills Drive
Los Angeles, CA 90046

Linda Kozlowski
151 El Camino Drive
Beverly Hills, CA 90212

Stepfanie Kramer
9300 Wilshire Blvd. #555
Beverly Hills, CA 90212

Brian Krause
10683 Santa Monica Blvd.
Los Angeles, CA 90025

Sylvia Kristal
8955 Norma Place
Los Angeles, CA 90069

Lisa Kudrow
10850 Wilshire Blvd. #400
Los Angeles, CA 90024

Kari Kupcinet
1730 N. Clark Street #3311
Chicago, IL 60614

Swoosie Kurtz
320 Central Park West
New York, NY 10025

L   L

Mathew Laborteaux
4555 Mariota Avenue
Toluca Lake, CA 91602

Patrick Laborteaux
1450 Belfast Drive
Los Angeles, CA 90069

Alana Ladd
1420 Moraga Drive
Los Angeles, CA 90049

Cheryl Ladd
P.O. Box 1329
Santa Ynez, CA 93460

Diane Ladd
P.O. Box 17111
Beverly Hills, CA 90209

Christine Lahti
500-25th Street
Santa Monica, CA 90402

Ricki Lake
401 Fifth Avenue
New York, NY 10016

Hedy Lamarr
568 Orange Drive #47
Altamonte Springs, FL 32701

Lorenzo Lamas
3727 West Magnolia Blvd. #807
Burbank, CA 91505

Martin Landau
7455 Palo Vista Drive
Los Angeles, CA 90046

Audrey Landers
3112 Nicka Drive
Los Angeles, CA 90077

Steve Landesberg
355 N. Genesee Avenue
Los Angeles, CA 90036

Nathan Lane
P.O. Box 1249
White River Junction, VT 05001

SueAne Langdon
12429 Laurel Terrace Drive
Studio City, CA 91604

Hope Lange
803 Bramble
Los Angeles, CA 90049

Jessica Lange
9830 Wilshire Blvd.
Beverly Hills, CA 90212

Ted Lange
15315 Magnolia Blvd. #429
Sherman Oaks, CA 91403

Frank Langella
1999 Avenue of the Starts #2850
Los Angeles, CA 90067

Heather Langenkamp
9229 Sunset Blvd. #311
Los Angeles, CA 90069

Angela Lansbury
635 Bonhill Road
Los Angeles, CA 90049

John Larroquette
5874 Dearhead Road
Malibu, CA 90265

Eva LaRue
11300 W. Olympic Blvd. #870
Los Angeles, CA 90064

John Laughlin
11815 Magnolia Blvd. #2
N. Hollywood, CA 91607

John Phillip Law
1339 Miller Drive
Los Angeles, CA 90069

Carol Lawrence
12337 Ridge Circle
Los Angeles, CA 90049

Martin Lawrence
3130 Benedict Canyon
Beverly Hills, CA 90210

Vicki Lawrence
6000 Lido Avenue
Long Beach, CA 90803

Robin Leach
1 Dag Hammarskjold Plaza, 21st Fl.
New York, NY 10017

Michael Learned
1600 N. Beverly Drive
Beverly Hills, CA 90210

Matt LeBlanc
11766 Wilshire Blvd., #1470
Los Angeles, CA 90025

Kelly LeBrock
344 E. 59th Street
New York, NY 10022

Christopher Lee
21 Golden Square, #200
London W1R 3PA ENGLAND

Hyapatia Lee
15127 Califa Street
Van Nuys, CA 91411

Peggy Lee
11404 Bellagio Road
Los Angeles, CA 90024

Janet Leigh
1625 Summitridge Drive
Beverly Hills, CA 90210

Jennifer Jason Leigh
2400 Whitman Place
Los Angeles, CA 90068

Chris Lemmon
80 Murray Drive
S. Glastonbury, CT 06073

Jack Lemmon
141 S. El Camino Drive #201
Beverly Hills, CA 90212

Jay Leno
P.O. Box 7885
Burbank, CA 91510

Rula Lenska
306 - 16 Eustin Road
London NW13 ENGLAND

Melissa Leo
853-7th Avenue #9A
New York, NY 10019

David Letterman
1697 Broadway
New York, NY 10019

Daniel Day Lewis
46 Albermarle Street
London W1X 4PP ENGLAND

Dawnn Lewis
P.O. Box 56718
Sherman Oaks, CA 91413

Jerry Lewis
3160 W. Sahara Avenue #816
Las Vegas, NV 89102

Richard Lewis
345 N. Maple Drive #300
Beverly Hills, CA 90210

Judith Light
1475 Sierra Vista Drive
Aspen, CO 81611

Audra Lindley
200 N. Swall Drive #58
Beverly Hills, CA 90211

Art Linkletter
1100 Bel Air Road
Los Angeles, CA 90077

Laura Linney
1450 W. 45th Street #1204
New York, NY 10036

Ray Liotta
16829 Monte Hermosa Drvie
Pacific Palisades, CA 90272

John Lithgow
1319 Warnall Avenue
Los Angeles, CA 90024

Rich Little
5485 W. Flamingo Road #105
Las Vegas, NV 89103

Christopher Lloyd
P.O. Box 491246
Los Angeles, CA 90049

Norman Lloyd
1813 Old Ranch Road
Los Angeles, CA 90049

Sondra Locke
11750 Sunset Blvd. #406
Los Angeles, CA 90049

June Lockhart
P.O. Box 3207
Santa Monica, CA 90403

Heather Locklear
151 El Camino Drive
Beverly Hills, CA 90212

Robert Loggia
544 Bellagio Terrace
Los Angeles, CA 90049

Julie London
16074 Royal Oaks
Encino, CA 91436

Shelly Long
15237 Sunset Blvd.
Pacific Palisades, CA 90272

Traci Lords
9150 Wilshire Blvd. #175
Beverly Hills, CA 90212

Sophia Loren
1151 Hidden Valley Road
Thousand Oaks, CA 91360

Lori Loughlin
9278 Sierra Mar Drive
Los Angeles, CA 90069

Tina Louise
310 E. 46th Street #18-T
New York, NY 10017

Linda Lovelace (Marciano)
120 Enterprise
Secaucus, NJ 07094

Jon Lovitz
4735 Viviana Drive
Tarzana, CA 91356

Dale Lowdermilk
P.O. Box 5743
Montecito, CA 93150

Chad Lowe
7920 Sunset Blvd., 4th Floor
Los Angeles, CA 90046

Rob Lowe
646 Romero Canyon Road
Santa Barbara, CA 93108

Susan Lucci
P.O. Box 621
Quogue, NY 11959

Lorna Luft
9100 Wilshire Blvd. #455
Los Angeles, CA 90212

Joan Lunden
1965 Broadway #400
New York, NY 10023

Kelly Lynch
1970 Mandeville Canyon Road
Los Angeles, CA 90049

M   M

Ali MacGraw
10345 W. Olympic Blvd. #200
Los Angeles, CA 90064

Stephen Macht
248 S. Rodeo Drive
Beverly Hills, CA 90212

Kyle MacLachlan
132 S. Rodeo Drive #300
Beverly Hills, CA 90212

Shirley MacLaine
25200 Old Malibu Road
Malibu, CA 90265

Patrick MacNee
P.O. Box 1685
Palm Springs, CA 92263

William H. Macy
924 Westwood Blvd. #900
Los Angeles, CA 90024

Michael Madsen
31336 Broadbeach Road
Malibu, CA 90265

Virginia Madsen
9830 Wilshire Blvd.
Beverly Hills, CA 90212

Debra Maffett
1525 McGavock Street
Nashville, TN 37203

Bill Maher
7800 Beverly Blvd. #D
Los Angeles, CA 90036

Robert Maheu
3523 Cochise Lane
Las Vegas, NV 89109

Lee Majors
3000 Holiday Drive PH #1
Ft. Lauderdale, FL 33316

Chris Makepeace
P.O. Box 1095, Station Q
Toronto, Ont. M4T 2P2 CANADA

Kristina Malandro
P.O. Box 491035
Los Angeles, CA 90049

Karl Malden
1845 Mandeville Canyon Road
Los Angeles, CA 90049

Nick Mancuso
3500 W. Olive Avenue #1400
Burbank, CA 91505

Howie Mandell
8942 Wilshire Blvd.
Beverly Hills, CA 90211

Marla Maples
721 Fifth Avenue
New York, NY 10022

Sophie Marceau
13 rue Madeleine Michelle
F-92200 Neuilly-sur-Seine FRANCE

Ann-Margret (Smith)
151 El Camino Drive
Beverly Hills, CA 90212

Julianne Margulies
8942 Wilshire Blvd.
Beverly Hills, CA 90211

Todd Marinovich
225 38th Street
Manhattan Beach, CA 90266

E.G. Marshall
RFD #2, Orego Road
Mount Kisco, NY 10549

Penny Marshall
8942 Wilshire Blvd.
Beverly Hills, CA 90212

Peter Marshall
16714 Oakview Drive
Encino, CA 91316

Jared Martin
15060 Ventura Blvd #350
Sherman Oaks, CA 91403

Pamela Sue Martin
P.O. Box 2278
Hailey, ID 83333

Steve Martin
P.O. Box 929
Beverly Hills, CA 90213

Wink Martindale
5744 Newcastle
Calabasas, CA 91302

A. Martinez
6835 Wild Life Road
Malibu, CA 90265

Marsha Mason
320 Galisted Street #305
Santa Fe, NM 87401

Tom Mason
853 - 7th Avenue #9A
New York, NY 10019

Mary Stuart Masterson
1724 N. Vista Street
Los Angeles, CA 90046

Jerry Mathers
31658 Rancho Viejo Road #A
San Juan Capistrano, CA 92675

Tim Matheson
10390 Santa Monica Blvd. #300
Los Angeles, CA 90025

Marlee Matlin
12304 Santa Monica Blvd. #119
Los Angeles, CA 90025

Walter Matthau
1999 Avenue of the Stars #2100
Los Angeles, CA 90067

Brad Maule
4136 Dixie Canyon
Sherman Oaks, CA 91423

Virginia Mayo
109 E. Avenue De Los Arboles
Thousand Oaks, CA 91360

David McCallum
91 The Grove
London N13 5J5 ENGLAND

Andrew McCarthy
8942 Wilshire Blvd
Beverly Hills, CA 90211

Jenny McCarthy
2112 Broadway
Santa Monica, CA 90404

Kevin McCarthy
14854 Sutton Street
Sherman Oaks, CA 91403

Nobu McCarthy
9229 Sunset Blvd., #311
Los Angeles, CA 90069

Mary McCormack
P.O. Box 5617
Beverly Hills, CA 90210

Matt McCoy
4526 Wilshire Blvd.
Los Angeles, CA 90010

James McDaniel
8730 Sunset Blvd. #480
Los Angeles, CA 90069

Roddy McDowell
3110 Brookdale Road
Studio City, CA 91604

Darren McGavin
P.O. Box 2939
Beverly Hills, CA 90213

Vonetta McGee
1801 Avenue of the Stars, #902
Los Angeles, CA 90067

Kelly McGillis
303 Whitehead Street
Key West, FL 33040

Ewan McGregor
2 Goodwin's Court
London WC2N 4LL ENGLAND

Patrick McGoohan
16808 Bollinger Drive
Pacific Palisades, CA 90272

Elizabeth McGovern
17319 Magnolia Blvd.
Encino, CA 91316

Dorothy McGuire
10351 Santa Monica Blvd. #300
Los Angeles, CA 90025

Michael McKean
833 Thornhill Road
Calabasas, CA 91302

Nancy McKeon
P.O. Box 6778
Burbank, CA 91510

Philip McKeon
P.O. Box 1830
Studio City, CA 91614

Rachel McLish
25 Judd Terrace
Rancho Mirage, CA 92270

Ed McMahon
12000 Crest Court
Beverly Hills, CA 90210

Kristy McNichol
151 El Camino Drive
Beverly Hills, CA 90212

Chad McQueen
8306 Wilshire Blvd. #438
Beverly Hills, CA 90211

Jayne Meadows (Allen)
15201 Burbank Blvd.
Van Nuys, CA 91411

Burgess Meredith
P.O. Box 757
Malibu, CA 90265

Lee Ann Meriwether
P.O. Box 260402
Encino, CA 91326

Laurie Metcalf
11845 Kling Street
N. Hollywood, CA 91607

Guy Michelmore
72 Goldsmith Avenue
London W3 6HN ENGLAND

Toshiro Mifune
9-30-7 Siejko, Setagaysku
Tokyo JAPAN

Joanna Miles
2062 N. Vine Street
Los Angeles, CA 90068

Sarah Miles
Chithurst Manor
Trotton nr. Petersfield
Hampshire GU31 5EU ENGLAND

Dennis Miller
40 West 57th Street
New York, NY 10019

Johnny Lee Miller
870 Sunset Blvd. #490
Los Angeles, CA 90069

Penelope Ann Miller
43-B Navy Street
Vencie, CA 90291

Donna Mills
2260 Benedict Canyon Drive
Beverly Hills, CA 90210

Hayley Mills
81 High Street
Hampton, Middlesex, ENGLAND

Yvette Mimieux
500 Perugia Way
Los Angeles, CA 90077

Kim Miyori
121 N. San Vicente Blvd.
Beverly Hills, CA 90211

Mary Ann Mobley
2751 Hutton Drive
Beverly Hills, CA 90210

Matthew Modine
9696 Culver Blvd. #203
Culver City, CA 90232

D.W. Moffett
450 N. Rossmore Avenue #401
Los Angeles, CA 90004

Richard Moll
1119 N. Amalfi Drive
Pacific Palisades, CA 90272

Ricardo Montalban
1423 Oriole Drive
Los Angeles, CA 90069

Clayton Moore
4720 Parkolivo
Calabasas, CA 91302

Demi Moore
1453 - 3rd Street #420
Santa Monica, CA 90401

Dudley Moore
73 Market Street
Venice, CA 90291

Mary Tyler Moore
510 E. 86th Street, #21A
New York, NY 10028

Melba Moore
7005 Kennedy Blvd. East #3250
Guttenberg, NJ 07093

Roger Moore
2-4 Noel Street
London, W1V 3RB, ENGLAND

Esai Morales
1147 S. Wooster Street
Los Angeles, CA 90035

Rick Moranis
285 Central Park West
New York, NY 10024

Rita Moreno
1620 Amalfi Drive
Pacific Palisades, CA 90272

Harry Morgan
13172 Boca De Canon Lane
Los Angeles, CA 90049

Jaye P. Morgan
1185 La Grange Avenue
Newbury park, CA 91320

Cathy Moriarty
9881 Carmelita Avenue
Beverly Hills, CA 90210

Michael Moriarty
200 W. 58th Street #3B
New York, NY 10019

Noriyuki "Pat" Morita
P.O. Box 491278
Los Angeles, CA 90049

Robert Morse
13830 Davana Terrace
Sherman Oaks, CA 91403

Kate Moss
205 West 39th Street #1200
New York , NY 10018

Bill Moyers
524 West 57th Street
New York, NY 10019

Armin Mueller-Stahl
c/o ZBF
Ordensmeisterstr. 15-16
D-12099 Berlin GERMANY

Patrick Muldoon
9300 Wilshire Blvd., #400
Beverly Hills, CA 90212

Chris Mulkey
918 Zenizia Avenue
Venice, CA 90291

Martin Mull
338 Chadbourne Avenue
Los Angeles, CA 90049

Richard Mulligan
145 S. Beachwood Drive
Los Angeles, CA 90004

Dermot Mulroney
1180 S. Beverly Drive #618
Los Angeles, CA 90035

Billy Mumy
8271 Melrose Avenue #202
Los Angeles, CA 90046

Ben Murphy
3601 Vista Pacifica #17
Malibu, CA 90265

Eddie Murphy
152 W. 57th Street #4700
New York, NY 10019

Bill Murray
RFD #1, Box 573
Palisades, NY 10964

Don Murray
1215-F De La Vina Street
Santa Barbara, CA 93101

N _____ N

Kathy Najimy
3366 Wrightwood Drive
Studio City, CA 91604

Hugo Napier
2207 N. Beachwood Drive
Los Angeles, CA 90068

Patricia Neal
45 E. End Avenue #4C
New York, NY 10028

Tracey Needham
9229 Sunset Blvd. #311
Los Angeles, CA 90069

Liam Neeson
150 S. Rodeo Drive #220
Beverly Hills, CA 90212

Craig T. Nelson
28872 Boniface Drive
Malibu, CA 90265

Judd Nelson
409 N. Camden Drive #202
Beverly Hills, CA 90210

Claudette Nevins
3500 W. Olive Avenue #1400
Burbank, CA 91505

Bob Newhart
420 Amapola Lane
Los Angeles, CA 90077

Paul Newman
555 Long Wharf Drive
New Haven, CT 06511

Phyllis Newman
529 W. 42nd Street #7F
New York, NY 10036

Julie Newmar
204 Carmelina Avenue
Los Angeles, CA 90049

Thomas Ian Nicholas
1801 Avenue of the Stars, #1250
Los Angeles, CA 90067

Nichelle Nichols
22647 Ventura Blvd.
Woodland Hills, CA 91364

Jack Nicholson
15760 Ventura Blvd. #1730
Encino, CA 91436

Julia Nickson
2232 Moreno Drive
Los Angeles, CA 90039

Brigitte Nielsen
P.O. Box 57593
Sherman Oaks, CA 91403

Leslie Nielsen
1622 Viewmont Drive
Los Angeles, CA 90069

Leonard Nimoy
2300 W. Victory Blvd., #C-384
Burbank, CA 91506

Nick Nolte
6174 Bonsall Drive
Malibu, CA 90265

Chuck Norris
P.O. Box 872
Navasota, TX 77868

Edward Norton
8000 Sunset Blvd. #300
Los Angeles, CA 90046

Deborah Norville
P.O. Box 426
Mill Neck, NY 11765

Michael Nouri
17616 Ravello Drive
Pacific Palisades, CA 90272

O   O

Hugh O'Brian
10880 Wilshire Blvd. #1500
Los Angeles, CA 90024

Conan O'Brien
30 Rockefeller Plaza
New York, NY 10012

Carrol O'Connor
30826 Broadbeach Road
Malibu, CA 90265

Donald O'Connor
P.O. Box 20204
Sedona, AZ 86341

Chris O'Donnell
2029 Century Park East #500
Los Angeles, CA 90067

Rosie O'Donnell
235 No. Broadway
Nyack, NY 10960

Maureen O'Hara
Box 1400, Christeansted
St. Croix, VI 00820

Miles O'Keeffe
P.O. Box 216
Malibu, CA 90265

Soon-Tech Oh
4231 W. Sarah Street
Burbank, CA 91505

Gary Oldman
76 Oxford Street
London W1N OAX ENGLAND

Ken Olin
5855 Topanga Canyon #410
Woodland Hills, CA 91367

Edward James Olmos
18034 Ventura Blvd. #228
Encino, CA 91316

Ryan O'Neal
21368 Pacific Coast Hwy.
Malibu, CA 90265

Jennifer O'Neil
15301 Ventura Blvd. #345
Sherman Oaks, CA 91403

Michael Ontkean
P.O. Box 1212
Malibu, CA 90265

Haley Joel Osment
4942 Vineland Avenue #200
North Hollywood, CA 91601

Bibi Osterwald
341 Carroll Park West
Long Beach, CA 90815

Annette O'Toole
360 Morton Street
Ashland, OR 97520

Peter O'Toole
31/32 Soho Square
London, W1V 5DG ENGLAND

Catherine Oxenberg
1526 N. Beverly Drive
Beverly Hills, CA 90210

P _____ P

Al Pacino
301 W. 57th Street #16
New York, NY 10019

Joanna Pacula
1465 Lindacrest Drive
Beverly Hills, CA 90210

Holly Palance
2753 Roscomare Avenue
Los Angeles, CA 90077

Jack Palance
P.O. Box 6201
Tehachapi, CA 93561

Chazz Palminteri
375 Greenwich Street
New York, NY 10013

Bruce Paltrow
304-21st Street
Santa Monica, CA 90402

Gwyneth Paltrow
9830 Wilshire Blvd.
Beverly Hills, CA 90212

Anna Paquin
P.O. Box 9585
Wellington NEW ZEALAND

Eleanor Parker
2195 La Paz Way
Palm Spring, CA 92262

Fess Parker
P.O. Box 908
Los Olivos, CA 93441

Jamerson Parker
1604 N. Vista Avenue
Los Angeles, CA 90046

Sarah Jessica Parker
P.O. Box 69646
Los Angeles, CA 90069

Mandy Patinkin
200 West 90th Street
New York, NY 10024

Jason Patric
10683 Santa Monica Blvd.
Los Angeles, CA 90025

Adrian Paul
16027 Ventura Blvd., #206
Encino, CA 91436

Jane Pauley
271 Central Park W. #10E
New York, NY 10024

David Paymer
1506 Pacific Street
Santa Monica, CA 90405

Gregory Peck
P.O. Box 837
Beverly Hills, CA 90213

Thaao Penghlis
7187 Macapa Drive
Los Angeles, CA 90068

Chris Penn
9560 Wilshire Blvd. #516
Beverly Hills, CA 90212

Sean Penn
2049 Central Park E. #2500
Los Angeles, CA 90067

Joe Penny
10453 Sarah
N. Hollywood, CA 91602

Rosie Perez
10683 Santa Monica Blvd.
Los Angeles, CA 90025

Ron Perlman
P.O. Box 5617
Beverly Hills, CA 90210

Valerie Perrine
Via Toscana 1
I-00187 Rome ITALY

Luke Perry
8484 Wilshire Blvd. #745
Beverly Hills, CA 90211

Joe Pesci
P.O. Box 6
Lavallette, NJ 08735

Donna Pescow
9300 Wilshire Blvd. #555
Beverly Hills, CA 90212

Bernadette Peters
323 West 80th Street
New York, NY 10024

Michelle Pfeiffer
721 Fairview Street
Burbank, CA 91505

Regis Philbin
101 W. 67th Street #51A
New York, NY 10023

Julianne Phillips
1999 Avenue of the Starts #2850
Los Angeles, CA 90067

Lou Diamond Phillips
11766 Wilshire Blvd. #1470
Los Angeles, CA 90025

Mitch Pileggi
9229 Sunset Blvd. #315
Los Angeles, CA 90069

Bronson Pinchot
9150 Wilshire Blvd. #350
Beverly Hills, CA 90212

Jada Pinkett
9560 Wilshire Blvd. #516
Beverly Hills, CA 90212

Brad Pitt
9150 Wilshire Blvd. #350
Beverly Hills, CA 90212

Mary Kay Place
2739 Motor Avenue
Los Angeles, CA 90064

Suzanne Pleshette
P.O. Box 1492
Beverly Hills, CA 90213

Amanda Plummer
160 Prince Street #2
New York, NY 10012

Christopher Plummer
49 Wampum Hill Road
Weston, CT 06883

Sidney Poitier
9255 Doheny Road
Los Angeles, CA 90069

Markie Post
10153 1/2 Riverside Drive #333
Toluca Lake, CA 91602

Annie Potts
7920 Sunset Blvd. #350
Los Angeles, CA 90046

CCH Pounder
121 N. San Vicente Blvd.
Beverly Hills, CA 90211

Maury Povich
250 W. 57th Street #26W
New York, NY 10019

Jane Powell
150 W. End Avenue #26C
New York, NY 10023

Stefanie Powers
P.O. Box 5087
Sherman Oaks, CA 91403

Paula Prentiss
719 N. Foothill Road
Beverly Hills, CA 90210

Priscilla Presley
1167 Summit Drive
Beverly Hills, CA 90210

Jason Priestly
132 S. Rodeo Drive #300
Beverly Hills, CA 90212

Victoria Principal
120 S. Spalding Drive #205
Beverly Hills, CA 90212

Andrew Prine
3364 Longridge Avenue
Sherman Oaks, CA 91403

Freddie Prinz, Jr
P.O. Box 5617
Beverly Hills, CA 90210

Richard Pryor
16847 Bosque Drive
Encino, CA 91436

Keshia Knight Pulliam
P.O. Box 866
Teaneck, NJ 07666

Bill Pullman
132 S. Rodeo Street #300
Beverly Hills, CA 90212

Linda Purl
10417 Ravenwood Court
Los Angeles, CA 90077

Q — Q

Dennis Quaid
9034 Sunset Blvd. #200
Los Angeles, CA 90069

Randy Quaid
721 N. Bedford Drive
Beverly Hills, CA 90210

Kathleen Quinlan
P.O. Box 861
Rockaway, OR 97136

Aiden Quinn
500 S. Buena Vista Ave. #206
Burbank, CA 91502

Anthony Quinn
P.O. Box 479
Bristol, RL 02809

Francesco Quinn
1230 N. Horn Avenue #730
Los Angeles, CA 90069

R — R

Steve Railback
P.O. Box 1308
Los Angeles, CA 90078

Tony Randall
1 West 81st Street #6D
New York, NY 10024

Theresa Randle
1018 Meadowbrook Avenue
Los Angeles, CA 90019

Sally Jessy Raphael
510 W. 57th Street #200
New York, NY 10019

Phylicia Rashad
888-7th Avenue #602
New York, NY 10106

Dan Rather
524 West 57th Street
New York, NY 10019

Stephen Rea
861 Sutherland Avenue
London W9 ENGLAND

Peter Reckell
8033 Sunset Blvd. #4016
Los Angeles, CA 90046

Robert Redford
1101-E Montana Avenue
Santa Monica, CA 90403

Lynn Redgrave
21342 Colina Drive
Topanga, CA 90290

Vanessa Redgrave
21 Golden Square
London, W1R 3PA, ENGLAND

Christopher Reeve
RR #2
Bedford, NY 10506

Keanu Reeves
9460 Wilshire Blvd., #700
Beverly Hills, CA 90212

Duncan Regehr
2501 Main Street
Santa Monica, CA 90405

Tim Reid
11342 Dona Lisa Drive
Studio City, CA 91604

Judge Reinhold
626 Santa Monica Blvd. #113
Santa Monica, CA 90405

Paul Reiser
11845 W. Olympic Blvd. #1125
Los Angeles, CA 90064

Burt Reynolds
16133 Jupiter Farm Road
Jupiter, FL 33478

Debbie Reynolds
305 Convention Center Drive
Las Vegas, NV 89109

Ving Rhames
751-24th Street
Santa Monica, CA 90402

Christina Ricci
8942 Wilshire Blvd.
Beverly Hills, CA 90211

Branscombe Richmond
5706 Calvin Avenue
Tarzana, CA 91356

Jason James Richter
10683 Santa Monica Blvd.
Los Angeles, CA 90025

Don Rickles
925 N. Alpine Drive
Beverly Hills, CA 90210

Molly Ringwald
9454 Wilshire Blvd. #405
Beverly Hills, CA 90212

John Ritter
15030 Ventura Blvd. #806
Sherman Oaks, CA 91403

Geraldo Rivera
555 W. 57th Street #1100
New York, NY 10019

Joan Rivers
1 E. 62nd Street
New York, NY 10021

Jason Robards
350 Willow Street
Southport, CT 06490

Jane Robelot
524 West 57th Street
New York, NY 10019

Eric Roberts
132 S. Rodeo Drive #300
Beverly Hills, CA 90212

Julia Roberts
6220 Del Valle Drive
Los Angeles, CA 90048

Pernell Roberts
20395 Seaboard Road
Malibu, CA 90265

Tanya Roberts
3500 W. Olive Avenue #1400
Burbank, CA 91505

Cliff Robertson
325 Dunemere Drive
La Jolla, CA 92037

Holly Robinson
10683 Santa Monica Blvd.
Los Angeles, CA 90025

Debbie Rochon
P.O. Box 1299
New York, NY 10007

Lela Rochon
250 W. 57th Street #1610
New York, NY 10107

Mimi Rogers
11693 San Vicente Blvd. #241
Los Angeles, CA 90049

Mr. Rogers (Fred)
4802 - 5th Avenue
Pittsburgh, PA 15213

Roy Rogers
19838 Tomahawk Road
Apple Valley, CA 92307

Tristan Rogers
8550 Holloway Drive #301
Los Angeles, CA 90069

Wayne Rogers
11828 La Grange Avenue
Los Angeles, CA 90025

Rolanda (Watts)
1456-2nd Avenue, #202
New York, NY 10021

Andy Rooney
254 Rowayton Avenue
Rowayton, CT 06853

Michael Rooker
P.O. Box 5617
Beverly Hills, CA 90210

Mickey Rooney
1400 Red Sail Circle
Westlake Village, CA 91361

Roseanne
9100 Wilshire Blvd. #1000W
Los Angeles, CA 90025

Katharine Ross
33050 Pacific Coast Hwy.
Malibu, CA 90265

Isabella Rossellini
745 Fifth Avenue #814
New York, NY 10151

Richard Roundtree
28843 Wagon Road
Agoura Hills, CA 91301

Mickey Rourke
9150 Wilshire Blvd., #350
Beverly Hills, CA 90212

Misty Rowe
50 Pierrepont Drive
Ridgefield, CT 06877

Gena Rowlands
7917 Woodrow Wilson Drive
Los Angeles, CA 90046

Jennifer Rubin
7920 Sunset Blvd. #400
Los Angeles, CA 90046

Zelda Rubinstein
1800 Avenue of the Starts #400
Los Angeles, CA 90067

Mercedes Ruehl
Box 178, Old Chelsea Station
New York, NY 10011

Jennifer Runyon
164 E. Hulls Ridge Court
Boise, ID 83702

Jane Russell
2934 Torito Road
Santa Barbara, CA 93108

Kurt Russell
1900 Avenue of the Stars #1240
Los Angeles, CA 90067

Meg Ryan
11718 Barrington Court #508
Los Angeles, CA 90049

Winona Ryder
10345 West Olympic Blvd.
Los Angeles, CA 90064

S _____ S

Morely Safer
51 West 52nd Street
New York, NY 10019

Katey Sagal
7095 Hollywood Drive #792
Los Angeles, CA 90028

Bob Saget
9150 Wilshire Blvd., #350
Beverly Hills, CA 90212

Eva Marie Saint
10590 Wilshire Blvd. #408
Los Angeles, CA 90024

Pat Sajak
3400 Riverside Drive
Burbank, CA 91505

Soupy Sales
245 E. 35th Street
New York, NY 10016

Emma Samms
2934 1/2 N. Beverly Glen Circle
Suite #417
Los Angeles, CA 90077

Altana Sanchez-Gijon
8730 Sunset Blvd. #490
Los Angeles, CA 90069

Paul Sand
924 Westwood Blvd., #900
Los Angeles, CA 90024

Adam Sandler
5420 Worster Avenue
Van Nuys, CA 91401

Julian Sands
1287 Ozeta Terrace
Los Angeles, CA 90069

Chris Sarandon
9540 Hidden Valley Road
Beverly Hills, CA 90210

Susan Sarandon
40 West 57th Street
New York, NY 10019

Paul Satterfield
P.O. Box 48886A
Los Angeles, CA 90048

Doug Savant
1015 E. Angeleno Avenue
Burbank, CA 91501

Diane Sawyer
77 West 66th Street
New York, NY 10023

Raphael Sbarge
4526 Wilshire Blvd.
Los Angeles, CA 90010

Roy Scheider
P.O. Box 364
Sagaponack, NY 11962

Rick Schroder
9560 Wilshire Blvd. #500
Beverly Hills, CA 90212

Arnold Schwarzenegger
3110 Main Street #300
Santa Monica, CA 90405

Eric Schweig
P.O. Box 5163
Vancouver, B.C. V7B 1MB
CANADA

David Schwimmer
1330 Londonderry Place
Los Angeles, CA 90069

Annabella Sciorra
132 S. Rodeo Drive, #300
Beverly Hills, CA 90212

Tracy Scoggins
3500 W. Olive Avenue #1400
Burbank, CA 91505

George C. Scott
3211 Retreat Court
Malibu, CA 90265

Lizabeth Scott
8277 Hollywood Blvd.
Los Angeles, CA 90069

Willard Scott
30 Rockefeller Plaza #304
New York, NY 10012

Steven Seagal
1021 Stone Canyon Road
Los Angeles, CA 90077

George Segal
8446 1/2 Melrose Place
Los Angeles, CA 90069

Jerry Seinfeld
147 El Camino Drive #205
Beverly Hills, CA 90212

Connie Selleca-Tish
9255 Sunset Blvd. #1010
Los Angeles, CA 90069

Tom Selleck
331 Sage Lane
Santa Monica, CA 90402

Jane Seymour
P.O. Box 548
Agoura, CA 91376

Ted Shackleford
12305 Valleyheart Drive
Studio City, CA 91604

Garry Shandling
9150 Wilshire Blvd., #350
Beverly Hills, CA 90212

Omar Sharif
18 rue Troyan
F-75017 Paris FRANCE

William Shatner
P.O. Box 7401725
Studio City, CA 91604

Helen Shaver
9171 Wilshire Blvd. #436
Beverly Hills, CA 90210

Ally Sheedy
P.O. Box 523
Topanga, CA 90290

Charlie Sheen
1845 Olivera Drive
Agoura Hills, CA 91301

Martin Sheen
6919 Dune Drive
Malibu, CA 90265

Cybill Shepherd
3930 Valley Meadow Road
Encino, CA 91436

Nicholette Sheridan
8730 Shoreham Drive #A
Los Angeles, CA 90069

Brooke Shields
2300 West Sahara #630
Las Vegas, NV 89192

Yoko Shimada
7245 Hillside Avenue #415
Los Angeles, CA 90046

Pauly Shore
8420 Cresthill Road
West Hollywood, CA 90069

Martin Short
760 N. La Cienega Blvd. #200
Los Angeles, CA 90069

Kathy Shower
8383 Wilshire Blvd. #954
Beverly Hills, CA 90211

Kin Shriner
3915 Benedict Canyon
Sherman Oaks, CA 91423

Wil Shriner
5313 Quakertown Avenue
Woodland Hills, CA 91364

Maria Shriver
3110 Main Street #300
Santa Monica, CA 90403

Elizabeth Shue
P.O. Box 464
South Orange, NJ 07079

Henry Silva
8747 Clifton Way #305
Beverly Hills, CA 90210

Ron Silver
6116 Tundall Avenue
Riverdale, NY 10471

Alicia Silverstone
60 McCreery Drive
Hillsborough, CA 94010

Jean Simmons
636 Adelaide Place
Santa Monica, CA 90402

Sinbad
21704 Devonshire #13
Chatsworth, CA 91311

Marc Singer
11218 Canton Drive
Studio City, CA 91604

Gary Sinise
9830 Wilshire Blvd.
Beverly Hills, CA 90212

Red Skelton
P.O. Box 390190
Anza, CA 92539

Tom Skerritt
P.O. Box 2095
Santa Monica, CA 90406

Christian Slater
9150 Wilshire Blvd. #350
Beverly Hills, CA 90212

Allison Smith
1999 Avenue of the Stars #2850
Los Angeles, CA 90067

Buffalo Bob Smith
500 Overlook Drive
Flat Rock, NC 28731

Jaclyn Smith
10398 Sunset Blvd.
Los Angeles, CA 90077

Keely Smith
28011 Paquet Place
Malibu, CA 90265

Wil Smith
330 Bob Hope Drive
Burbank, CA 91523

Jimmy Smits
Box 49922, Barrington Station
Los Angeles, CA 90049

Dick Smothers
6442 Coldwater Canyon Ave. #107-B
North Hollywood, CA 91606

Tom Smothers
6442 Coldwater Canyon Ave. #107-B
North Hollywood, CA 91606

Wesley Snipes
9701 Wilshire Blvd., 10th Floor
Beverly Hills, CA 90212

Carrie Snodgress
16650 Schoenborn
Sepulveda, CA 91343

Tom Snyder
1225 Beverly Estates Drive
Beverly Hills, CA 90210

Suzanne Somers
8899 Beverly Blvd., #713
Los Angeles, CA 90048

Elke Sommer
Atzelaberger Street 46
D-19080 Maloffstein, GERMANY

David Soul
4337 Tioga Street
Duluth, MN 55804

Sissy Spacek
Beau Val Farm
Route 22, #640
Cobham, VA 22929

Kevin Spacey
120 W. 45th Street #3600
New York, NY 10036

David Spade
9150 Wilshire Blvd. #350
Beverly Hills, CA 90212

James Spader
9530 Heather Road
Beverly Hills, CA 90210

Robert Stack
321 St. Pierre Road
Los Angeles, CA 90077

Leslie Stahl
524 West 57th Street
New York, NY 10019

Frank Stallone
10668 Eastborne Avenue #206
Los Angeles, CA 90025

Sylvester Stallone
100 SE 32nd Road
Coconut Grove, FL 33129

John Stamos
9255 Sunset Blvd. #1010
Los Angeles, CA 90069

Florence Stanley
P.O. Box 48876
Los Angeles, CA 90048

Harry Dean Stanton
14527 Mulholland Drive
Los Angeles, CA 90077

Jean Stapleton
5757 Wilshire Blvd. #512
Los Angeles, CA 90036

Mary Steenburgen
165 Cooper Cliff Lane
Sedona, AZ 86336

Andrew Stevens
9300 Wilshire Blvd. #400
Beverly Hills, CA 90212

Stella Stevens
2180 Coldwater Canyon
Beverly Hills, CA 90210

Parker Stevenson
4526 Wilshire Blvd.
Los Angeles, CA 90010

Ben Stiller
9660 Wilshire Blvd. #516
Beverly Hills, CA 90212

Dean Stockwell
9630 Keokuk Avenue
Chatsworth, CA 91311

Guy Stockwell
6652 Coldwater Canyon Avenue
North Hollywood, CA 91606

John Stockwell
344 S. Rossmore Avenue
Los Angeles, CA 90029

Madeleine Stowe
10345 W. Olympic Blvd. #200
Los Angeles, CA 90064

Marcia Strassman
4928 Bluebell Avenue
Valley Villagte, CA 91607

Meryl Streep
9830 Wilshire Blvd.
Beverly Hills, CA 90212

Sally Struthers
9100 Wilshire Blvd., #1000 West
Beverly Hills, CA 90212

Donald Sutherland
760 N. La Cienega Blvd. #300
Los Angeles, CA 90069

Kiefer Sutherland
132 So. Rodeo Drive, #300
Beverly Hills, CA 90212

Bo Svenson
15332 Antioch Street #356
Pacific Palisades, CA 90272

Michael Swan
15315 Magnolia Blvd. #429
Sherman Oaks, CA 91403

Don Swayze
247 S. Beverly Drive #102
Beverly Hills, CA 90212

Patrick Swayze
132 So. Rodeo Drive, #300
Beverly Hills, CA 90212

D.B. Sweeney
25144 Malibu Road
Malibu, CA 90265

Loretta Swit
10100 Santa Monica Blvd. #2490
Los Angeles, CA 90067

T _____ T

Mr. T
395 Green Bay Road
Lake Forest, IL 60045

George Takei
4368 W. 8th Street #17
Los Angeles, CA 90005

Elizabeth Taylor
P.O. Box 55995
Sherman Oaks, CA 91413

Leigh Taylor-Young
9229 Sunset Blvd. #710
Los Angeles, CA 90069

Meshach Taylor
10100 Santa Monica Blvd., 25th Flr.
Los Angeles, CA 90067

Noah Taylor
P.O. Box 5617
Beverly Hills, CA 90210

John Tesh
14755 Ventura Blvd. #1-916
Sherman Oaks, CA 91403

Lauren Tewes
2739-31st Avenue South
Seattle, WA 98144

Alan Thicke
10505 Sarah
Toluca Lake, CA 91602

Tiffani-Amber Thiessen
3500 W. Olive Avenue #1400
Burbank, CA 91505

Roy Thinnes
15301 Ventura Blvd. #345
Sherman Oaks, CA 91403

Heather Thomas
1433 San Vicente Blvd.
Santa Monica, CA 90402

Henry Thomas
9805 Elmendorf Lavernia Road
San Antonio, TX 78223

Marlo Thomas
420 E. 54th Street #22F
New York, NY 10022

Melody Thomas-Scott
20620 Kingsboro Way
Woodland Hills, CA 91364

Philip Michael Thomas
12615 West Dixie Hwy.
N. Miami, FL 33161

Richard Thomas
4963 Los Feliz Blvd.
Los Angeles, CA 90027

Emma Thompson
56 King's Road
Kingston-upon -Thames
KT2 5HF ENGLAND

Lea Thompson
P.O. Box 5617
Beverly Hills, CA 90210

Linda Thompson
151 El Camino Drive
Beverly Hills, CA 90212

Gordon Thomson
2411 Yonge Street #202
Toronto, Ontario
M4P 2E7 CANADA

Uma Thurman
9830 Wilshire Blvd.
Beverly Hills, CA 90212

Meg Tilly
321 S. Beverly Drive #M
Beverly Hills, CA 90212

Charlene Tilton
22059 Galvez Street
Woodland Hills, CA 91364

Lily Tomlin
P.O. Box 27700
Los Angeles, CA 90027

Angel Tompkins
9812 Video Drive, #101
Los Angeles, CA 90035

Rip Torn
130 W. 42nd Street #2400
New York, NY 10036

Fred Travalena
4515 White Oak Place
Encino, CA 91316

Daniel J. Travanti
1077 Melody Road
Lake Forest, IL 60045

Nancy Travis
231 S. Cliffwood Avenue
Los Angeles, CA 90049

John Travolta
159 Park Avenue
Parkridge, NJ 07656

Alex Trebek
10202 W. Washington Blvd.
Culver City, CA 90232

Christy Turlington
344 E. 59th Street
New York, NY 10022

Kathleen Turner
163 Amsterdam Avenue #210
New York, NY 10023

Nicholas Turturro
5201 Calvin Avenue
Tarzana, CA 91356

Shannon Tweed
9300 Wilshire Blvd., #410
Beverly Hills, CA 90212

Cicely Tyson
315 West 70th Street
New York, NY 10023

Richard Tyson
9200 Sunset Blvd. #625
Los Angeles, CA 90069

U _____ U

Anneliese Uhlig
1519 Escalona Drive
Santa Cruz, CA 95060

Dr. Art Ulene
10810 Via Verona
Los Angeles, CA 90024

Liv Ullman
Hafrsfjordgst 7
0273 Oslo, NORWAY

Blair Underwood
5200 Lankershim Blvd. #260
N. Hollywood, CA 90036

Jay Underwood
111 Screenland Drive
Burbank, CA 91505

Robert Urich
P.O. Box 1645
Park City, UT 84060

Bonnie Urseth
9255 Sunset Blvd., #515
Los Angeles, CA 90069

Peter Ustinov
11 Rue de Silly
92100, Boulogne, FRANCE

V   V

Karen Valentine
P.O. Box 1410
Washington Depot, CT 06793

Joan Van Ark
10950 Alta View Drive
Studio City, CA 91604

Jean-Claude Van Damme
P.O. Box 4149
Chatsworth, CA 91313

Mamie Van Doren
428 - 31st Street
Newport Beach, CA 92663

Dick Van Dyke
23215 Mariposa De Oro
Malibu, CA 90265

Jerry Van Dyke
10500 Camarillo Street
Toluca Lake, CA 91602

Dick Van Patten
13920 Magnolia Blvd.
Sherman Oaks, CA 91423

Vincent Van Patten
13926 Magnolia Blvd.
Sherman Oaks, CA 91423

Robert Vaughn
162 Old W. Mountain Road
Ridgefield, CT 06877

Abe Vigoda
8500 Melrose Avenue #208
W. Hollywood, CA 90069

Jan-Michael Vincent
11693 San Vicente Blvd., #296
Los Angeles, CA 90049

Jon Voight
13340 Galewood Drive
Sherman Oaks, CA 91423

Max Von Sydow
avd C-G Rissbery, Box 5209
Stockholm, 10245 SWEDEN

Lark Voorhies
10635 Santa Monica Blvd., #130
Los Angeles, CA 90025

W   W

Lindsay Wagner
P.O. Box 188
Pacific Palisades, CA 90272

Robert Wagner
P.O. Box 933339
Los Angeles, CA 90093

Ken Wahl
480 Westlake Blvd.
Malibu, CA 90265

Christopher Walken
142 Cedar Road
Wilton, CT 06897

Mike Wallace
555 West 57th Street
New York, NY 10019

Barbara Walters
33 West 60th Street
New York, NY 10023

Jamie Walters
4702 Ethel Avenue
Sherman Oaks, CA 91423

Judge Joseph Wapner
16616 Park Lane Place
Los Angeles, CA 90049

Fred Ward
1214 Cabrillo Avenue
Venice, CA 90291

Megan Ward
1999 Avenue of the Stars #2850
Los Angeles, CA 90067

Sela Ward
289 S. Robertson Blvd. #469
Beverly Hills, CA 90211

Marsha Warfield
P.O. Box 691713
Los Angeles, CA 90069

Julie Warner
9830 Wilshire Blvd.
Beverly Hills, CA 90212

Malcolm-Jamal Warner
15303 Ventura Blvd. #1100
Sherman Oaks, CA 91403

Lesley Ann Warren
2934 Beverly Glen Circle #372
Los Angeles, CA 90077

Denzel Washington
4701 Sancola
Toluca Lake, CA 91602

Keenan Ivory Wayans
16405 Mulholland Drive
Los Angeles, CA 90049

Shawn Weatherly
12203 Octagon Street
Los Angeles, CA 90049

Carl Weathers
10960 Wilshire Blvd. #826
Los Angeles, CA 90024

Dennis Weaver
P.O. Box 257
Ridgeway, CO 81432

Sigourney Weaver
200 W. 57th Street #1306
New York, NY 10019

Bruce Weitz
5030 Arundel Drive
Woodland Hills, CA 91364

Raquel Welch
540 Evelyn Place
Beverly Hills, CA 90210

Tahnee Welch
134 Duane Street #400
New York, NY 10013

Tuesday Weld
40 West 57th Street
New York, NY 10019

George Wendt
3856 Vantage Avenue
Studio City, CA 91604

Patricia Wettig
5855 Topanga Canyon #410
Woodland Hills, CA 91367

Wil Wheaton
2820 Honolulu #255
Verdugo City, CA 91043

Lisa Whelchel
30408 Olympic Street
Castaic, CA 91384

Forest Whitaker
1990 S. Bundy Drive #200
Los Angeles, CA 90025

Jaleel White
151 El Camino Drive
Beverly Hills, CA 90212

Vanna White
3400 Riverside Drive
Burbank, CA 91505

Stuart Whitman
749 San Ysidro Road
Santa Barbara, CA 93108

James Whitmore
4990 Puesta Del Sol
Malibu, CA 90265

Gene Wilder
1511 Sawtelle Blvd. #155
Los Angeles, CA 90025

Billy Dee Williams
9255 Sunset Blvd. #404
Los Angeles, CA 90069

Cindy Williams
7023 Birdview Avenue
Malibu, CA 90265

Jobeth Williams
9911 W. Pico Blvd. #PH1
Los Angeles, CA 90035

Kimberly Williams
151 El Camino Drive
Beverly Hills, CA 90212

Montel Williams
435 W. 53rd Street
New York, NY 10019

Robin Williams
1100 Wall Road
Napa, CA 94558

Bruce Willis
1453 Third Street #420
Santa Monica, CA 90401

Star Guide 1998-1999   TV/Movies

Flip Wilson
21970 Pacific Coast Hwy.
Malibu, CA 90265

Mara Wilson
3500 West Olive, #1400
Burbank, CA 91505

Rita Wilson
23414 Malibu Colony Road
Malibu, CA 90265

Paul Winfield
5693 Holly Oak Drive
Los Angeles, CA 90068

Oprah Winfrey
P.O. Box 909715
Chicago, IL 60690

Debra Winger
P.O. Box 9078
Van Nuys, CA 91409

Henry Winkler
P.O. Box 49914
Los Angeles, CA 90049

Kate Winslet
503/504 Lotts Road
The Chambers, Chelsea Harbour
London SWIO OXF, ENGLAND

Y

Amy Yasbeck
606 N. Larchmont Blvd. #309
Los Angeles, CA 90004

Jonathan Winters
4310 Arcola Avenue
Toluca Lake, CA 91602

Shelly Winters
457 N. Oakhurst Drive
Beverly Hills, CA 90210

Billy Wirth
9255 Sunset Blvd., #1010
Los Angeles, CA 90069

Elijah Wood
9150 Wilshire Blvd., #350
Beverly HIlls, CA 90212

James Woods
760 N. La Cienega Blvd.
Los Angeles, CA 90069

Edward Woodward
Ravens Court
Calstock, Cornwall
PL18 9ST ENGLAND

Joanne Woodward
555 Long Wharf Drive
New Haven, CT 06511

Jane Wyman
56 Kavendish Drive
Rancho Mirage, CA 92270

Y

Robert Young
31589 Saddletree Drive
Westlake Village, CA 91361

Sean Young
P.O. Box 20547
Sedona, AZ 86341

Henny Youngman
77 West 55th Street
New York, NY 10019

Z _____ Z

Grace Zabriskie
1800 S. Robertson Blvd. #426
Los Angeles, CA 90035

Jacklyn Zeman
6930 Dume Drive
Malibu, CA 90265

Pia Zadora
9560 Wilshire Blvd.
Beverly Hills, CA 90212

Ian Ziering
2700 Jalmia Drive
West Hollywood, CA 90046

Paula Zahn
524 West 57th Street
New York, NY 10019

Efrem Zimbalist, Jr.
1448 Holsted Drive
Solvang, CA 93463

Steve Zahn
2372 Veteran Avenue #102
Los Angeles, CA 90064

Stephanie Zimbalist
16255 Ventura Blvd. #1011
Encino, CA 91436

Roxana Zal
1450 Belfast Drive
Los Angeles, CA 90069

Kim Zimmer
25561 Almendra Drive
Santa Clarita, CA 91355

Billy Zane
450 N. Rossmore Avenue #1001
Los Angeles, CA 90004

Adrian Zmed
22103 Avenida Morelos
Woodland Hills, CA 91364

Carmen Zapata
6107 Ethel Avenue
Van Nuys, CA 91405

Daphne Zuniga
P.O. Box 1249
White River Junction, VT 05001

Music

A   A

Paula Abdul
14755 Ventura Blvd., #I-710
Sherman Oaks, CA 91403

AC/DC
46 Kensington Ct. St.
London W8 5DP ENGLAND

Bryan Adams
406 - 68 Water Street
Vancouver, BC, V6B 1A3 CANADA

ADC Band
17397 Santa Barbara
Detroit, MI 48221

Aerosmith
P.O. Box 882494
San Francisco, CA 94188

Air Supply
14755 Ventura Blvd. #1-710
Sherman Oaks, CA 91403

Alabama
P.O. Box 529
Ft. Payne, AL 35967

Brick Alan
976 Murfreesboro Road, #93
Nashville, TN 37217

Alice In Chains
207 1/2 First Avenue So., #300
Seattle, WA 98104

Mose Allison
34 Dogwood Street
Smithtown, NY 11787

Greg Allman
650 California Street, #900
San Francisco, CA 94108

Herb Alpert
31930 Pacific Coast Hwy.
Malibu, CA 90265

America
345 N. Maple Drive, #300
Beverly Hills, CA 90210

Tori Amos
P.O. Box 8456
Clearwater, FL 34618

Lynn Anderson
514 Fairlane Drive
Nashville, TN 37211

Julie Andrews
P.O. Box 666
Beverly Hills, CA 90213

Patti Andrews
9823 Aldea Avenue
Northridge, CA 91354

Paul Anka
10573 W. Pico Blvd., #159
Los Angeles, CA 90064

Adam Ant
503 The Chambers
Chelsea Harbour, Lots Road
London SW10 OXF ENGLAND

Ray Anthony
9288 Kinglet Drive
Los Angeles, CA 90069

Arrested Development
9380 SW 72nd Street #B-220
Miami, FL 33174

Ashford & Simpson
254 W. 72nd Street #1A
New York, NY 10023

Vladimir Ashkenazv
Sonnenhof 4
6004, Lucerne, SWITZERLAND

Asleep At The Wheel
P.O. Box 463
Austin, TX 75767

Rick Astley
4-7 The Vineyard Sanctuary
London SE1 1QL ENGLAND

Frankie Avalon
4303 Spring Forest Lane
Westlake Village, CA 91362

Hoyt Axton
102 Bedford Street, #102
Hamilton, MT 59840

Charles Aznavour
76-78 ave. des Champs Elysses
F-75008 Paris FRANCE

B _____ B

B-52's
P.O. Box 60468
Rochester, NY 14606

Babyface
8255 Beverly Blvd.
Los Angeles, CA 90048

Burt Bacharach
10 Ocean Park Blvd. #4
Santa Monica, CA 90405

Joan Baez
P.O. Box 1026
Menlo Park, CA 94025

Anita Baker
8216 Tivoli Cove Drive
Las Vegas, NV 89128

Hank Ballard
11457 Harrisburg Road
Los Alamitos, CA 90720

Kaye Ballard
P.O. Box 922
Rancho Mirage, CA 92270

Shirley Bassey
24 Avenue Princess Grace #1200
Monte Carlo MONACO

Kathleen Battle
165 West 57th Street
New York, NY 10019

Bay City Rollers
27 Preston Grange
Road Preston Pans. East
Lothian, SCOTLAND

Beach Boys
4860 San Jacinto Circle #F
Fallbrook, CA 92028

Beastie Boys
3575 Cahuenga Blvd. West, #450
Los Angeles, CA 90068

Beavis & Butt-Head
1515 Braodway #400
New York, NY 10036

Beck
1325 Avenue of the Americas
New York, NY 10019

The Bee-Gees
1801 Bay Road
Miami Beach, FL 33139

Harry Belafonte
300 West End Avenue, #5A
New York, NY 10023

Archie Bell
P.O. Box 11669
Knoxville, TN 37939

Bell Biv Devoe
P.O. Box 604
San Francisco, CA 94101

Bellamy Brothers
13917 Restless Lane
Dade City, FL 33525

Pat Benatar
5721 Bonsall Road
Malibu, CA 90265

Tony Bennett
101 W. 55th Street #9A
New York, NY 10019

George Benson
519 Next Day Hill Drive
Englewood, NJ 07631

Chuck Berry
Buckner Road - Berry Park
Wentzville, MO 63385

Clint Black
6255 Sunset Blvd., #1111
Hollywood, CA 90028

Black Oak Arkansas
1487 Red Fox Run
Lilburn, GA 30247

Blood, Sweat & Tears
43 Washington Street
Groveland, MA 01834

Blur
20 Manchester Square
London W1A 1ES ENGLAND

Suzy Bogguss
33 Music Square W., #110
Nashville, TN 37203

Michael Bolton
92 Snowberry Lane
New Canaan, CT 06840

Jon Bon Jovi
250 W. 57th Street, #603
New York, NY 10107

Gary "US" Bonds
141 Dunbar Avenue
Fords, NJ 08863

Debbie Boone
4334 Kester Avenue
Sherman Oaks, CA 91403

Pat Boone
904 N. Beverly Drive
Beverly Hills, CA 90210

Victor Borge
Fieldpoint Park
Greenwich, CT 06830

David Bowie
76 Oxford Street
London WIN OAX ENGLAND

Boxcar Willie
199 E. Garfield Road
Aurora, OH 44202

The Boys
P.O. Box 5482
Carson, CA 90746

Boyz II Men
5750 Wilshire Blvd., #300
Los Angeles, CA 90036

Toni Braxton
3350 Peachtree Road #1500
Atlanta, GA 30326

Garth Brooks
3322 West End Avenue #1100
Nashville, TN 37203

James Brown
1217 West Medical Park Road
Augusta, GA 30909

Les Brown
1417 Capri Drive
Pacific Palisades, CA 90272

T. Graham Brown
P.O. Box 50337
Nashville, TN 37205

Jackson Browne
2745 Kling Street
Studio City, CA 91604

Dave Brubeck
221 Millstone Road
Wilton, CT 06807

Lindsey Buckingham
900 Airole Way
Los Angeles, CA 90077

Jimmy Buffett
500 Duval Street #B
Key West, FL 33040

Bush
10900 Wilshire Blvd., #1230
Los Angeles, CA 90024

C _____ C

Glen Campbell
28 Biltmore Est.
Phoenix, AZ 85016

Luther Campbell
8400 N.E. 2nd Avenue
Miami, FL 33138

Freddie Cannon
18641 Cassandra Street
Tarzana, CA 91356

Irene Cara
1560 Broadway, #1308
New York, NY 10036

Mariah Carey
P.O. Box 4450
New York, NY 10101

Belinda Carlisle
23922 De Ville Way
Malibu, CA 90265

Kim Carnes
2031 Old Natchez Terrace
Franklin, TN 37064

Mary-Chapin Carpenter
1250-6th Street #401
Santa Monica, CA 90401

Richard Carpenter
9386 Raviller Drive
Downey, CA 90240

Vikki Carr
3102 Iron Stone Lane
San Antonio, TX 78203

Jose Carreras
via Augusta 59
E-08006 Barcelona SPAIN

Betty Carter
307 Lake Street
San Francisco, CA 94118

Carlene Carter
50 W. Main Street
Ventura, CA 93001

Deana Carter
9830 Wilshire Blvd.
Beverly Hills, CA 90212

Johnny Cash
700 E. Main Street
Hendersonville, TN 37075

David Cassidy
3799 Las Vegas Blvd. South
Las Vegas, NV 89109

Shaun Cassidy
19425 Shirley Court
Tarzana, CA 91356

Peter Cetera
1880 Century Park East #900
Los Angeles, CA 90067

Ray Charles
2107 W. Washington Blvd., #200
Los Angeles, CA 90018

Chubby Checker
1646 Hilltop Road
Birchrunville, PA 19421

Cher
P.O. Box 960
Beverly Hills, CA 90213

Mark Chestnut
P.O. Box 128031
Nashville, TN 37212

Eric Clapton
46 Kensington Court
London WE8 5DT ENGLAND

Dick Clark
3003 W. Olive Avenue
Burbank, CA 91505

Roy Clark
1800 Forrest Blvd.
Tulsa, OK 74114

Van Cliburn
455 Wilder Place
Shreveport, LA 71104

Rosemary Clooney
1019 N. Roxbury Drive
Beverly Hills, CA 90210

The Coasters
4905 S. Atlantic Avenue
Daytona Beach, FL 32127

Iron Eyes Cody
2013 Griffith Park Blvd.
Los Angeles, CA 90039

Natalie Cole
955 South Carrillo Drive #200
Los Angeles, CA 90048

Mark Collie
3322 West End Avenue #520
Nashville, TN 37203

Judy Collins
450-7th Avenue #603
New York, NY 10123

Phil Collins
729 Seventh Avenue #1600
New York, NY 10019

Jessie Colter
1117 - 17th Avenue South
Nashville, TN 37212

Perry Como
305 Northern Blvd. #3A
Great Neck, NY 11021

Harry Connick, Jr.
260 Brookline Street
Cambridge, MA 02139

Rita Coolidge
1330 N. Wetherly Drive
Los Angeles, CA 90069

Alice Cooper
4135 E. Keim Street
Paradise Valley, AZ 85253

Chick Corea
2635 Griffith Park Blvd.
Los Angeles, CA 90039

Christopher Cross
P.O. Box 63
Marble Falls, TX 78654

Elvis Costello
9028 Great Guest Road
Middlesex TW8 9EW, ENGLAND

Sheryl Crow
10345 W. Olympic Blvd., #200
Los Angeles, CA 90064

Billy "Crash" Craddock
3007 Old Martinsville Road
Greensboro, NC 27455

Rodney Crowell
1111 - 16th Avenue South #302
Nashville, TN 37212

David Crosby
P.O. Box 9008
Solvang, CA 93464

Cherie Currie
3050 N. Chandelle Road
Los Angeles, CA 90046

Crosby, Stills, & Nash
14930 Ventura Blvd., #206
Sherman Oaks, CA 91403

Billy Ray Cyrus
P.O. Box 1206
Franklin, TN 37065

D   D

Roger Daltry
18/21 Jermyn Street #300
London SW1Y 6HP ENGLAND

John Davidson
6051 Spring Valley Road
Hidden Hills, CA 91302

Vic Damone
P.O. Box 2999
Beverly Hills, CA 90213

Jimmy Dean
8000 Centerview Parkway #400
Cordova, TN 38018

Charlie Daniels Band
17060 Central Pike
Lebanon, TX 37087

Deep Purple
3 E. 54th Street, #1400
New York, NY 10022

Terence Trent D'Arby
9830 Wilshire Blvd.
Beverly HIlls, CA 90212

Rick Dees
3400 Riverside Dr., #800
Burbank, CA 91505

Def Leppard
72 Chancellor's Road
London W6 9QB ENGLAND

John Denver
P.O. Box 1587
Aspen, CO 81612

Depeche Mode
P.O. Box 1281
London, N1 9UX, ENGLAND

Neil Diamond
10345 W. Olympic Blvd., #200
Los Angeles, CA 90064

Diamond Rio
242 W. Main Street #236
Hendersonville, TN 37075

Bo Diddley
1560 Broadway, #1308
New York, NY 10036

Joe Diffie
P.O. Box 479
Velma, OK 73091

Celine Dion
C.P. 65 Repentiguy
Quebec J6A 5H7 CANADA

Dire Straits
509 Hartnell Street
Monterey, CA 93940

Mickey Dolenz
9000 Sunset Blvd. #1200
Los Angeles, CA 90069

Placido Domingo
150 Central Park South
New York, NY 10019

Fats Domino
5515 Marais Street
New Orleans, LA 70117

Doobie Brothers
15140 Sonoma Hwy.
Glen Ellen, CA 95442

The Doors
3011 Ledgewood Drive
Los Angeles, CA 90068

The Drifters
10 Chelsea Court
Neptune, NJ 07753

Peter Duchin
305 Madison Avenue #956
New York, NY 10165

Sandy Duncan
44 W. 77th Street, #1B
New York, NY 10024

Holly Dunn
209 10th Avenue So., #347
Nashville, TN 37203

Duran Duran
P.O. Box 21
London, W10 6XA, ENGLAND

Bob Dylan
P.O. Box 870, Cooper Station
New York, NY 10276

E   E

Duane Eddy
1228-17th Avenue South #2
Nashville, TN 37111

Electric Light Orchestra
9850 Sandalfoot Blvd., #458
Boca Raton, FL 33428

Larry Elgart
2065 Gulf Of Mexico Drive
Longboat Key, FL 34228

En Vogue
151 El Camino
Beverly Hills, CA 90212

John Entwhistle
1705 Queen Court
Los Angeles, CA 90068

Gloria Estefan
555 Jefferson Avenue
Miami Beach, FL 33139

Melissa Etheridge
P.O. Box 884563
San Francisco, CA 94188

Kevin Eubanks
173 Brighton Avenue
Boston, MA 02134

Everly Brothers
277 Comroe Road
Nashville, TN 37211

Extreme
189 Carlton Street
Toronto, Ontario
M5A 2K7 CANADA

F   F

Faith No More
5550 Wilshire Blvd., #202
Los Angeles, CA 90036

Marianne Faithfull
Yew Tree Cottage
Aidworth, Berks., ENGLAND

Lola Falana
1201 "N" Street, NW #A-5
Washington DC 20005

Donna Fargo
P.O. Box 150527
Nashville, TN 37215

Fat Boys
250 W. 57th Street, #1723
New York, NY 10107

Dr. Feelgood
3 E. 54th Street
New York, NY 10022

Jose Feliciano
266 Lyons Plain Road
Weston, CT 06883

Freddy Fender
P.O. Box 270540
Corpus Christi, TX 78427

Maynard Ferguson
P.O. Box 716
Ojai, CA 93023

Ferrante & Teicher
12224 Avila Drive
Kansas City, MO 64145

The Firm
57A Great Titchfield Street
London, W1P 7FL, ENGLAND

Eddie Fisher
10000 North Point Street #1802
San Francisco, CA 94109

Roberta Flack
1 West 72nd Street
New York, NY 10023

Flash Cadillac
433 E. Cucharras Street
Colorado Springs, CO 80903

Mick Fleetwood
4905 S. Atlantic Avenue
Daytona Beach, FL 32127

Myron Floren
26 Georgeff Road
Rolling Hills, CA 90274

Dan Fogelberg
P.O. Box 2399
Pagosa Springs, CO 81147

Foreigner
640 Lee Road, #106
Wayne, PA 19087

Forester Sisters
P.O. Box 1456
Trenton, GA 30752

Pete Fountain
237 North Peters Street #400
New Orleans, LA 71030

The Four Seasons
P.O. Box 262
Carteret, NJ 07008

Peter Frampton
7411 Center Bay Drive
North Bay Village, FL 33141

Connie Francis
50 Sullivan Drive
West Orange, NJ 07052

Aretha Franklin
P.O. Box 12137
Birmingham, MI 48012

Glen Frey
5020 Brent Knoll Lane
Suwanee, GA 30174

Janie Fricke
P.O. Box 798
Lancaster, TX 75146

G   G

Kenny G
3500 W. Olive Avenue #680
Burbank, CA 91505

Art Garfunkel
9 East 79th Street
New York, NY 10021

Larry Gatlin
Fantasy Harbour, Waccamaw
Myrtle Beach, SC 29577

Crystal Gayle
51 Music Square East
Nashville, TN 37203

Gloria Gaynor
P.O. Box 374
Fairview, NJ 07010

David Geffen
9110 Sunset Blvd., #3
Los Angeles, CA 90069

Sir Bob Geldof
Davington Priory, Faversham
Kent, ENGLAND

Genesis
25 Ives Street
London, SW3, ENGLAND

Bobby Gentry
8 Tidewater Way
Savannah, GA 31411

Boy George (O'Dowd)
7 Pepy's Ct., 84 The Chase
Clapham, London SW4 0NF
ENGLAND

Barry Gibb
3088 South Mann
Las Vegas, NV 89102

Debbie Gibson
300 Main Street #201
Huntington, NY 11743

Johnny Gill
17539 Corinthian Drive
Encino, CA 91316

Mickey Gilley
P.O. Box 1242
Pasadena, TX 77501

Philip Glass
231 - 2nd Avenue
New York, NY 10003

Bobby Goldsboro
P.O. Box 5250
Ocala, FL 32678

Berry Gordy
878 Stradella Road
Los Angeles, CA 90077

Lesley Gore
170 E. 77th Street #2A
New York, NY 10021

Eydie Gorme
820 Greenway Drive
Beverly Hills, CA 90210

Robert Goulet
3110 Monte Rosa
Las Vegas, NV 89120

Amy Grant
2910 Poston Avenue
Nashville, TN 37203

Grateful Dead
P.O. Box 1073-C
San Rafael, CA 94915

Rev. Al Green
P.O. Box 456
Memphis, TN 38083

Lee Greenwood
P.O. Box 430
Kodak, TN 37764

Guns & Roses
83 Riverside Drive
New York, NY 10024

Arlo Guthrie
The Farm
Washington, MA 01223

H   H

Sammy Hagar
8502 Fathom Drive
Baldwinsville, CA 13027

Merle Haggard
3009 East Street
Sevierville, TN 37862

Hall & Oates
130 W. 57th Street #2A
New York, NY 10019

Tom T. Hall
P.O. Box 1246
Franklin, TN 37065

Marvin Hamlisch
970 Park Avenue #501
New York, NY 10028

Lionel Hampton
575 Laramie Lane
Mahwah, NJ 07430

Herbie Hancock
3 East 28th Street #600
New York, NY 10016

EmmyLou Harris
P.O. Box 158568
Nashville, TN 37215

George Harrison
Friar Park Road
Henly-On-Thames, ENGLAND

Deborah Harry
156 W. 56th Street, Fifth Floor
New York, NY 10019

Corey Hart
81 Hymus Blvd.
Montreal, PQ Que. H9R 1E2
CANADA

Richie Havens
123 West 44th Street #11A
New York, NY 10036

Edwin Hawkins
2041 Locust Street
Philadelphia, PA 19103

Isaac Hayes
504 W. 168th Street
New York, NY 10032

Heart
9220 Sunset Blvd., #320
Los Angeles, CA 90069

Don Henley
13601 Ventura Blvd., #99
Sherman Oaks, CA 91423

Faith Hill
480 Glen Arbor Circle
Cordova, TN 37018

Al Hirt
3530 Rue Delphine
New Orleans, LA 70131

Hole
955 S. Carrillo Drive, #200
Los Angeles, Ca 90048

Hootie & the Blowfish
2321 Devine Street
Columbia, SC 29205

Linda Hopkins
382 N. Lemon
Walnut, CA 91789

Lena Horne
23 East 74th Street
New York, NY 10021

Bruce Hornsby
P.O. Box 3545
Williamsburg, VA 23187

Thelma Houston
4296 Mt. Vernon
Los Angeles, CA 90008

Whitney Houston
2160 N. Central Road
Ft. Lee, NJ 07024

Englebert Humperdinck
10100 Sunset Blvd.
Los Angeles, CA 90077

I   I

Ice Cube
6809 Victoria Avenue
Los Angeles, CA 90043

Ice-Tea
2287 Sunset Plaza Drive
Los Angeles, CA 90069

Billy Idol
7314 Woodrow Wilson Drive
Los Angeles, CA 90046

Julio Iglesias
5 Indian Creek Drive
Miami, FL 33154

Indigo Girls
755 1st National Bank Bldg.
Decatur, GA 30030

The Isley Brothers
1211 Sunset Plaza Drive #110
Los Angeles, CA 90069

J _____ J

Alan Jackson
1101-17th Avenue South
Nashville, TN 37212

Freddie Jackson
231 W. 58th Street
New York, NY 10019

Janet Jackson
14755 Ventura Blvd. #1-170
Sherman Oaks, CA 91403

Jermaine Jackson
4641 Hayvenhurst Avenue
Encino, CA 91316

Joe Jackson
6 Pembridge Road
Trinity House #200
London, W11, ENGLAND

Marlon Jackson
4641 Hayvenhurst Avenue
Encino, CA 91316

Michael Jackson
Neverland Ranch
Los Olivos, CA 93441

Tito Jackson
23726 Long Valley Road
Hidden Hills, CA 91302

Mick Jagger
304 West 81st Street
New York, NY 10024

Etta James
4031 Panama Court
Piedmont, CA 94611

Janes's Addiction
8800 Sunset Blvd. #401
Los Angeles, CA 90069

Al Jarreau
1543-7th Street #3
Santa Monica, CA 90401

Waylon Jennings
824 Old Hickory Blvd.
Brentwood, TN 37027

Jethro Tull
2 Wansdown Pl., Fulham
London SW6 ENGLAND

Joan Jett
155 E. 55th Street, #6H
New York, NY 10022

Jewel
P.O. Box 33494
San Diego, CA 92163

Billy Joel
280 Elm Street
Southampton, NY 11968

Elton John
2660 Peachtree Street NW, P.H.
Atlanta, GA 30305

Davey Jones
P.O. Box 400
Beavertown, PA 17813

Jesus Jones
729-7th Avenue #1600
New York, NY 10019

Quincy Jones
3800 Barham Blvd. #503
Los Angeles, CA 90068

Rickie Lee Jones
476 Broome Street #6A
New York, NY 10013

Tom Jones
363 Copa de Oro Road
Los Angeles, CA 90077

Montel Jordan
629 Fifth Avenue
Pelham, NY 10803

Journey
650 California Street #900
San Francisco, CA 94108

Naomi Judd
P.O. Box 682068
Franklin, TN 37068

K   K

K.C. & the Sunshine Band
4550 Biscayne Blvd., PH
Miami, FL 33137

Casey Kasem
138 N. Mapleton Drive
Los Angeles, CA 90077

Hal Ketchum
1700 Hayes Street #304
Nashville, TN 37203

Chaka Khan
P.O. Box 16680
Beverly Hills, CA 90209

B.B. King
1414 Sixth Avenue
New York, NY 10019

Ben E. King
P.O. Box 1094
Teaneck, NJ 07666

Carole King
509 Hartnell Street
Monterey, CA 93940

Kiss
P.O. Box 827
Hagerstown, MD 21741

Gladys Knight
2801 Yorkshire Avenue
Henderson, NV 89014

Mark Knopfler
10 Southwick Mews
London SW2 ENGLAND6

Kool & The Gang
89 Fifth Avenue, #700
New York, NY 10003

Alison Krauss
1017-16th Avenue South
Nashville, TN 37212

Lenny Kravitz
14681 Harrison Street
Miami, FL 33176

Kris Kristofferson
P.O. Box 2147
Malibu, CA 90265

L _____ L

Patti LaBelle
1212 Grennox Road
Wynnewood, PA 19096

K.D. Lang
Box 33800, Station D
Vancouver B.C.
V6J 5C7 CANADA

Cyndi Lauper
2211 Broadway #10F
New York, NY 10024

Tracy Lawrence
2100 West End Avenue #1000
Nashville, TN 37203

Chris Ledoux
4205 Hillsboro Road #208
Nashville, TN 37215

Brenda Lee
2175 Carson Street
Nashville, TN 37210

Julian Lennon
12721 Mulholland Drive
Beverly Hills, CA 90210

Sean Lennon
1 W. 72nd Street
New York, NY 10023

LeVert
110 - 112 Lantoga Road #D
Wayne, PA 19087

Huey Lewis
P.O. Box 779
Mill Valley, CA 94942

Jerry Lee Lewis
P.O. Box 3864
Memphis, TN 38173

Gordon Lightfoot
1365 Yonge Street #207
Toronto, Ont. M4T 2P7 CANADA

LL Cool J
160 Varick Street
New York, NY 10013

Kenny Loggins
670 Oak Springs Lane
Santa Barbara, CA 93108

Lost Boys
1775 Broadway #433
New York, NY 10019

Courtney Love
33401 NE 78th Street
Carnation, WA 98014

Patty Loveless
1908 Wedgewood Avenue
Nashville, TN 37212

Lyle Lovett
c/o General Delivery
Klein, TX 77391

Loretta Lynn
P.O. Box 120369
Nashville, TN 37212

Lynyrd Skynyrd
3423 Piedmont Road NE, #220
Atlanta, GA 30305

M   M

Madonna
4519 Cockerham Drive
Los Angeles, CA 90027

Taj Mahal
1671 Appian Way
Santa Monica, CA 90401

The Mamas & The Papas
108 E. Matilija Street
Ojai, CA 93023

Melissa Manchester
15822 High Knoll Road
Encino, CA 91436

Barbara Mandrell
605-C N. Main Street
Ashland City, TN 37015

Erline Mandrell
605-C N. Main Street
Ashland City, TN 37015

Louise Mandrell
P.O. Box 800
Hendersonville, TN 37077

Barry Manilow
5443 Beethoven Street
Los Angeles, CA 90066

Marilyn Manson
83 Riverside Drive
New York, NY 10024

Marky Mark
63 Pilgrim Road
Braintree, MA 02184

Ziggy Marley
Jack's Hill
Kingston, JAMAICA

Branford Marsalis
3 Hastings Square
Cambridge, MA 02139

Wynton Marsalis
3 Lincoln Center #2911
New York, NY 10023

Richard Marx
15250 Ventura Blvd. #900
Sherman Oaks, CA 91403

Johnny Mathis
3500 W. Olive Avenue #750
Burbank, CA 91505

Paul McCartney
Waterfall Estate Peamarsh
St. Leonard on the Sea
Sussex, ENGLAND

Marilyn McCoo
2639 Lavery Court #5
Newbury Park, CA 91320

"Country Joe" McDonald
17337 Ventura Blvd. #208
Encino, CA 91316

Reba McEntyre
40 Music Square West
Nashville, TN 37203

Bobby McFerrin
826 Broadway, #400
New York, NY 10003

Maureen McGovern
163 Amsterdam Avenue, #174
New York, NY 10023

Tim McGraw
3310 West End Avenue #500
Nashville, TN 37203

The McGuire Sisters
100 Rancho Circle
Las Vegas, NV 89119

Zubin Mehta
27 Oakmont Drive
Los Angeles, CA 90049

John Mellencamp
Rt. 1, Box 361
Nashville, IN 47448

Sergio Mendez
4849 Encino Avenue
Encino, CA 91316

Menudo
2895 Biscayne Blvd., #455
Miami, FL 33137

Sir Yehudi Menuhin
Buhlstr
CH-3780 Gstaad-Neueret
SWITZERLAND

Metallica
729 7th Avenue, #1400
New York, Ny 10019

Pat Metheny
173 Brighton Avenue
Boston, MA 02134

George Michael
338 N. Foothill Road
Beverly Hills, CA 90210

Bette Midler
135 Watts Street #400
New York, NY 10013

Mitch Miller
345 W. 58th Street
New York, NY 10019

Ronnie Milsap
3015 Theater Drive
Myrtle Beach, SC 29577

Liza Minnelli
P.O. Box 790039
Middle Village, NY 11379

Joni Mitchell
1505 West 2nd Avenue #200
Vancouver BC V6H 3Y4 CANADA

Eddie Money
P.O. Box 429094
San Francisco, CA 94142

Lorrie Morgan
P.O. Box 78
Spencer, TN 37212

Alanis Morissette
75 Rockefeller Plaza #2100
New York, NY 10019

Mark Morrison
28 Kensington Church Street
London W8 4EP ENGLAND

Van Morrison
12304 Santa Monica Blvd. #300
Los Angeles, CA 90025

Motley Crue
40/42 Newman Street
London, W1P 3PA, ENGLAND

Maria Muldaur
311 Oakdale Road
Charlotte, NC 28216

Anne Murray
4950 Yonge Street #2400
Toronto, Ontario, M2N 6K1 CANADA

N   N

Graham Nash
14930 Ventura Blvd., #205
Sherman Oaks, CA 91403

Naughty by Nature
155 Morgan Street
Jersey City, NJ 07302

Star Guide 1998-1999

Music

Willie Nelson
Rt. #1, Briarcliff TT
Spicewood, TX 78669

Peter Nero
11806 N. 56th Street #B
Tampa, FL 33617

Michael Nesmith
2828 Donald Douglas Loop N. #15
Santa Monica, CA 90405

Aaron Neville
P.O. Box 750187
New Orleans, LA 70130

New Edition
151 El Camino Drive
Beverly Hills, CA 90212

New Kids on the Block
27 Dudley Street
Roxbury, MA 02132

Tommy Newsom
19315 Wells Drive
Tarzana, CA 91356

Juice Newton
P.O. Box 3035
Rancho Santa Fe, CA 92067

Wayne Newton
3422 Happy Lane
Las Vegas, NV 89120

Olivia Newton-John
P.O. Box 2710
Malibu, CA 90265

Nirvana
151 El Camino Drive
Beverly Hills, CA 90212

Ted Nugent
8000 Eckert
Concord, MI 49237

O _____ O

Oak Ridge Boys
2102 W. Linden Avenue
Nashville, TN 37212

Billy Ocean
Ascot
Berkshire ENGLAND

The O'Jays
1995 Broadway #501
New York, NY 10023

Mike Oldfield
115-A Glenthorne Road
London W6 0LJ ENGLAND

Yoko Ono (Lennon)
One W. 72nd Street
New York, NY 10023

Tony Orlando
3220 Falls Parkway
Branson, MO 65616

Ozzy Osbourne
66 Malibu Colony Road
Malibu, CA 90265

K. T. Oslin
1103 - 16th Avenue
Nashville, TN 37212

Donny Osmond
36 Avignon
Newport Beach, CA 92657

Marie Osmond
P.O. Box 1990
Branson, MO 65615

Paul Overstreet
P.O. Box 2977
Hendersonville, TN 37077

Buck Owens
3223 Sillect Avenue
Bakersfield, CA 93308

P _____ P

Pablo Cruise
P.O. Box 779
Mill Valley, CA 94941

Patti Page
71537 Hwy. 111 #K
Rancho Mirage, CA 92270

Robert Palmer
584 Broadway #1201
New York, NY 10012

Johnny Paris
1764 Parkway Drive South
Maumee, OH 43537

Dolly Parton
P.O. Box 150307
Nashville, TN 37215

Les Paul
78 Deerhaven Road
Mahwah, NJ 07430

Luciano Pavarotti
Via Giardini
I-41040 Saliceto
Panaro, ITALY

Johnny Paycheck
P.O. Box 121377
Nashville, TN 37212

Peaches & Herb
7319-C Hanover Parkway
Greenbelt, MD 20770

Pearl Jam
417 Denny Way, #200
Seattle, WA 98109

Teddy Pendergrass
1505 Flat Rock Road
Narberth, PA 19072

The Penguins
708 West 137th Street
Gardena, CA 90247

Carl Perkins
27 Sunnymeade Drive
Jackson, TN 38305

Peter, Paul & Mary
301 W. 53rd Street
New York, NY 10019

Oscar Peterson
2421 Hammond Road
Mississagua, Ont. L5K 1T3 CANADA

Tom Petty
4626 Encino Avenue
Encino, CA 91316

Chynna Phillips
10557 Troon Avenue
Los Angeles, CA 90064

Michelle Phillips
9150 Wilshire Blvd. #175
Beverly Hills, CA 90212

Sam Phillips
639 Madison Avenue
Memphis, TN 38103

Wilson Pickett
1560 Broadway #1308
New York, NY 10036

Ray Pillow
Route 4, New Hwy. 96 West
Franklin, TN 37064

Pink Floyd
729 7th Avenue, #1600
New York, NY 10019

The Platters
2756 N. Green Valley Parkway #449
Las Vegas, NV 89014

Poison
1750 North Vine Street
Hollywood, CA 90028

The Police
194 Kensington Park Road
London, W11 2ES, ENGLAND

Iggy Pop
P.O. Box 561
Pine Bush, NY 12565

Billy Preston
4271 Garthwaite Avenue
Los Angeles, CA 90008

Andre Previn
8 Sherwood Lane
Bedford Hills, NY 10507

Leontyne Price
9 Van Dam Street
New York, NY 10003

Charlie Pride
3198 Royal Lane #204
Dallas, TX 75229

Prince (formely known)
9401 Kiowa Trail
Chanhassen, MN 55317

Public Enemy
298 Elizabeth Street
New York, NY 10012

Q _____ Q

Queen
16A High Street Barnes
London SW13 9LW ENGLAND

Quiet Riot
P.O. Box 24455
New Orleans, LA 70184

R _____ R

Eddie Rabbitt
1915 Church Street
Nashville, TN 37203

R.E.M.
P.O. Box 128288
Nashville, TN 37212

Bonnie Raitt
1344 N. Spaulding
Los Angeles, CA 90046

Paul Revere and the Raiders
P.O. Box 544
Grangeville, ID 83530

Eddy Raven
P.O. Box 1402
Hendersonville, TN 37075

Cliff Richard
Portsmouth Road
Box 46A, Esher
Surrey KT10 9AA ENGLAND

Lou Rawls
109 Fremont Place
Los Angeles, CA 90005

Little Richard (Penniman)
Hyatt Sunset Hotel
8401 Sunset Blvd
Los Angeles, CA 90069

Red Hot Chili Peppers
11116 Aqua Vista #39
North Hollywood, CA 91602

Keith Richards
"Redlands"
West Wittering
Chichester, Sussex, ENGLAND

Helen Reddy
820 Stanford
Santa Monica, CA 90403

Lionel Richie
P.o. Box 9055
Calabasas, CA 91372

Martha Reeves
P.O. Box 1987
Paramount, CA 90723

Righteous Brothers
9841 Hot Springs Drive
Huntington Beach, CA 92646

Jeannie C. Riley
P.O. Box 23256
Nashville, TN 37202

Axl Rose
15250 Ventura Blvd. #900
Sherman Oaks, CA 91403

LeAnn Rimes
6060 N. Central Expressway #816
Dallas, TX 75206

Rosemarie
6916 Chisholm Avenue
Van Nuys, CA 91406

Smokey Robinson
17085 Rancho Street
Encino, CA 91316

Diana Ross
Box 11059, Glenville Station
Greenwich, CT 06831

Johnny Rodriquez
P.O. Box 23162
Nashville, TN 37202

David Lee Roth
455 Bradford Street
Pasadena, CA 91105

Kenny Rogers
Rt. 1, Box 100
Colbert, GA 30628

Billy Joe Royal
204 Cherokee Road
Hendersonville, TN 37075

Rolling Stones
P.O. Box 6152
New York, NY 10128

Run-D.M.C.
160 Varick Street
New York, NY 10013

Sonny Rollins
193 Brighton Avenue
Boston, MA 02134

Rupaul
6671 Sunset Blvd. #1590
Hollywood, CA 90028

Linda Ronstadt
644 North Doheny
Los Angeles, CA 90069

Bobby Rydell
917 Bryn Mawr Avenue
Narberth, PA 19072

S _____ S

Sade
41-45 Beak Street
London W1R 3LE ENGLAND

Carole Bayer Sager
10761 Bellagio Road
Los Angeles, CA 90077

Buffy Sainte-Marie
2729 Westshire Drive
Los Angeles, CA 90068

Salt & Pepper
215 East Orangethorpe Ave. #363
Fullerton, CA 92632

Carlos Santana
121 Jordan Street
San Rafael, CA 94901

Boz Scaggs
8900 Wilshire Blvd. #300
Beverly Hills, CA 90211

Lalo Schifrin
710 N. Hillcrest Road
Beverly Hills, CA 90210

Earl Scruggs
P.O. Box 66
Madison, TN 37115

John Sebastian
3520 Hayden Avenue
Culver City, CA 90232

Jon Secada
P.O. Box 4417
Miami, FL 33269

Neil Sedaka
888 - 7th Avenue #1600
New York, NY 10106

Pete Seeger
Duchess Junction, Box 431
Beacon, NY 12508

Bob Seger
567 Purdy
Birmingham, MI 48009

Doc Severinsen
4275 White Pine Lane
Santa Ynez, CA 93460

Sha Na Na
1720 N. Ross Street
Santa Ana, CA 92706

Paul Shaffer
1697 Broadway
New York, NY 10019

Shanice
8455 Fountain Avenue #530
Los Angeles, CA 90069

Artie Shaw
2127 W. Palos Court
Newbury Park, CA 91320

Tommy Shaw
6025 The Comers Parkway #202
Norcross, GA 30092

Shenandoah
1028-B 18th Avenue So.
Nashville, TN 37212

T. G. Sheppard
3341 Arlington Avenue #F-206
Toledo, OH 43614

Bobby Sherman
1870 Sunset Plaza Drive
Los Angeles, CA 90069

Beverly Sills
211 Central Park West #4F
New York, NY 10024

Gene Simmons
2650 Benedict Canyon
Beverly Hills, CA 90210

Paul Simon
110 W. 57th Street #300
New York, NY 10019

Nina Simone
7250 Franklin Avenue #115
New York, NY 10046

Frank Sinatra
915 N. Foothill Road
Beverly Hills, CA 90210

Frank Sinatra, Jr.
2211 Florian Place
Beverly Hills, CA 90210

Nancy Sinatra
P.O. Box 69453
Los Angeles, CA 90069

Tina Sinatra
30966 Broad Beach Road
Malibu, CA 90265

Ricky Skaggs
380 Forest Retreat
Hendersonville, TN 37075

Grace Slick
2548 Laurel Pass
Los Angeles, CA 90046

Smashing Pumpkins
8380 Melrose Avenue, #210
Los Angeles, CA 90069

Vince Smith
P.O. Box 1221
Pottsville, PA 17901

Snoop Doggy Dog
10900 Wilshire Blvd. #1230
Los Angeles, CA 90024

Hank Snow
P.O. Box 1084
Nashville, TN 37202

Sir Georg Solti
Chalet Haut Pre
1884 Villars-sur Ollon
SWITZERLAND

Soundgarden
207 1/2 First Avenue So., #300
Seattle, WA 98104

Phil Spector
1210 South Arroyo Blvd.
Pasadena, CA 91101

Ronnie Spector
39B Mill Plan Road #233
Danbury, CT 06811

Spinal Tap
15250 Ventura Blvd., #1215
Sherman Oaks, Ca 91403

Rick Springfield
9200 Sunset Blvd. #PH 15
Los Angeles, CA 90069

Bruce Springsteen
1224 Benedict Canyon
Beverly Hills, CA 90210

Spyro Gyro
926 Horseshoe Road
Suffern, NY 10301

Billy Squier
P.O. Box 1251
New York, NY 10023

Lisa Stansfield
Box 59, Ashwall
Herfordshire SG7 5NG ENGLAND

Ringo Starr
1541 Ocean Avenue, #200
Santa Monica, CA 90401

Statler Brothers
P.O. Box Box 492
Hernando, MS 38632

Isaac Stern
211 Central Park West
New York, NY 10024

Connie Stevens
8721 Sunset Blvd. #PH 1
Los Angeles, CA 90069

Ray Stevens
1708 Grand Avenue
Nashville, TN 37212

Shadoe Stevens
2570 Benedict Canyon
Beverly Hills, CA 90210

Rod Stewart
3500 W. Olive Avenue #920
Burbank, CA 91505

Sting
2 The Grove,
Highgate Village
London, N6, ENGLAND

Sly Stone
250 West 57th Street #407
New York, NY 10019

George Strait
1000 18th Avenue South
Nashville, TN 37212

Barbra Streisand
301 North Carolwood
Los Angeles, CA 90077

Marty Stuart
119 W. 17th Avenue So.
Nashville, TN 37203

Donna Summer
18165 Eccles
Northridge, CA 91324

Joan Sutherland
c/o Colbert Artists
111 W. 57th Street
New York, NY 10019

Keith Sweat
40 West 57th Street
New York, NY 10019

SWV
35 Hart Street
Brooklyn, NY 11206

T   T

Bernie Taupin
2905 Roundtop Road
Santa Ynez, CA 93460

James Taylor
644 N. Doheny Drive
Los Angeles, CA 90069

The Temptations
1325 Avenue of the Americas
New York, NY 10019

Toni Tennille
3612 Lake View Road
Carson City, NV 89703

Clark Terry
24 Westland Drive
Glen Cove, NY 11542

B.J. Thomas
24 Music Square West #208
Nashville, TN 37203

The Thompson Twins
9 Eccleston Street
London, SW1, ENGLAND

Hank Thompson
5 Rushing Creek Court
Roanoke, TX 76262

Three Degrees
19 The Willows
Maidenhead Road
Windsor, Berk, ENGLAND

Tiffany
2165 East Lemon Heights Drive
Santa Ana, CA 92705

Mel Tillis
P.O. Box 1626
Branson, MO 65616

Pam Tillis
P.O. Box 25304
Nashville, TN 37202

TLC
1325 Avenue of the Americas
New York, NY 10019

Aaron Tippin
P.O. Box 41689
Nashville, TN 37204

Tony! Tony! Tony!
484 Lake Park Avenue #21
Oakland, CA 94610

Mel Torme
1734 Coldwater Canyon
Beverly Hills, CA 90210

Liz Torres
1206 Havenhurst Drive
Los Angeles, CA 90046

Toto
50 West Main Street
Ventura, CA 93001

Randy Travis
P.O. Box 121712
Nashville, TN 37212

Joey Travolta
4975 Chimineas Avenue
Tarzana, CA 91356

Travis Tritt
1112 N. Sherbourne Drive
Los Angeles, CA 90069

Marshall Tucker Band
315 S. Beverly Drive, #206
Beverly Hills, CA 90212

Tanya Tucker
5200 Maryland Way, #202
Brentwood, TN 37027

Tina Turner
3377 Fryman Place
Studio City, CA 91604

2 Live Crew
8400 N.E. 2nd Avenue
Miami, FL 33138

Bonnie Tyler
17 - 19 Soho Square
London W1 ENGLAND

U   U

U2
119 Rockland Center, Box 350
Nanuet, NY 10954

UFO
10 Sutherland
London W9 24Q ENGLAND

Leslie Uggams
3 Lincoln Center
New York, NY 10023

Tracey Ullman
3800 La Crescenta Avenue #209
La Crescenta, CA 91214

V   V

Jerry Vale
1100 N. Alta Loma Road, #1404
Los Angeles, CA 90069

Frankie Valli
25934 W. Manley Ct.
Calabasas, CA 91302

Richard Van Allen
18 Octavia Street
London, SW11 3DN, ENGLAND

Eddie Van Halen
31736 Broad Beach Road
Malibu, CA 90265

Music

Luther Vandross
P.O. Box 5542
Beverly Hills, CA 90209

Vanilla Ice
1290 Avenue of the Americas #4200
New York, NY 10104

Vanity
1871 Messino Drive
San Jose, CA 95132

Steve Van Zandt
322 West 57th Street
New York, NY 10019

Bobby Vee
P.O. Box 41
Sauk Rapids, MN 56379

Suzanne Vega
30 W. 21st Street, #700
New York, NY 10010

The Village People
1560 Broadway, #1308
New York, NY 10036

Bobby Vinton
P.O. Box 6010
Branson, MO 65616

W ———————————————————— W

Porter Wagoner
P.O. Box 290785
Nashville, TN 37229

Tom Waits
P.O. Box 498
Valley Ford, CA 94972

Clay Walker
1000-18th Avenue South
Nashville, TN 37212

Junior Walker
141 Dunbar Avenue
Fords, NJ 08863

Steve Wariner
320 Main Street #240
Franklin, TN 37064

Dionne Warwick
1583 Lindacrest Drive
Beverly Hills, CA 90210

Jody Watley
P.O. Box 6339
Beverly HIlls, CA 90212

Andre Watts
205 West 57th Street
New York, NY 10019

Kitty Wells
240 Old Hickory Blvd.
Madison, TN 35115

Barry White
3395 South Jones Blvd., #176
Las Vegas, NV 89102

Karyn White
3300 Warner Blvd.
Burbank, CA 91505

Slim Whitman
1300 Division Street #103
Nashville, TN 37203

Roger Whittaker
P.O. Box 1655-GB
London, W8 5HZ ENGLAND

Andy Williams
2500 West Highway 76
Branson, MO 65616

Deniece Williams
1414 Seabright
Beverly Hills, CA 90210

Hank Williams, Jr.
Hwy. 79 East
Box 1350
Paris, TN 38242

Joe Williams
3337 Knollwood Court
Las Vegas, NV 89121

John Williams
333 Loring Avenue
Los Angeles, CA 90024

Paul Williams
8545 Franklin Avenue
Los Angeles, CA 90069

Vanessa Williams
P.O. Box 858
Chappaqua, NY 10514

Brian Wilson
14042 Aubrey Road
Beverly Hills, CA 90210

Carnie Wilson
13601 Ventura Blvd. #286
Sherman Oaks, CA 91423

Mary Wilson
163 Amsterdam Avenue #125
New York, NY 10023

Nancy Wilson
202 San Vicente Blvd., #4
Santa Monica, CA 90402

Wilson Phillips
1290 Avenue of the Americas #4200
New York, NY 10104

The Winans
P.O. Box 150245
Nashville, TN 37215

Steve Winwood
9200 Sunset Blvd., PH 15
Los Angeles, CA 90069

Bobby Womack
1048 Tatnall Street
Macon, GA 31201

Stevie Wonder
4616 Magnolia Blvd.
Burbank, CA 91505

Tammy Wynette
P.O. Box 121926
Nashville, TN 37212

Y   Y

"Weird" Al Yankovic
8842 Hollywood Blvd.
Los Angeles, CA 90069

Yanni
509 Hartnell Street
Monterey, CA 93940

Glen Yarborough
P.O. Box 158
Malibu, CA 90265

Trisha Yearwood
P.O. Box 65
Monticello, GA 31064

Yellowjackets
9220 Sunset Blvd. #320
Los Angeles, CA 90069

Dwight Yoakum
1250-6th Street #401
Santa Monica, CA 90401

Jesse Colin Young
P.O. Box 31
Lancaster, NG 03584

Neil Young
1026 S. Robertson Blvd., #200
Los Angeles, CA 90035

Z   Z

Dweezil Zappa
P.O. Box 5265
North Hollywood, CA 91616

Moon Zappa
P.O. Box 5265
North Hollywood, CA 91616

Pinchas Zuckerman
711 West End Avenue #5K-N
New York, NY 10025

ZZ Top
P.O. Box 19744
Houston, TX 77024

Sports

A _____ A

Henry "Hank" Aaron
1611 Adams Drive S.W.
Atlanta, GA 30311

Kareem Abdul-Jabbar
1436 Summitridge Drive
Beverly Hills, CA 90210

Akeem Abdul-Olajuwon
10 Greenway Plaza East
Houston, TX 77046

Andre Agassi
8921 Andre Drive
Las Vegas, NV 89113

Troy Aikman
1000 Creekside Court
Irving, TX 75063

Danny Ainge
2910 N. Central
Phoenix, AZ 85012

Marv Albert
30 Rockefeller Plaza #1411
New York, NY 10020

Muhammad Ali
P.O. Box 187
Berrien Springs, MI 49103

Marcus Allen
433 Ward Parkway #29
Kansas City, MO 64112

Roberto Alomar
333 West Camden Street
Baltimore, MD 21201

George "Sparky" Anderson
P.O. Box 6415
Thousand Oaks, CA 91359

Mario Andretti
53 Victory Lane
Nazareth, PA 18064

Michael Andretti
471 Rose Inn Avenue
Nazareth, PA 18604

Rocky Aoki
8685 NW 53rd Terrace
Miami, FL 33155

Luis Aparicio
P.O. Box 590
Cooperstown, NY 13325

Eddie Arcaro
11111 Biscayne Blvd.
Miami, FL 33161

Red Auerbach
P.O. Box 8607
Boston, MA 02114

Paul Azinger
4520 Bent Tree Blvd.
Sarasota, FL 34241

B   B

Tai Babilonia
13889 Valley Vista Blvd.
Sherman Oaks, CA 91423

Wally Bachman
160 SE 39th Street
Hillsboro, OR 97123

Donovan Bailey
625 Hales Chapel Road
Gray, TN 37615

Ernie Banks
16161 Ventura Blvd., #814
Encino, CA 91436

Sir Roger Bannister
21 Bardwell Road
Oxford OX2 6SV ENGLAND

Charles Barkley
10 Greenway Plaza East
Houston, TX 77046

Don Baylor
56325 Riviera
La Quinta, CA 92253

Boris Becker
Nusslocher Strasst 51
D-69181, Leiman, GERMANY

Albert Bell
333 West 35th Street
Chicago, IL 60616

George Bell
333 West 35th Street
Chicago, IL 60616

Johnny Bench
661 Reisling Knoll
Cincinnati, OH 45226

Yogi Berra
P.O. Box 462
Caldwell, NJ 07006

Gary Bettenhausen
2550 Tree Farm Road
Martinsville, IN 46151

Tony Bettenhausen
4941 McCrary Street
Speedway, IN 46224

Jerome Bettis
300 Stadium Circle
Pittsburgh, PA 15212

Craig Biggio
P.O. Box 288
Houston, TX 77001

Matt Biondi
1404 Rimer Drive
Moraga, CA 94556

Larry Bird
RR #1-Box 77A
West Baden Springs, IN 47469

Bonnie Blair
306 White Pine Road
Delafield, WI 53018

George Blanda
P.O. Box 1153
La Quinta, CA 92253

Jeff Blauser
1 CNN Center
Sourth Tower #405
Atlanta, GA 30303

Drew Bledsoe
Sullivan Stadium-Route 1
Foxboro, MA 02035

Rocky Bleier
580 Squaw Run Road East
Pittsburgh, PA 15238

Vida Blue
P.O. Box 1449
Pleasanton, CA 94566

Brian Boitano
101 First Street #370
Los Altos, CA 94022

Barry Bonds
9595 Wilshire Blvd., #711
Beverly Hills, CA 90212

Bobby Bonilla
390 Round Hill Road
Greenwich, CT 06831

Bjorn Borg
One Erieview Plaza #1300
Cleveland, OH 44114

Riddick Bowe
1025 Vermnot Ave. NW#1025
Washington, DC 20005

Christopher Bowman
5653 Kester Avenue
Van Nuys, CA 91405

Terry Bradshaw
8911 Shady Lane Drive
Shreveport, LA 71118

George Brett
P.O. Box 419969
Kansas City, MO 64141

Lou Brock
P.O. Box 28398
St. Louis, MO 63146

Jim Brown
1851 Sunset Plaza Drive
Los Angeles, CA 90069

Bill Buckner
2425 West Victory Blvd.
Meridian, ID 83642

Zola Budd
1 Church Row, Wandsworth Plain
London, SW18, ENGLAND

Leroy Burrell
1801 Ocean Park Blvd. #112
Santa Monica, CA 90405

Dr. Jerry Buss
P.O. Box 10
Inglewood, CA 90306

C _____ C

Hector "Macho" Camacho
4751 Yaradarm Lane
Boynton Beach, FL 33436

Bert Campaneris
P.O. Box 5096
Scottsdale, AZ 85261

Earl Campbell
P.O. Box 909
Austin, TX 78767

Jose Canseco
4525 Sheridan Avenue
Miami Beach, FL 33140

John Cappelletti
28791 Brant Lane
Laguna Niguel, CA 92677

Jennifer Capriati
5435 Blue Heron Lane
Wesley Chapel, FL 33543

Rod Carew
5144 E. Crescent Drive
Anaheim, CA 92807

Steve Carlton
P.O. Box 736
Durango, CO 81302

Peter & Kitty Carruthers
22 E. 71st Street
New York, NY 10021

Rosie Casals
P.O. Box 537
Sausalito, CA 94966

Pat Cash
281 Clarence Street
Sydney NSW, 2000, AUSTRALIA

Billy Casper
P.O. Box 1088
Chula Vista, CA 91912

Tracy Caulkins
1750 E. Boulder Street
Colorado Springs, CO 80909

Steve Cauthen
Cauthen Ranch
Boone County
Walton, KY 41094

Orlando Cepeda
331 Brazelton Court
Suison City, CA 94505

Rick Cerrone
63 Eisenhower
Cresskill, NJ 07626

Ron Cey
22714 Creole Road
Woodland Hills, CA 91364

Michael Chang
P.O. Box 6080
Mission Viejo, CA 92690

Julio Ceasar Chavez
539 Telegraph Canyon Rd. #253
Chula Vista, CA 91910

Joey Chitwood
4410 West Alva Street
Tampa, FL 33614

Amy Chow
1751 Pinnacle Drive #1500
McLean, VA 22102

Roger Clemens
8582 Katy Freeway, #121
Houston, TX 77024

Sebastian Coe
16 Upper Woburn Place
London WC1H OOP ENGLAND

Paul Coffey
633 Hawthorne Street
Birmingham, MI 48009

Nadia Comaneci
4421 Hidden Hills Road
Norman, OK 73072

Jimmy Connors
200 S. Refugio Road
Santa Ynez, CA 93460

Bob Costas
c/o NBC Sports
30 Rockefeller Plaza
New York, NY 10112

Fred Couples
8251 Greensboro Drive #530
McLean, VA 22102

Jim Courier
1 Erieview Plaza #1300
Cleveland, OH 44114

Robin Cousins
2887 Hollyridge Drive
Los Angeles, CA 90068

Bob Cousy
459 Salisbury Street
Worcester, MA 01609

Ben Crenshaw
2905 San Gabriel #213
Austin, TX 78703

Denny Crumm
23015 Third Street
Louisville, KY 40292

Randall Cunningham
5020 Spanish Heights Drive
Las Vegas, NV 89118

D _____ D

Tim Daggett
53 Harmon Street
Long Beach, NY 11561

John Daly
P.O. Box 109601
Palm Beach Garden, FL 33418

Ron Darling
19 Woodland Street
Millbury, MA 01527

Lindsay Davenport
1101 Wilson Blvd. #1800
Arlington, VA 22209

Al Davis
332 Center Street
El Segundo, CA 90245

Dominique Dawes
129 Ritchie Avenue
Silver Spring, MD 20910

Oscar De La Hoya
637 N. 1st Street
Montebello, CA 90640

Mary Decker (Slaney)
2923 Flintlock Street
Eugene, OR 97401

Bucky Dent
2606 Varandah Lane #816
Arlington, TX 76006

Gail Devers
20214 Leadwell
Canoga Park, CA 91304

Rob Dibble
54 Summitt Farms Road
Southington, CT 06489

Dan Dierdorf
13302 Buckland Hall Road
St. Louis, MO 63131

Joe DiMaggio
3233 - 34th Street N.E.
Ft. Lauderdale, FL 33308

Mike Ditka
1 Dunsinane Lane
Bannockburn, IL 60015

Tom Dolan
1751 Pinnacle Drive #1500
McLean, VA 22102

Terry Donohue
11918 Laurelwood
Studio City, CA 91604

Tony Dorsett
6005 Kettering Court
Dallas, TX 75248

James "Buster" Douglas
465 Waterbury Court #A
Gahanna, OH 43230

Clyde Drexler
10 Greenway Plaza East
Houston, TX 77277

Joe Dumars
c/o The Palace
Auburn Hills, MI 48057

Angelo Dundee
11264 Pines Blvd.
Hollywood, FL 33026

Lenny Dykstra
236 Chester Road
Devon, PA 19333

E   E

Dale Earnhardt
Rt. 10, Box 595-B
Mooresville, NC 28115

Dennis Eckersley
39 Plympton Road
Sudburg, MA 01776

Stefan Edberg
Spinnaregaten 6
S-59300, Vastervik, SWEDEN

Lee Elder
1725 K Street N.W. #1202
Washington, DC 20006

Sean Elliott
P.O. Box 530
San Antonio, TX 78292

Jimmy Ellis
7507 Nachand Lane
Louisville, KY 40218

John Elway
4763 South Elizabeth
Englewood, CO 80110

Dick Enberg
Box 710
Rancho Santa Fe, CA 92067

Julius Erving
64 William Street
Hempstead, NY 11550

Janet Evans
424 Brower
Placentia, CA 92670

Chris Everett
500 N.E. 25th Street
Wilton Manors, FL 33305

Patrick Ewing
37 Summit Street
Englewood Cliffs, NJ 07632

F   F

Brett Favre
1265 Lombardi Avenue
Green Bay, WI 54304

Bob Feller
P.O. Box 157
Gates Mills, OH 44040

Mary Jo Fernandez
133-1st Street NE
St. Petersburg, FL 33701

Mark Fidrych
260 West Street
Northboro, MA 01532

Cecil Fielder
c/o Yankee Stadium
Bronx, NY 10451

Rollie Fingers
4894 Eastcliff Court
San Diego, CA 92130

Carlton Fisk
16612 Catawba Road
Lockport, IL 60441

Christian Fittipaldi
282 Alphaville Barueri 064500
Sao Paulo BRAZIL

Emerson Fittipaldi
950 S. Miami Avenue
Miami, FL 33130

Peggy Fleming
1122 S. Robertson Blvd., #15
Los Angeles, CA 90035

Raymond Floyd
29 Indian Creek Island,
Miami, FL 33154

Whitey Ford
38 Schoolhouse Lane
Lake Success, NY 11020

George Foreman
7639 Pine Oak Drive
Humble, TX 77397

A.J. Foyt
6415 Toledo
Houston, TX 77008

Joe Frazier
2917 N. Broad Street
Philadelphia, PA 19132

Walt Frazier
400 Central Park West #7W
New York, NY 10025

G _____ G

Roman Gabriel
16817 McKee Road
Charlotte, NC 28278

Joe Garagiola
6221 East Huntress Drive
Paradise Valley, AZ 85253

Randy Gardner
4640 Glencove Avenue #6
Marina Del Rey, CA 90291

Zina Garrison
P.O. Box 272305
Houston, TX 77277

Steve Garvey
11718 Barrington Court #6
Los Angeles, CA 90049

Mark Gastineau
1717 South Dorsey Lane
Tempe, AZ 85281

Cito Gaston
1 Blue Jays Way #3200
Toronto, Ont., M5V 1J1, CANADA

Willie Gault
33-26th Place
Venice, CA 90291

Jeff George
1 Georgia Drive
Atlanta, GA 30313

Althea Gibson (Darbeu)
275 Prospect Street #768
East Orange, NJ 07017

Kirk Gibson
15135 Charlevois Street
Grosse Pointe, MI 48230

Frank Gifford
625 Madison Avenue #1200
New York, NY 10022

Tom Glavine
1 CNN Center
South Tower #405
Atlanta, GA 30303

Dwight Gooden
6700-30th Street South
St. Petersburg, FL 33712

Ekaterina Gordeeva
1375 Hopmeadow Street
Simsbury, CT 06070

Jeff Gordon
P.O. Box 9
Harrisburg, NC 28075

Curt Gowdy
300 Boylston Street #506
Boston, MA 02116

Mark Grace
1060 West Addison Street
Chicago, IL 60613

Steffi Graff
Luftschiffring 8
D-68782, Bruhl, GERMANY

Otto Graham
2216 Riviera Drive
Sarasota, FL 34232

Horace Grant
One Magic Place
Orlando, FL 32801

Dennis Green
9520 Viking Drive
Eden Prairie, MN 55344

Bob Greise
3250 Mary Street
Miami, FL 33133

Wayne Gretzky
9100 Wilshire Blvd., #1000W
Beverly Hills, CA 90212

Rosey Grier
P.O. Box "A"
Santa Ana, CA 92711

Ken Griffey, Jr.
P.O. Box 4100
Seattle, WA 98104

Ken Griffey, Sr.
5385 Cross Birdge Road
Westchester, OH 45069

Lou Groza
5287 Parkway Drive
Berea, OH 44017

Archie Griffin
4965 St. Andrews Drive
Westerville, OH 43082

Ron Guidry
P.O. Box 278
Scott, LA 70583

Florence Griffith-Joyner
27758 Santa Margarita #385
Mission Viejo, CA 92691

Greg Gumbel
347 W. 57th Street
New York, NY 10019

Marquis Grissom
1 CNN Center
South Tower #405
Atlanta, GA 30303

Tony Gwynn
15643 Boulder Ridge Lane
Poway, CA 92064

H   H

Marvin Hagler
112 Island Street
Stoughton, MA 02072

Tim Hardaway
701 Areana Blvd.
Miami, FL 33136

Dorothy Hamill
75490 Fairway Drive
Indian Wells, CA 92210

Tonya Harding
121 Morrison Street SW #1100
Portland, OR 97204

Scott Hamilton
3674 W. Amherst Avenue
Denver, CO 80236

Harlem Globetrotters
1000 S. Fremont Avenue
Alhambra, CA 91803

Jim Harbaugh
100 South Capitol Avenue
Indianapolis, IN 46225

Franco Harris
200 Chauser Court South
Sewickley, PA 15143

Anfernee Hardaway
One Magic Place
Orlando, FL 32801

Bret "Hit Man" Hart
435 Patina Place SW
Calgary Alb. T3H 2P5 CANADA

John Havlicek
24 Beech Road
Weston, CT 02193

Bob Hayes
13901 Preston Valley Place
Dallas, TX 75240

Tommy Hearns
19785 W. 12 Mile Road
Southfield, MI 48076

Beth & Eric Heiden
3505 Blackhawk Drive
Madison, WI 53705

Rickey Henderson
10561 Englewood Drive
Oakland, CA 94621

Thomas "Hollywood" Henderson
7 Seafield Lane
Westhampton Beach, NY 11978

Keith Hernandez
255 East 49th Street #28-D
New York, NY 10017

Orel Hershiser
1638 Via Tuscany
Winter Park, FL 32789

Martina Hingus
Seidenbbaum Truebbach
CH-15234 SWITZERLAND

Ben Hogan
P.O. Box 15006
Richmond, VA 23227

Hulk Hogan
130 Willadel Drive
Belleair, FL 34616

Larry Holmes
101 Larry Holmes Drive, #500
Easton, PA 18042

Lou Holtz
P.O. Box 518
Notre Dame, IN 46556

Evander Holyfield
794 Highway 279
Fairburn, GA 30213

Jeff Hostetler
332 Center Street
El Segundo, CA 90245

Paul Hornung
325 W. Main Street#1116
Louisville, KY 40202

Ralph Houk
3000 Plantation Road
Winter Haven, FL 33884

Gordie Howe
6645 Peninsula Drive
Traverse City, MI 49684

Bobby Hull
115 E. Maple Street
Hinsdale, IL 60521

Jim 'Catfish' Hunter
RR #1, Box 895
Hertford, NC 27944

I   I

Michael Irvin
1 Cowboys Parkway
Irving, TX 78063

Hale Irwin
2801 Stonington Place
St. Louis, MO 63131

J   J

Bo Jackson
1765 Old Shell Road
Mobile, AL 36604

Gordon Johncock
1042 Becker Road
Hastings, MI 49056

Keith Jackson
c/o ABC Sports
1330 Avenue of Americas
New York, NY 10019

Ben Johnson
926 Stonehaven Avenue
New Market, Ont. L3X 1K7
CANADA

Phil Jackson
980 N. Michigan Avenue #1600
Chicago, IL 60611

Ervin "Magic" Johnson
13100 Mulholland Drive
Beverly Hills, CA 90210

Reggie Jackson
305 Amador Avenue
Seaside, CA 93955

Jimmy Johnson
2269 N.W. 199th Street
Miami, FL 33056

Dan Jansen
5040 S. 76th Street
Greenfield, WI 53220

Kevin Johnson
201 East Jefferson
Phoenix, AZ 85004

Bruce Jenner
P.O. Box 11137
Beverly Hills, CA 90213

Michael Jordan
3700 Point Lane
Highland Park, IL 60035

Tommy John
51 Isla Bahia
Ft. Lauderdale, FL 33316

Jackie Joyner-Kersee
P.O. Box 2220
Winnetka, CA 91396

K _____ K

Al Kaline
945 Timberlake Drive
Bloomfield Hills, MI 48302

Bela Karolyi
RR #1-Box 140
Huntsville, TX 77340

Anatoly Karpov
Luzhnetskaya 8
Moscow, 119270 RUSSIA

Alex Karras
7943 Woodrow Wilson Drive
Los Angeles, CA 90046

George Kell
P.O. Box 70
Swifton, AR 72471

Shawn Kemp
190 Queen Anne Avenue, N.
Suite #200
Seattle, WA 98109

Nancy Kerrigan
7 Cedar Avenue
Stoneham, MA 02180

Jason Kidd
777 Sports Street
Dallas, TX 75207

Harmon Killebrew
P.O. Box 14550
Scottsdale, AZ 85267

Jeane-Claude Killey
13 Chemin Bellefontaine
1223 Cologny GE SWITZERLAND

Billie Jean King
445 North Wells #404
Chicago, IL 60610

Don King
871 West Oakland Blvd.
Oakland Park, FL 33311

Tom Kite
3512 Riva Ridge Road
Austin, TX 78746

Franz Klammer
Mooswald 22
A-9712, Friesach, AUSTRIA

Evel Knievel
160 E. Flamingo Road
Las Vegas, NV 89109

Bobby Knight
Indiana University Basketball
Bloomington, IN 47405

Chuck Knox
11220 NE 53rd Street
Kirkland, WA 98033

Olga Korbut
4705 Masters Ct.
Duluth, MN 30136

Bernie Kosar
6969 Ron Park Place
Youngstown, OH 44512

Mike Krzyzewski
Duke University Basketball
Durham, NC 27706

Sandy Koufax
P.O. Box 88
Carpinteria, CA 93014

Tony Kubek
8323 North Shore Road
Menosha, WI 54252

Jack Kramer
231 N. Glenroy Place
Los Angeles, CA 90049

Toni Kukoc
980 N. Michigan Avenue #1600
Chicago, IL 60611

L   L

Christian Laettner
1 CNN Center #405
Atalanta, GA 30303

Tom Landry
5336 Rock Cliff Place
Dallas, TX 75209

Jack LaLanne
P.O. Box 1926
Morro Bay, CA 93442

Bernhard Langer
1120 S.W. 21st Lane
Boca Raton, FL 33486

Donny Lalonde
12001 Ventura Place #404
Studio City, CA 91604

Barry Larkin
100 Riverfront Stadium
Cincinnati, OH 45202

Jack Lambert
222 Highland Drive
Carmel, CA 93921

Tommy LaSorda
1473 W. Maxzim Avenue
Fullerton, CA 92633

Jake LaMotta
235 Beacon Drive
Phoenixville, PA 19460

Rod Laver
P.O. Box 4798
Hilton Head Island, SC 29928

Jim Lampley
3347 Tareco Drive
Los Angeles, CA 90068

Buddy Lazier
8135 W. Crawfordsville
Indianapolis, IN 46224

Mario Lemieux
630 Academy Street
Sewickley, PA 15143

Bob Lemon
95 Fairway Lakes
Myrtle Beach, SC 29577

Greg Lemond
1101 Wilson Blvd., #1800
Arlington, VA 22209

Ivan Lendl
60 Arch Street
Greenwich, CT 06830

Sugar Ray Leonard
4401 East West Hwy., #303
Bethesda, MD 20914

Marv Levy
One Bill Drive
Orchard Park, NY 14127

Carl Lewis
P.O. Box 571990
Houston, TX 77082

Lenno Lewis
811 Totowa Road #100
Totowa, NJ 07512

Eric Lindros
1 Pattison Place
Philadelphia, PA 19148

Nancy Lopez
2308 Tara Drive
Albany, GA 31707

Ronnie Lott
11342 Canyon View Circle
Cupertino, CA 95014

Greg Louganis
P.O. Box 4130
Malibu, CA 90264

Johnny Lujack
6321 Crow Valley Drive
Bettendorf, IA 52722

Greg Luzinski
620 Jackson Road
Medford, NJ 08055

M _____ M

John Madden
5304 Blackhawk Drive
Danville, CA 94506

Bill Madlock
453 East Decautur Street
Decautur, IL 62521

Phil Mahre
White Pass
Naches, WA 98937

Steve Mahre
2408 N. 52nd Avenue
Yakima, WA 98908

Karl Malone
301 West South Temple
Salt Lake City, UT 84101

Ray "Boom Boom" Mancini
12524 Indianapolis Street
Los Angeles, CA 90066

Danny Manning
1 CNN Center #405
Atlanta, GA 30303

Nigel Mansell
Station Road Box 1
Ballasalle
Isle of Man ENGLAND

Diego Maradona
Eduardo Dato
E-41005 Seville SPAIN

Jaun Marichal
9458 NW 54 Doral Circle Lane
Miami, FL 33128

Dan Marino
3415 Stallion Lane
Ft. Lauderdale, FL 33331

Russell Maryland
c/o Texas Stadium
Irving, TX 75062

Don Mattingly
RR #5, Box 74
Evansville, IN 47711

Gene Mauch
71 Princeton
Rancho Mirage, CA 92270

Willie Mays
P.O. Box 2410
Menlo Park, CA 94026

Tim McCarver
1518 Youngford Road
Gladwnne, PA 19035

John McEnroe
27312 Malibu Colony
Malibu, CA 90265

Tug McGraw
2595 Wallingford Road
San Marino, CA 91108

Mark McGwire
1704 Alamo Plaza #322
Alamo, CA 94507

Jim McKay
2805 Sheppard Road
Monkton, MD 21111

Denny McLain
11994 Hyne Road
Brighton, MI 48116

Steve McNair
335 South Hollywood
Memphis, TN 38104

Rick Mears
204 Spyglass Lane
Jupiter, FL 33477

Don Meredith
P.O. Box 597
Santa Fe, NM 87504

Al Michaels
47 W. 66th Street
New York, NY 10023

Cheryl Miller
6767 Forest Lawn Drive #115
Los Angeles, CA 90068

Johnny Miller
P.O. Box 2260
Napa, CA 94558

Reggie Miller
11116 Catamaran Court
Indianapolis, IN 46236

Shannon Miller
3728 Summer Cloud Drive
Edmond, OK 73013

Rick Mirer
11220 NE 53rd Street
Kirkland, WA 98033

Larry Mize
P.O. Box 109601
Palm Beach Garderns, FL 33410

Rick Monday
149 42nd Avenue
San Mateo, CA 94403

Joe Montana
P.O. Box 7342
Menlo Park, CA 94026

Warren Moon
1 Lakeside Estate Drive
Missouri City, TX 77459

Archie Moore
3517 East Street
San Diego, CA 92102

Alonzo Morning
701 Areana Blvd.
Miami, FL 33136

Edwin Moses
P.O. Box 120
Indianapolis, IN 46206

Manny Mota
3926 Los Olivos Lane
La Crescenta, CA 91214

Shirley Muldowney
79559 North Avenue
Armada, MI 48005

Bobby Murcer
P.O. Box 75089
Oklahoma City, OK 73147

Brent Musburger
47 West 66th Street
New York, NY 10023

Stan Musial
1655 Des Peres Road #125
St. Louis, MO 63131

Thomas Muster
370 Felter Avenue
Hewlett, NY 11557

Dikembe Mutombo
1 CNN Center #405
Atlanta, GA 30303

N   N

Joe Namath
7 Bay Harbor Road
Tequesta, FL 33469

Ille Nastase
15 East 69th Street
New York, NY 10021

Martina Navratilova
1266 E. Main Street #44
Stamford, CT 06902

Byron Nelson
Rt.3, Box 5 Litsey Road
Roanoke, TX 76262

Bobby Nichols
8681 Glenlyon Ct.
Ft. Meyers, FL 33912

Jack Nicklaus
11760 U.S. Highway 1 #6
N. Palm Beach, FL 33408

Joe Niekro
39 Shadow Lane
Lakeland, FL 33813

Phil Niekro
6382 Nichols Road
Flowery Branch, GA 30542

Chuck Noll
201 Grang Street
Sewickley, PA 15143

Hideo Nome
1000 Elysian Park Avenue
Los Angeles, CA 90012

Greg Norman
218 US Hwy. One #302
Tequesta, FL 33469

Ken Norton
4 Cantilena
San Clemente, CA 92673

O   O

Pat O'Brien
c/o CBS Sports
51 W. 52nd Street
New York, NY 10019

Shaquille O'Neal
501 John Street
Manhattan Beach, CA 90266

Bobby Orr
1800 W. Madison Street
Chicago, IL 60612

Tom Osburne
University of Nebraska Football
Lincoln, NE 68588

P   P

Billy Packer
c/o CBS Sports
51 W. 52nd Street
New York, NY 10019

Arnold Palmer
P.O. Box 52
Youngstown, PA 15696

Jim Palmer
P.O. Box 590
Cooperstown, NY 13325

Jack Pardee
2706 Peninsula Drive
Missouri City, TX 77459

Dave Parker
7864 Ridge Road
Cincinnati, OH 45237

Ara Parseghien
240 Seaview Court PH A
Marco, FL 33937

Joe Paterno
830 McKee Street
State College, PA 16803

Floyd Patterson
Springtown Road
Box 336
New Paltz, NY 12561

Corey Paven
2515 McKinney #930, Box 10
Dallas, TX 75201

Walter Payton
300 No. Martingale Road #340
Schaumburg, IL 60195

Rodney Peete
10683 Santa Monica Blvd.
Los Angeles, CA 90025

Pele
Praca dos Tres Poderes
palacio de Planalto BR
70150900 Brasilia DF BRAZIL

Roger Penske
13400 Outer Drive West
Detroit, MI 48239

Joe Pepitone
32 Lois Lane
Farmingdale, NY 11735

Gaylord Perry
P.O. Box 1958
Kill Devil Hills, NC 27948

Kyle Petty
135 Longfield Drive
Mooresville, NC 28115

Richard Petty
Rt #4, Box 86
Randleman, NC 27317

Mary Pierce
1 Erieview Plaza, #1300
Cleveland, OH 44114

Lou Piniella
P.O. Box 4100
Seattle, WA 98104

Vada Pinson
710-31st Street
Oakland, CA 94609

Scottie Pippen
2320 Shady Lane
Highland Park, IL 60035

Gary Player
3930 RCA Blvd., #3001
Palm Beach Gardens, FL 33410

Jim Plunkett
51 Kilroy Way
Atherton, CA 90425

Nick Price
300 South Beach Road
Hobe Sound, FL 33455

R   R

Bobby Rahal
P.O. Box 39
Hillard, OH 43026

Willie Randolph
648 Juniper Place
Franklin Lakes, NJ 07417

Ahmad Rashad
30 Rockefeller Plaza #1411
New York, NY 10020

Pee Wee Reese
1400 Willow Avenue
Louiseville, KY 40204

Mary Lou Retton
322 Vista Del Mar
Redondo Beach, CA 90277

Dusty Rhodes
8577A Boca Glades Blvd. West
Boca Raton, FL 33434

Jerry Rice
2 Brittany Meadows
Atherton, CA 94025

Jim Rice
RR #8
Anderson, SC 29621

Bobby Richardson
P.O. Box 2000
Lynchburg, VA 24506

Dot Richarson
USC Medical Center
1200 N. State Street #GH-3900
Los Angeles, CA 90033

Cathy Rigby
110 E. Wilshire #200
Fullerton, CA 92632

Jim Riggleman
1060 West Addison Street
Chicago, IL 60613

Pat Riley
P.O. Box 12819
Albany, NY 12212

Cal Ripken, Jr.
2330 W. Juppa Road #333
Lutherville, MD 21093

Cal Ripken, Sr.
410 Clover Street
Aberdeen, MD 21001

Mariano Rivera
Shea Stadium
Flushing, NY 11368

Mickey Rivers
350 NW 48th Street
Miami, FL 33127

Phil Rizzuto
912 Westminster Avenue
Hillside, NJ 07205

Oscar Robertson
621 Tuschulum Avenue
Cincinnati, OH 45226

Brooks Robinson
36 S. Charles Street #2000
Baltimore, MD 21201

David Robinson
P.O. Box 530
San Antonio, TX 78292

Eddie Robinson
Grambling Football
Grambling, LA 71245

Frank Robinson
15557 Aqua Verde Drive
Los Angeles, CA 90024

Glen Robinson
1001 North Fourth Street
Milwaukee, WI 53203

Dennis Rodman
4809 Seashore Drive
Newport Beach, CA 92663

Alex Rodriquez
P.O. Box 4100
Seattle, WA 98104

Chi Chi Rodriguez
P.O. Box 5118
Akron, OH 44334

Ivan Rodriguez
P.O. Box 90111
Arlington, TX 76004

Bill Rogers
353 The Marketplace
Fanuil Hall
Boston, MA 02109

Pete Rose
8570 Crescent Drive
Los Angeles, CA 90046

Ken Rosewall
111 Pentacost Avenue
Turramurra, NSW
2074, AUSTRALIA

Kyle Rote
24700 Deepwater Point Drive #14
St. Michaels, MD 21663

Pete Rozelle
P.O. Box 9686
Rancho Santa Fe, CA 92067

Johnny Rutherford
4919 Black Oak Lane
Ft. Worth, TX 76114

Bill Russell
P.O. Box 1200
Mercer Island, WA 98040

Nolan Ryan
719 Dezzo Drive
Alvin, TX 77512

S _____ S

Gabriela Sabatini
Ap. Int 14 Suc. 27
1427 Buenos Aires, ARGENTINA

Gale Sayers
624 Buck Road
Northbrook, IL 60062

Brett Saberhagen
5535 Amber Circle
Calabasas, CA 91302

Mike Schmidt
373 Eagle Drive
Jupiter, FL 33477

Pete Sampras
6352 MacLaurin Drive
Tampa, FL 33647

Mrs. Marge Schott
100 Riverfront Stadium
Cincinnati, OH 45202

Barry Sanders
1200 Featherstone Road
Pontiac, MI 48057

Tex Schramm
9355 Sunnybrook
Dallas, TX 75220

Deion Sanders
P.O. Box 4064
Atlanta, GA 30302

Vin Scully
1555 Capri Drive
Pacific Palisades, CA 90272

Summer Sanders
730 Sunrise Avenue
Roseville, CA 95661

Junior Seau
9449 Friars Road
San Diego, CA 92108

Ron Santo
1303 Somerset
Glenview, IL 60025

Tom Seaver
Larkspur Lane
Greenwich, CT 06830

Monica Seles
7751 Beeridge Road
Sarasota, FL 34241

Bud Selig
c/o County Coliseum
Milwaukee, WI 53214

Gary Sheffield
2267 NW 199th Street
Miami, FL 33056

Bill Shoemaker
2553 Fairfield Place
San Marino, CA 91108

Pam Shriver
2324 W. Joppa Road #650
Lutherville-Timonium, MD 21093

Don Shula
16 Indian Creek Island
Miami Lakes, FL 33154

Phil Simms
252 W. 71st Street
New York, NY 10023

O.J. Simpson
360 Rockingham Avenue
Los Angeles, CA 90049

Bruce Smith
One Bill Drive
Orchard Park, NY 14127

Dean Smith
U.N.C. Basketball
Chapel Hill, NC 27599

Emmitt Smith
1 Cowboys Parkway
Irving, TX 78063

J.C. Snead
P.O. Box 2047
Ponte Verde Beach, FL 32082

Sam Snead
P.O. Box 741
Hot Springs, VA 24445

Tom Sneva
3301 E. Valley Vista Lane
Paradise Valley, AZ 85253

Annika Sorenstam
1000 Avenue of the Champions
Palm Beach Gardens, FL 33418

Warren Spahn
Route #2
Hartshorne, OK 74547

Leon Spinks
330 S. President Street #202
Carol Stream IL 60188

Michael Spinks
250 W. 57th Street
New York, NY 10107

Mark Spitz
383 Dalehurst
Los Angeles, CA 90077

Steve Spurrier
P.O. Box 14485
Gainesville, FL 32661

Ken Stabler
Rt. Box, General Delivery
Orange Beach, AL 36561

Eddie Stanky
2100 Spring Hill Road
Mobile, AL 36607

Willie Stargell
1616 Shipyard Blvd. #278
Wilmington, NC 28412

Bart Starr
2065 Royal Fern Lane
Birmingham, AL 35244

Roger Staubach
6750 LBJ Freeway
Dallas, TX 75109

George Steinbrenner
River Ave. & E. 161st Street
Bronx, NY 10451

Jan Stephenson
1231 Garden Street #204
Titusville, FL 32769

David Stern
645 - 5th Avenue
New York, NY 10022

Jackie Stewart
24 Rte. de Divonne
1260, Lyon, SWITZERLAND

Payne Stewart
390 N. Orange Avenue #2600
Orlando, FL 32801

Michael Stich
Ernst-Barlach Street 44
D-25336 Elmshorn GERMANY

John Stockton
301 West South Temple
Salt Lake City, UT 84101

Hank Stram
194 Belle Terre Blvd.
Covington, LA 70483

Darryl Strawberry
P.O. Box 17868
Encino, CA 91316

Danny Sullivan
1614 East Cliff Road
Burnsville, MN 55337

Pat Summerall
10036 Sawgrass Drive
Ponte Verde, FL 32082

Don Sutton
2261 Liane Lane
Santa Ana, CA 92705

Lynn Swann
600 Grant Street #4800
Pittsburgh, PA 15219

Barry Switzer
1 Cowboy Parkway
Irving, TX 78063

Sheryl Swoopes
1751 Pinnacle Drive #1500
McLean, VA 22102

T _____ T

Paul Tagliabue
410 Park Avenue
New York, NY 10022

Roscoe Tanner
1109 Gnome Trail
Lookout Mountain, TN 37350

Fran Tarkington
1431 Garmon Ferry Road NW
Atlanta, GA 30327

Lawrence Taylor
367 Delano Place
Fairview, NJ 07022

Ernie Terrell
11136 South Parnell
Chicago, IL 60628

Vinny Testaverde
936 Crenshaw Lake Road
Lutz, FL 33549

Joe Theisman
5912 Leesburg Pike
Falls Church, VA 22041

Debi Thomas
22 E. 71st Street
New York, NY 10021

Frank Thomas
c/o Comiskey Park
Chicago, IL 60616

Isaiah Thomas
710 Lone Pine Road
Bloomfield, MI 48304

Thurman Thomas
One Bill Drive
Orchard Park, NY 14127

John Thompson
Georgetown University Basketball
Washington, DC 20057

Y.A. Tittle
2595 East Bayshore Road
Palo Alto, CA 94303

Alberto Tomba
I-40068 Castel de Britti
ITALY

Mike Tomczak
c/o Three River Stadium
Pittsburgh, PA 15212

James Toney
6305 Wellesley
West Bloomfield, MI 48322

Joe Torre
c/o Yankee Stadium
Bronx, NY 10451

Gwen Torrence
P.O. Box 361965
Decatur, GA 30036

Torville & Dean
Box 16, Beeston
Nottingham NG9 ENGLAND

Lee Trevino
1901 W. 47th Place #200
Westwood, KS 66205

Mark Tuinei
1 Cowboy Place
Irving, TX 78063

Mike Tyson
6740 Tomiyasu Lane
Las Vegas, NV 89120

U   U

Bob Uecker
201 South 46th Street
Milwaukee, WI 53214

Johnny Unitas
5607 Patterson Road
Baldwin, MD 21013

Al Unser
7625 Central N.W.
Albuquerque, NM 87105

Al Unser, Jr
3243 Calle de Deborah N.W.
Albuquerque, NM 87104

Bobby Unser
7700 Central S.W.
Albuquerque, NM 87105

Gene Upshaw
1102 Pepper Tree Drive
Great Falls, VA 22066

V   V

Fernando Valenzuela
3004 N. Beachwood Drive
Los Angeles, CA 90027

Mo Vaugh
c/o Fenway Park
Boston, MA 62215

Ken Venturi
P.O. Box 5118
Akron, OH 44334

Dick Vermeil
51 W. 52nd Street
New York, NY 10019

Guillermo Vilas
Avenue Foch 86
Paris, FRANCE

Frank Viola
844 Sweetwater Island Circle
Longwood, FL 32779

W   W

Virginia Wade
Sharstead Court
Sittingbourne, Kent, ENGLAND

Lanny Wadkins
6002 Kettering Court
Dallas, TX 75248

Greta Waitz
Postboks 51, Jjan
1113 Oslo NORWAY

Doak Walker
P.O. Box 77329
Steamboat Springs, CO 80477

Bill Walsh
Stanford University Football
Stanford, CA 94305

Bill Walton
1010 Myrtle Way
San Diego, CA 92103

Darrell Waltrip
P.O. Box 855
Franklin, TN 37065

Malivai Washington
1101 Wilson Blvd., #1800
Arlington, VA 22209

Tom Watson
1901 West 47th Place #200
Westwood, KS 66205

Ricky Watters
c/o Veterans Stadium
Philadelphia, PA 19148

Earl Weaver
501 Cypress Pt. Drive W.
Pembroke Pines, FL 33027

Chris Webber
One Harry S. Truman Drive
Landover, MD 20785

Tom Weiskopf
7580 East Gray Road
Scottsdale, AZ 85260

Jerry West
1210 Moraga Avenue
Los Angeles, CA 90049

Reggie White
P.O. Box 10628
Green Bay, WI 54307

Mats Wilander
Vickersvagen 2
Vaxjo, SWEDEN

Hoyt Wilhelm
3102 N. Himes Avenue
Tampa, FL 33607

Lanny Wilkens
2660 Peachtree Road NW #39F
Atlanta, GA 30305

Jamaal Wilkes
7846 West 81st Street
Playa del Rey, CA 90291

Billy Williams
586 Prince Edward
Glen Ellyn, IL 60137

Matt Williams
c/o Candlestick Park
San Francisco, CA 94124

Ted Williams
2455 N. Citrus Hills Blvd.
Hernando, FL 33442

Dave Winfield
11809 Gwynne Lane
Los Angeles, CA 90077

Katarina Witt
Lindenstr. 8
16244 Altenhof, GERMANY

Mark Wohlers
P.O. Box 4064
Atlanta, GA 30302

Todd Woodbridge
1751 Pinnacle Drive #1500
McLean, VA 22102

John Wooden
17711 Margate St. #102
Encino, CA 91316

Tiger Woods
6704 Teakwood Street
Cypress, CA 90630

Y _____ Y

Kristi Yamaguchi
3650 Montecito Drive
Fremont, CA 94536

Caleb Yarborough
9617 Dixie River Road
Charlotte, NC 28270

Carl Yastrzemski
4621 S. Ocean Blvd.
Highland Beach, FL 33431

Steve Young
261 East Broadway
Salt Lake City, UT 84111

Z _____ Z

Kim Zmeskal
17203 Bamwood
Houston, TX 77090

"Fuzzy" Zoeller
418 Deer Run Terrace
Floyd's Knobs, IN 47119

Politics

A _____ A

Bella Abzug
2 Fifth Avenue
New York, NY 10011

Gerry Adams
51/55 Falls Road
Belfast BT 12
NORTHERN IRELAND

King Bhumibol Adulyadey
Villa Chitralada
Bangkok, THAILAND

Sen. Daniel K. Akaka (HI)
Senate Hart Bldg. #720
Washington, DC 20510

Emperor Akihoto
The Imperial Palace
Tokyo, JAPAN

President Hafez Al-Assad
Office of the President
Damascus, SYRIA

Prince Albert of Monaco
Palais De Monace
Boite Postal 518
98015 Monte Carlo, MONACO

Medeleine Albright
1318-34th Street NW
Washington, DC 20007

Ex-Gov. Lamar Alexander
1109 Owen Place N.E.
Washington, DC 20008

Idi Amin
P.O. Box 8948,
Jidda 21492 Saudi Arabia

Prince Andrew of England
Sunninghill Park
Windsor, ENGLAND

Kofi Annan
799 United Nations Plaza
New York, NY 10017

Princess Anne of England
Gatcombe Park
Gloucestershire, ENGLAND

Yassir Arafat
P.O. Box 115
Jericho PALESTINE

Rep. Bill Archer (TX)
House Longworth Bldg. #1236
Washington, DC 20515

Dennis Archer
2 Woodward Avenue
Detroit, MI 49226

Moshe Arens
49 Hagderat
Savyon, ISREAL

Jean-Bertrand Aristide
425-8th Street NW
Washington, DC 20004

B _____ B

Sec. Bruce Babbitt
5169 Watson Street NW
Washington, DC 20016

Ex-Sen. Howard Baker
P.O. Box 8
Huntsville, TN 37756

Marion Barry
161 Raleigh Street SE
Washington, DC 20032

Birch Bayh
1575 "I" Street #1025
Washington, DC 20005

Abraham Beame
1111-20th Street NW
Washington, D.C. 20575

Queen Beatrix of Holland
Kasteel Drakesteijn
Lage Vuursche, 3744 BA
HOLLAND

Griffen Bell
206 Townsend Place NW
Atlanta, GA 30727

Sen. Robert F. Bennett (UT)
Senate Dirksen Bldg., #431
Washington, D.C. 20510

HRH Prince Bertil
Hert av Halland Kunglslottet
11130, Stockholm, SWEDEN

P.M. Benazir Bhutto
70 Clifton Road
Karachi, Pakistan

Sen. Joseph Biden, Jr. (DL)
221 Russel, Sen. Office Bldg.
Washington, DC 20510

Sen. Jeff Bingaman (NM)
Senate Hart Building #703
Washington, DC 20510

Tony Blair
#10 Downing Street
London SW1 ENGLAND

Julian Bond
361 W. View Drive
Atlanta, GA 30310

Rep. David Bonior (MI)
House Rayburn Building #2207
Washington, DC 20515

Rep. Sonny Bono (CA)
House Cannon Building #512
Washington, DC 20515

Sen. Barbara Boxer (CA)
Senate Hart Bldg. #112
Washington, DC 20510

Bill Bradley
4 Hawthorn Avenue
Princeton, NJ 08540

Ex-Mayor Tom Bradley
3631 Mt. Vernon Drive
Los Angeles, CA 90008

James & Sarah Brady
1255 "I" Street #1100
Washington, DC 20005

Sen. John Breaux (LA)
Senate Hart Building #516
Washington, DC 20510

Justic Steven Breyer
1 - 1st Street N.E.
Washington, DC 20543

Rep. George E. Brown (CA)
2300 Rayburn, Hse. Office Bldg.
Washington, DC 20515

Sen. Hank Brown (CO)
Senate Hart Building #716
Washington, DC 20510

Ex-Gov. Jerry Brown
295 Third Street
Oakland, CA 94607

Sec. Jesse Brown
810 Vermont Avenue N.W.
Washington, DC 20420

Willie L. Brown, Jr.
401 Van Ness Avenue #336
San Francisco, CA 94102

Sen. Richard Bryan (NV)
Senate Russell Building #364
Washington, DC 20510

Zbigniew Brzezinski
1800 "K" Street NW #400
Washington, DC 20006

Patrick J. Buchanan
1017 Saville Lane North
McLean, VA 22101

Sen. Dale Bumpers (AR)
7613 Honesty Way
Bethesda, MD 20817

Jim Bunning
4 Fairway Drive
Southgate, KY 41071

Sen. Conrad Burns (MT)
Senate Dirksen Building #187
Washington, DC 20510

Barbara Bush
9 West Oak Drive
Houston, TX 77056

Ex-President George Bush
9 West Oak Drive
Houston, TX 77056

Gov. George Bush, Jr. (TX)
P.O. Box 12404
Austin, TX 78711

Gatsha Mangosuthu Buthelezi
Union Bldg
Petoria 0001 SOUTH AFRICA

Sen. Robert Byrd (WV)
311 Hart, Sen. Office Bldg.
Washington, DC 20510

C   C

Sen. Ben Campbell (CO)
456 New Jersey Avenue SE
Washington, DC 20003

Ex-PM Kim Campbell
P.O. Box 1575 , Postal Station B
Ottawa, Ontario
K1P 5R5 CANADA

King Juan Carlos
Palace De La Carcuela
Madrid, SPAIN

Gov. Arne Carlson (MN)
130 State Capitol
St. Paul, MN 55155

Caroline, Princess of Monaco
80 Avenue Foch
F-75016 Paris, FRANCE

Ex-Pres. Jimmy Carter
1 Woodland Drive
Plains, GA 31780

Rosalynn Carter
1 Woodland Drive
Plains, GA 31780

Dr. Fidel Castro
Palacio del Gobierno
Havana, CUBA

Sen. John H. Chafee (RI)
506 Dirksen, Sen. Office Bldg.
Washington, DC 20510

Violeta Chamarrol
Presidential Palace
Managua, NICARAGUA

HRH Prince Charles
Highgrove House
Gloucestershire ENGLAND

Dick Cheny
500 N. Akard Street, #3600
Dallas, TX 75201

Gov. Lawton Chiles (FL)
The Capitol
Tallahassee, FL 32301

Jacques Chirac
Palais de l'Elysses
55 rue du Faubourg-St. Honore
F-75008 Paris FRANCE

Shirley Chisholm
80 Wentworth Lane
Palm Coast, FL 32137

Jean Chretien
24 Sussex Drive
Ottawa, Ontario
K1M 0MS CANADA

Warren Christopher
400 S. Hope Street #1060
Los Angeles, CA 90071

Sec. Henry Cisneros
5026 Reno Road NW
Washington, DC 20008

Ramsey Clark
36 E. 12th Street
New York, NY 10003

Clark Clifford
9421 Rockville Pike
Bethesda, MD 20814

President Bill Clinton
1600 Pennsylvania Avenue
Washington, DC 20505

Chelsea Clinton
1600 Pennsylvania Avenue
Washington, DC 20505

Hillary Rodham Clinton
1600 Pennsylvania Avenue
Washington, DC 20505

Sen. Dan Coats (IN)
Senate Russell Bldg. #404
Washington, DC 20510

Sen. Thad Cochran (MS)
Senate Russell Building #326
Washington, DC 20510

Sec. William S. Cohen
202 Harlow Street #204
Bangor, ME 04401

Rep. Cardiss Collins (IL)
2308 Rayburn, Hse. Office Bldg.
Washington, DC 20515

Sen. Kent Conrad (ND)
Senate Dirksen Building #724
Washington, DC 20510

Ex-King Constantine
4 Linnell Drive
Hampstead Way
London, NW11, ENGLAND

Rep. John Conyers (MI)
2426 Rayburn, Hse. Office Bldg.
Washington, DC 20515

Sen. Paul Coverdell (GA)
Senate Russell Building #200
Washington, DC 20510

Archibald Cox
Glesen Lane
Weyland, MA 01778

Sen. Larry Craig (ID)
Senate Hart Building #313
Washington, DC 20510

Rep. Phillip Crane (IL)
House Cannon Building #233
Washington, DC 20515

Ex-Sen. Alan Cranston
2024 Camden Avenue
Los Angeles, CA 90025

Jean Cretien
24 Sussex Drive
Ottawa, Ontario
K1M 0MS CANADA

Sec. Andrew Cuomo
Department of Housing & Urban
Development
Washington, DC 20410

Ex-Gov. Mario Cuomo
60 East 42nd Street
New York, NY 10165

D   D

Mayor Richard Daley
City Hall, 5th Floor
121 N. Lasalle Street
Chicago, IL 60602

Sec. William Daley
Department of Commerce
Washington, DC 20230

Sen. Alfonse M. D'Amato (NY)
Senate Hart Building #520
Washington, DC 20510

Sen. Thomas Daschle (SD)
Senate Hart Building #509
Washington, DC 20510

Ex-Sen. Dennis DeConcini
6014 Chesterbrook Road
MacLean, VA 22101

1st Deputy Pres. W. F. deKlerk
Tuynhuys
Capetown 8000 South Africa

Rep. Ronald V. Dellums (CA)
2108 Rayburn, Hse. Office Bldg.
Washington, DC 20515

Ex-Gov. George Deukmejian
555 West 5th Street
Los Angeles, CA 90013

Sen. Mike DeWine (OH)
Senate Russell Building #140
Washington, DC 20510

Rep. John Dingell (MI)
2328 Rayburn, Hse. Office Bldg.
Washington, DC 20515

David Dinkins
576 Main Street
New York, NY 10044

Sen. Christopher Dodd (CT)
Senate Russell Building #444
Washington, DC 20510

Elizabeth Dole
9909 Collins Avenue
Bal Harbour, FL 33154

Ex-Sen. Robert Dole
9909 Collins Avenue
Bal Harbour, FL 33154

Sen. Pete Domenici (NM)
328 Dirksen Senate Office Bldg.
Washington, DC 20510

Ex-Rep. Robert Dornan
12387 Lewis Street #203
Garden Grove, CA 92640

Ex-Gov. Michael Dukakis
85 Perry Street
Brookline, MA 02146

Ex-Gov. Pierre duPont
Patterns
Rockland, DE 19732

E _____ E

Lawrence Eagleburger
350 Park Avenue #2600
New York, NY 10022

Ex-Sen. Thomas Eagleton
1 Mercantile Center
St. Louis, MO 63101

Gov. Jim Edgar (IL)
Office of the Governor
State House
Springfield, IL 62706

Prince Edward
Buckingham Palace
London, SW1, ENGLAND

Dr. Joycelyn Elders
800 Marshall Street
Little Rock, AR 72202

HRH Queen Elizabeth II
Buckingham Palace
London, SW1, ENGLAND

HRH Elizabeth, Queen Mother
Clarence House
London, SW1, ENGLAND

Emir of Bahrain
721 Fifth Avenue, 60th Floor
New York, NY 10022

Emir of Kuwait
Bayan Palace
Kuwait City, KUWAIT

Gov. John Engler (MI)
101 N. Capitol
Lansing, MI 48909

Rep. Anna G. Eshoo (CA)
House Cannon Building #308
Washington, DC 20515

Charles Evers
416 West County Line Road
Tougaloo, MS 39174

Myrlie Evers-Williams
4805 Mt. Hope Drive
Baltimore, MD 21215

Sen. James Exon (NE)
Senate Hart Building #528
Washington, DC 20510

F _____ F

King Fahd
Royal Palace
Riyadh, SAUDI ARABIA

Dante Fascell
6300 SW 99th Terrace
Miami, FL 33156

Sen. Russell Feingold (WI)
Senate Hart Building #SH-502
Washington, DC 20510

Sen. Dianne Feinstein (CA)
Senate Hart Building #331
Washington, DC 20510

Geraldine Ferraro
22 Deepdene Road
Forest Hills, NY 11375

Marlin Fitzwater
2001 Swan Terrace
Alexandria, VA 22307

Ex- Rep. Thomas Foley
601 West 1st Avenue #2W
Spokane, WA 99204

Betty Ford
40365 San Dune Road
Rancho Mirage, CA 92270

Ex-Pres. Gerald R. Ford
40365 San Dune Road
Rancho Mirage, CA 92270

Sen. Wendell Ford (KY)
Senate Russell Building #173A
Washington, DC 20510

Rep. Barney Frank (MA)
House Rayburn Building #2210
Washington, DC 20515

William Freeh
Federal Bureau of Investigation
Washington, DC 20535

G _____ G

Col. Mu' ammar Gaddafi
State Office/Babel Aziziya
Tripoli, LIBYA

Rep. Richard Gephart (MO)
House Longworth Building #1226
Washington, DC 20515

Rep. Newt Gingrich (GA)
House Rayburn Building #2428
Washington, DC 20515

Ruth Bader Ginsburg
700 New Hampshire Avenue NW
Washington, DC 20037

Mayor Rudolph Giuliani
City Hall
New York, NY 10007

Sen. John Glenn (OH)
Senate Hart Bldg. #503
Washington, DC 20510

Ex-Sen. Barry Goldwater
6250 Hogahn
Paradise Valley, AZ 85253

Ex-Chmn. Mikhail Gorbachev
49 Leningradsky Prospekt 209
Moscow RUSSIA.

V.P. Albert Gore, Jr.
34th & Massachusetts
Washington, DC 20005

Tipper Gore
34th & Massachusetts
Washington, DC 20005

Sen. Slade Gorton (WA)
Senate Hart Bldg. #730
Washington, DC 20510

Sen. Bob Graham (FL)
Senate Hart Building #524
Washington, DC 20510

Sen. Phil Gramm (TX)
Senate Russell Building #370
Washington, DC 20510

Ex- Rep. Fred Grandy
9417 Spruce Tree Circle
Bethesda, MD 20814

Sen. Charles E. Grassley (IA)
Senate Hart Bldg. #135
Washington D.C. 20510

Alan Greenspan
Federal Reserve System
20th St. & Constitution Ave. NW
Washington, DC 20551

H   H

Sen. Chuck Hager (NE)
Hart Senate Office Bldg. #528
Washington, DC 20515

Gen. Alexander Haig, Jr.
6041 Crimson Court
McLean, VA 22101

Gus Hall
235 W. 23rd Street
New York, NY 10011

Rep. Lee Hamilton (IN)
House Rayburn Building #2314
Washington, DC 20515

Sen. Tom Harkin (IA)
Senate Hart Building #531
Washington, DC 20515

Ex-Sen. Gary Hart
P.O. Box 1988
Denver, CO 80201

King Hassan II
Royal Palace
Rabat, MOROCCO

Rep. Alcee Hastings (FL)
House Longworth Building #1039
Washington, DC 20515

Sen. Orrin G. Hatch (UT)
Senate Russell Building #131
Washington, DC 20510

Pres. Vaclav Havel
Hradecek CR-11908
Prague 1 CZECH REPUBLIC

Tom Hayden
10951 West Pico Blvd. #202
Los Angeles, CA 90064

Howell Heflin
311 E. 6th Street
Tuscumbia, AL 35674

Sen. Jesse Helms (NC)
Senate Dirken Building #403
Washington, DC 20510

Rep. Wally Herger (CA)
Rayburn House Office Bldg. #2433
Washington, DC 20515

Sec. Alexis M. Herman
Department of Labor
Washington, DC 20210

Sen. Ernest F. Hollings (SC)
Russell Senate Office Bldg. #125
Washington, DC 20510

Herbert Hoover III
200 S. Los Robles Avenue #520
Pasadena, CA 91101

Ex-Rep. Michael Huffington
3005-45th Street NW
Washington, DC 20016

Hubert H. Humphrey III
555 Park Street #310
St. Paul, MN 55103

Douglas Hurd
5 Mitford Cottage, Westwell
Burford OXON ENGLAND

Saddam Hussein
Al-Sijoud Palace
Baghdad, IRAQ

King Hussein I
Box 1055
Amman, JORDAN

Sen. Kay Bailey Hutchinson (TX)
Russell Senate Office Bldg. #283
Washington, DC 20515

Rep Henry J. Hyde (IL)
Rayburn House Office Bldg. #2110
Washington, DC 20515

J _____ J

Rev. Jesse Jackson
400 "T" Street NW
Washington, DC 20001

Rep. Jesse Jackson, Jr. (IL)
House Cannon Bldg. #312
Washington, D.C. 20515

Maynard Jackson
68 Mitchell
Atlanta, GA 30303

Lady Bird Johnson
LBJ Ranch
Stonewall, TX 78671

Sen. Tim Johnson (SD)
Russell Senate Office Bldg. #243
Washington, DC 20510

Vernon Jordan, Jr.
4610 Kenmore Drive NW
Washington, DC 20007

K   K

Mickey Kantor
5019 Klingle Street, NW
Washington, DC 20016

Jack Kemp
1776 "I" Street NW #800
Washington, DC 20006

Sen. Dirk Kempthorne (ID)
Senate Dirksen Building #367
Washington, DC 20510

Justice Anthony Kennedy
1 - 1st Street, N.E.
Washington, DC 20543

Rep. Joseph P. Kennedy II (MA)
House Rayburn Building #2242
Washington, DC 20515

Rep. Patrick Kennedy (RI)
House Longworth Building #1505
Washington, DC 20515

Sen. Ted Kennedy (MA)
Senate Russell Building #315
Washington, DC 20510

Sen. Bob Kerry (NE)
Senate Hart Building #303
Washington, DC 20510

Sen. John F. Kerry (MA)
Senate Russell Building #421
Washington, DC 20510

Dr. Alan Keyes
1030-15th Street NW #700
Washington, DC 20005

Coretta Scott King
234 Sunset Avenue N.W.
Atlanta, GA 30314

Lane Kirkland
815 - 16th Street N.W.
Washington, DC 20006

Dr. Henry Kissinger
435 E. 52nd Street
New York, NY 10022

Ex-Mayor Edward I. Koch
1290 Avenue of the Americas
New York, NY 10104

Chancellor Helmut Kohl
Marbacher Strasse II
D-6700, Ludwigshafen
Rhein, GERMANY

Sen. Herbert Kohl (WI)
Senate Hart Building #330
Washington, DC 20510

Mayor Teddy Kollek
22 Jaffa Road
Jerusalem, ISRAEL

L   **L**

Ex-Gov. Richard Lamm
University of Denver
Center for Public Policy
Denver, CO 80208

Bert Lance
P.O. Box 637
Calhoun, GA 30701

Sen. Mary Landrieu (LA)
Hart Senate Office Bldg. #136
Washington, DC 20510

Rep. Tom Lantos (CA)
Rayburn House Office Bldg #2217
Washington, DC 20515

Rep. Steve Largent (OK)
Cannon House Office Building #410
Washington, DC 20515

Sen. Frank Lautenberg (NJ)
Senate Hart Building #506
Washington, DC 20510

Paul Laxalt
1455 Pennsylvania Avenue NW
Washington, D.C. 20004

Rep. Jim Leach (IA)
House Rayburn Building #2186
Washington, DC 20515

Sen. Jon Kyl (AZ)
Hart Senate Office Bldg. #702
Washington, DC 20510

Sen. Patrick J. Leahy (VT)
Senate Russell Building #433
Washington, DC 20510

Gov. Mike Leavitt (UT)
210 State Capitol
Salt Lake City, UT 84114

Sen. Carl Levin (MI)
459 Russell, Sen. Office Bldg.
Washington, DC 20510

Rep. Jerry Lewis (CA)
House Rayburn Building #2112
Washington, DC 20515

Rep. John Lewis (GA)
House Cannon Building #229
Washington, DC 20515

Sen. Joseph I Lieberman (CT)
Senate Hart Building #316
Washington, DC 20510

Premier Li Peng
Office of the Premie
Beijing (Peking)
People Republic of China

Sen. Trent Lott (MS)
Senate Russell Building #487
Washington, DC 20510

Rep. Nita Lowey (NY)
House Rayburn Building #2421
Washington, DC 20515

Sen. Richard Lugar (IN)
Senate Hart Building #306
Washington, DC 20510

M   M

Sen. Connie Mack (FL)
Senate Hart Building #517
Washington, DC 20510

Sen. John McCain (AZ)
Russell, Sen. Office Bldg. #241
Washington, DC 20515

Ex. Gov. Lester Maddox
3155 Johnson Ferry NE
Marietta, GA 30062

Ex-Sen. Eugene J. McCarthy
271 Hawlin Road
Woodville, VA 22749

John Major
8 Stuckley Road
Huntingdon, Cambs. ENGLAND

Ex-Rep. Paul McCloskey
2220 Geng Road
Palo Alto, CA 94303

Charles T. Manatt
4814 Woodway Lane N.W.
Washington, DC 20016

Rep. Bill McCollum (FL)
House Rayburn Bldg. #2266
Washington, DC 20515

President Nelson Mandela
51 Plain Street
Johannesburg, SOUTH AFRICA

Sen. Mitch McConnell (KY)
Senate Russell Building #361A
Washington, DC 20510

Winnie Mandela
Orlando West, Soweto
Johannesbury SOUTH AFRICA

Ex-Sen. George McGovern
4012 Linnean Avenue NW
Washington, DC 20008

Imelda Marcos
Leyte Providencia Department
Tolosa, Leyte PHILIPPINES

Rep. Cynthia McKinney (GA)
House Cannon Bldg., #124
Washington, D.C. 20515

Princess Margaret
Kensington Palace
London, N5, ENGLAND

Ex-Sen. Howard Metzenbaum
4512 Foxhill Crescent NW
Washington, DC 20007

Kweisi Mfume
3000 Druid Park Drive
Baltimore, MD 21215

Ex-Rep. Bob Michael
1029 N. Glenwood Street
Peoria, IL 61606

Sen. Barbara Mikulski (MD)
Senate Hart Building #709
Washington, DC 20510

Rep. Patsy Mink (HI)
House Rayburn Bldg., #2135
Washington, D.C. 20515

Ambassador Walter Mondale
2116 Irving Avenue So.
Minneapolis, MN 55405

Sen. Carol Moseley-Braum (IL)
Senate Hart Building #320
Washington, DC 20510

Sen. Daniel Moynihan (NY)
Senate Russell Building #464
Washington, DC 20510

President Hosni Mubarak
Royal Palace
Cairo, EGYPT

Sen. Frank Murkowowski (AK)
Senate Hart Building #706
Washington, DC 20510

Sen. Patty Murray (WA)
Senate Russell Building #111
Washington, DC 20510

N _____ N

Benjamin Netanyahu
38 Rehou King George
Tel Aviv 61231 ISRAEL

Sen. Don Nickles (OK)
Senate Hart Building #133
Washington, DC 20510

General Manuel A. Noriega
#38699-079
P.O. Box 979132
Miami, FL 33197

Sam Nunn
915 Main Street
Perry, GA 31060

O _____ O

Justice Sandra Day O'Connor
1 - 1st Street N.E.
Washington, DC 20543

Rep. David Obey (WI)
House Rayburn Building #2462
Washington, DC 20515

Pres. Adolf Ogi
Bundeshaus
300 Bern SWITZERLAND

Rep. Solomon P. Ortiz (TX)
Rayburn House Office Bldg. #2136
Washington, DC 20515

P   P

Rep. Ron Packard (CA)
House Rayburn Building #2372
Washington, DC 20515

Princess Ashraf Pahlavi
12 Avenue Montaigne
75016, Paris, FRANCE

Reverend Ian Paisley
"The Parsonage"
17 Cyprus Avenue
Belfast, 5T5 5NT
NORTHERN IRELAND

Rep Mike Papas (NJ)
House Cannon Bldg. #228
Washington, DC 20515

Gov. George Pataki (NY)
State Capital Bldg.
Albany, NY 12247

Gov. Paul E. Patton (KY)
State Capiton
Frankfort, KY 40601

Rep. Bill Paxon (NY)
House Rayburn Building #2436
Washington, DC 20515

Rep. Nancy Pelosi (CA)
House Rayburn Building #2457
Washington, DC 20515

Sec. Federico Pena
Department of Energy
1000 Independence Avenue SW
Washington, DC 20585

Ex-Sen Charles Percy
1691-34th Street NW
Washington, DC 20007

Shimon Peres
10 Hayarkon Street, #3263
Tel-Aviv, 63571 ISRAEL

Mme. Isabel Peron
Moreto 3, Los Jeronimos
E-28014 Madrid, SPAIN

William Perry
8017 Rising Ridge Road
Bethesda, MD 20817

HRH Prince Philip
Buckingham Palace
London, ENGLAND

Donald Pickering
Back Court, Manor House
Eastleach, Glos. ENGLAND

Rep. Richard Pombo (LA)
Longworth House Office Bldg. #1519
Washington, DC 20515

Q ──────────────────────────── Q

Ex-Vice Pres. Dan Quayle
6263 N. Scottsdale Road #292
Scottsdale, AZ 85250

Marilyn Tucker Quayle
6263 Scottsdale Road #292
Scottsdale, AZ 85250

R ──────────────────────────── R

President Fidel Ramos
Malacanang Palace
Manila, PHILIPPINES

Rep. Charles B. Rangel (NY)
House Rayburn Building #2354
Washington, DC 20515

Crown Prince Ranier II
Grimaldi Palace
Monte Carlo, MONACO

Nancy Reagan
668 St. Cloud Road
Los Angeles, CA 90077

Ex-Pres. Ronald Reagan
668 St. Cloud Road
Los Angeles, CA 90077

Chief Justice Wm. Rehnquist
111-2nd Street NE
Washington, DC 20002

Sec. Janet Reno
Department of Justice
Washington, DC 20530

Ex-Sen. Abraham Ribicott
425 Park Avenue
New York, NY 10022

Ex-Gov. Ann Richards
P.O. Box 684746
Austin, TX 78768

Bill Richardson
799 United Nation Plaza
New York, NY 10017

Sec. Richard W. Riley
Department of Education
Washington, DC 20202

Mayor Richard Riordan
200 North Spring Street
Los Angeles, CA 90012

Sen. Charles Robb (VA)
Senate Russell Building #154
Washington, DC 20510

Sen. John Rockefeller (WV)
Senate Hart Building #109
Washington, DC 20510

Ex-Rep. Dan Rostenkowski
1372 West Evergreen Avenue
Chicago, IL 60622

Sec. Robert Rubin
Department of Treasury
Washington, DC 20220

S   S

Mme. Jehan El-Sadat
2310 Decatur Place N.W.
Washington, DC 20008

Saltan Hassanal Bokiah
Hassanal Bolkiah Nuda
Bandar Seri Begawan, BRUNEI

HRH Sarah, Dutchess Of York
Sunninghill Park
Windsor, Berks. ENGLAND

Justice Antonin Scalia
6713 Wemberly Way
McLean, VA 22101

Phyllis Schlafly
68 Fairmont
Alton, IL 62002

Mayor Kurt Schmoke
City Hall, 100 Holliday Street
Baltimore, MD 21201

Patricia Schroeder
1600 Emerson
Denver, CO 80218

Rep. Charles Schumer (NY)
House Rayburn Building #2211
Washington, DC 20515

Gen. Brent Scowcroft
6114 Wynnwood Road
Bethesda, MD 20816

Sec. Donna Shalala
Health and Human Services
200 Independence Avenue SW
Washington, DC 20201

Gen. John Shalikashvili
The Pentagon, Room 2E872
Washington, DC 20301

Sen. Richard Shelby (AL)
Senate Hart Building #110
Washington, DC 20510

Eduard Shevardnadze
State Council
Tbilisi GEORGIA

Ex-Sen. Paul Simon
Southern Illinois University
Carbondale, IL 62901

Sec. Rodney Slater
Department of Transportation
Washington, DC 20590

Sen. Olympia Snowe (ME)
Senate Russell Building #495
Washington, DC 20510

Ted Sorenson
1285 Avenue of the Americas
New York, NY 10019

Justice David Souter
1 - 1st Street N.E.
Washington, DC 20543

Sen. Arlen Specter (PA)
Senate Hart Building #530
Washington, DC 20510

Princess Stephanie
Maison Clos St. Martin
F-St. Remy de Provence FRANCE

George Stephanopoulos
1511 Connecticut Avenue NW
Washington, DC 20036

Justice John P. Stevens
1 - 1st Street N.E.
Washington, DC 20543

Sen. Ted Stevens (AK)
Senate Hart Building #522
Washington, DC 20510

Ex-Sen Adlai Stevenson III
10 South LaSalle Street, #3610
Chicago, IL 60604

Vice Adm. James Stockdale
Hoover Institute
Stanford, CA 94305

Rep. Louis Stokes (OH)
Rayburn, Hse. Office Bldg. #2365
Washington, DC 20515

Robert Strauss
1333 New Hampshire Ave. NW #400
Washington, DC 20536

John Sununu
24 Samoset Drive
Salem, NH 03079

T   T

Amb. Shirley Temple (Black)
115 Lakeview Drive
Woodside, CA 94062

Pres. Lee Teng-Hui
Chaehshou Hall
Chung King South Road
Taipei 10728 TAIWAN

Baroness Margaret Thatcher
Chester Square, Belgravia
London, ENGLAND

Justice Clarence Thomas
1 - 1st Street N.E.
Washington, DC 20543

Gov. Tommy Thompson
P.O. Box 7863
Madison, WI 53707

Sen. Strom Thurmond (SC)
Senate Russell Building #217
Washington, DC 20510

Star Guide 1998-1999 Politics

Kathleen Kennedy Townsend
100 State Circle
Annapolis, MD 21401

Bishop Desmond Tutu
Bishopcourt
Claremont 7700
Johannesburg, SOUTH AFRICA

U _____ U

Ex-Rep. Morris K. Udall
142 Calle Chaparita
Tucson, AZ 85716

Rep. Fred Upton (MI)
House Rayburn Building #2333
Washington, DC 20515

V _____ V

Cyrus Vance
425 Lexington Avenue
New York, NY 10017

Rep. Bruce Vento
Rayburn House Office Bldg. #2304
Washington, DC 20515

Rep. Nydia Velazquez (NY)
Cannon House Office Bldg. #132
Washington, DC 20515

Gov. George Voinovich (OH)
Office of the Governor
Columbus, OH 43266

W _____ W

Kurt Waldheim
1 Lobkowitz Platz
1010 Vienna, AUSTRIA

Sen. John Warner (VA)
Senate Russell Building #225
Washington, DC 20510

Lech Walesa
Polskistr 53
Gdansk, POLAND

Rep. Maxine Waters (CA)
Rayburn House Office Bldg. #2344
Washington, DC 20515

Ex-Gov. George Wallace
P.O. Box 667
Montgomery, AL 36101

James G. Watt
P.O. Box 3705
Jackson Hole, WY 83001

Rep. J.C. Watts, Jr. (OK)
House Longworth Building #1713
Washington, DC 20515

Rep. Henry Waxman (CA)
House Rayburn Building #2204
Washington, DC 20515

William H. Webster
9409 Brooke Drive
Bethesda, MD 20817

Gov. William Weld (MA)
State Capitol, Room #373
Boston, MA 02135

Sen. Paul Wellstone (MN)
Senate Hart Building #717
Washington, DC 20510

Gen. William Westmoreland
107 1/2 Tradd St.
Box 1059
Charleston, SC 29401

Ex-Justice Byron White
6801 Hampshire Road
McLean, VA 22101

Prince William
Kensington Palace
London W8 ENGLAND

Gov. Pete Wilson (CA)
Office of the Governor, State Captol
Sacramento, CA 95814

Ex-Rep. James Wright, Jr.
Lanham Federal Building
819 Taylor Street, #9A10
Ft. Worth, TX 76102

Y-Z _____ Y-Z

Boris Yeltsin
Uliza Twerskaya
Jamskaya 2 Moscow RUSSIA

Ex-Mayor Sam Yorty
12797 Blairwood Drive
Studio City, CA 91604

Ex-Mayor Andrew Young
1088 Veltrie Circle S.W.
Atlanta, GA 30311

Ex-Mayor Coleman A. Young
2 Woodward Avenue
Detroit, MI 48226

Others

They're Not A Star Until
They're A Star In Star Guide™

A _____ A

Leslie Abramson
4929 Wilshire Blvd.
Los Angeles, CA 90010

Red Adair
P.O. Box 747
Bellville, TX 77418

Richard Adams
26 Church Street
Whitechurch, Hants., ENGLAND

Louis Adler
3969 Villa Costera
Malibu, CA 90265

Roger Ailes
440 Park Avenue South
New York, NY 10016

Edward Albee
P.O. Box 697
Montauk, NY 11954

Amy Alcott
1411 Fifth Street #1400
Santa Monica, CA 90401

Ginger Alden
6554 Whitetail Lane
Memphis, TN 38115

Dr. Edwin "Buzz" Aldrin
838 N. Doheny Drive #1407
West Hollywood, CA 90069

Kim Alexis
345 North Maple Drive #185
Beverly Hills, CA 90210

Gloria Allred
6380 Wilshire Blvd. #1404
Los Angeles, CA 90048

Hollis Alpert
P.O. Box 142
Shelter Island, NY 11964

Robert Altman
502 Park Avenue #15G
New York, NY 10019

Christiane Amanpour
25 rue de Ponthieu
75008 Paris FRANCE

Rodney Amateau
133 1/2 S. Linden Drive
Beverly Hills, CA 90212

Aldrich Ames
P.O. Box 3000
White Deer, PA 17887

Rachel Ames
303 S. Crescent Heights
Los Angeles, CA 90048

Cleveland Amory
200 W. 57th Street
New York, NY 10019

Brad Anderson
13022 Wood Harbour Drive
Montgomery, TX 77356

Jack Anderson
7810 Kachina Lane
Potomac, MD 20854

Terry Anderson
50 Rockefeller Plaza
New York, NY 10020

Maya Angelou
3240 Valley Road
Winston-Salem, NC 28106

Wallis Annenberg
10273 Century Woods Place
Los Angeles, CA 90067

Army Archerd
442 Hilgard Avenue
Los Angeles, CA 90024

Ted Arison
3915 Biscayne Blvd.
Miami, FL 33137

Samuel Z. Arkoff
3205 Oakdell Lane
Studio City, CA 91604

Roone Arledge
535 Park Avenue, #13A
New York, NY 10021

Giorgio Armani
Palazzo Durini 24
I-20122 Milan ITALY

Garner Ted Armstrong
P.O. Box 2525
Tyler, TX 75710

Neil Armstrong
777 Columbus Avenue
Lebanon, OH 45036

Mary Kay Ash
2708 Fairmont Street
Dallas, TX 75201

Richard Avedon
407 East 75th Street
New York, NY 10021

B _____ B

Don Bachardy
145 Adelaide Drive
Santa Monica, CA 90402

Max Baer, Jr.
10433 Wilshire Blvd. #103
Los Angeles, CA 90024

F. Lee Bailey
1400 Centre Park Blvd. #909
West Palm Beach, FL 33401

Beryl Bainbridge
42 Albert Street
London NW1 7NU ENGLAND

Jim Bakker
P.O. Box 94
Largo, FL 33649

Tammy Faye Bakker
72727 Country Club Drive
Rancho Mirage, CA 92270

Bob Banner
2409 Briarcrest Drive
Beverly Hills, CA 90210

Joseph Barbera
12003 Briarvale Lane
Studio City, CA 91604

Barney
P.O. Box 8000
Allen, TX 75002

Mikhail Baryshnikov
157 West 57th Street #502
New York, NY 10019

Alan Bean
26 Sugarberry Circle
Houston, TX 77024

Marilyn Beck
P.O. Box 11079
Beverly Hills, CA 90213

Saul Bellow
1126 East 59th Street
Chicago, IL 60637

Peter Bencheley
35 Boudinot Street
Princeton, NJ 08540

William Bennett
20 West Lenox Street
Chevy Chase, MD 20815

Ingmar Bergman
P.O. Box 27127
S-10252 Stockholm, SWEDEN

David Berkowitz #78A1976
Sullivan Correctional Facility
Box AG
Fallsburg, NY 12733

Jay Bernstein
9360 Beverly Crest Drive
Beverly Hills, CA 90210

Mr. Blackwell
531 South Windsor Blvd.
Los Angeles, CA 90005

Nina Blanchard
3610 Wrightwood Drive
Studio City, CA 91604

Bill Blass
550 - 7th Avenue
New York, NY 10019

Linda Bloodworth-Thompson
9220 Sunset Blvd. #311
Los Angeles, CA 90069

Betsy Bloomingdale
131 Delfern Drive
Los Angeles, CA 90077

Judy Blume
40 E. 48th Street #1001
New York, NY 10017

John Wayne Bobbitt
7226 Westpark Avenue
Las Vegas, NV 89117

Lorena Bobbitt
709 Gray Avenue
Durham, NC 27701

Peter Bogdanovich
12451 Mulholland Drive
Beverly Hills, CA 90210

Yelena Bonner
Uliza Tschakalowa 48
Moscow, RUSSIA

Charley Boorman
Glebe, Annanoe County
Wicklow, IRELAND

Robert Bork
5171 Palisade Lane
Washington, DC 20016

Benjamin Bradlee
3014 "N" Street NW
Washington, DC 20007

Christie Brinkley
2124 Broadway, #104
New York, NY 10023

Edgar Bronfman
375 Park Avenue
New York, NY 10152

Dr. Joyce Brothers
235 East 45th Street
New York, NY 10017

Helen Gurley Brown
One West 81st Street #220
New York, NY 10024

Carla Bruni
62, Bd de Sebastopol
75003 Paris, FRANCE

Anita Bryant
P.O. Box 7300
Branson, MO 65615

Art Buchwald
4327 Hawthorne Street NW
Washington, DC 20016

William F. Buckley, Jr.
150 E. 35th Street
New York, NY 10016

Warren Buffett
1440 Kiewit Plaza
Omaha, NE 68131

Vincent T. Bugliosi
1926 W. Mountain Street
Glendale, CA 91201

Ken Burns
Maple Grove Road
Walpole, NH 03608

Joey Buttafuoco
1 Adam Road West
Massapequa, NY 11158

Dick Button
250 W. 57th Street #1818
New York, NY 10107

C _____ C

Lt. William Calley
c/o V.V. Vicks Jewelry
Cross Country Plaza
Columbus, GA 31903

James Cameron
919 Santa Monica Blvd.
Santa Monica, CA 90401

Stephen Cannell
7083 Hollywood Blvd.
Los Angeles, CA 90028

Pierre Cardin
59 Rue du Faubourg
St. Honore
F-75008 Paris, FRANCE

A.J. Carothers
2110 The Terrace
Los Angeles, CA 90049

Scott Carpenter
P.O. Box 3161
Vail, CO 81658

Allan Carr
1203 N. Sweezer #101
West Hollywood, CA 90069

Hodding Carter III
211 South St. Asaph
Alexandria, VA 22314

Barbara Cartland
Camfield Place Hatfield
Hertfordshire AL9 6JE, ENGLAND

Oleg Cassini
3 West 57th Street
New York, NY 10019

Engene Cernan
900 Town & Country Lane #300
Houston, TX 77024

Charles Champlin
2169 Linda Flora Drive
Los Angeles, CA 90024

Mark David Chapman
#81 A 3860, Box 149
Attica Correctional Facility
Attica, NY 14011

Suzette Charles
3680 Madrid Street
Las Vegas, NV 89121

Benjamin Chavis
P.O. Box 1661
Ellicott City, MD 21041

Julia Child
103 Irving Street
Cambridge, MA 02138

Michael Cimino
9015 Alto Cedro
Beverly Hills, CA 90210

Liz Claiborne
650 Fifth Avenue
New York, NY 10019

Marcia Clark
151 El Camino Drive
Beverly Hills, CA 90212

Mary Higgins Clark
210 Central Park South
New York, NY 10019

Arthur C. Clarke
4715 Gregory's Road
Colombo SRI LANKA

Eldridge Cleaver
935 NW 15th Avenue
Miami, FL 33125

Johnnie Cochran, Jr.
2373 Hobart Blvd.
Los Angeles, CA 90027

Jackie Collins
616 N. Beverly Drive
Beverly Hills, CA 90210

Marva Collins
4146 West Chicago Avenue
Chicago, IL 60651

Charles (Chuck) Colson
P.O. Box 17500
Washington, DC 20041

Charles T. Conrad, Jr.
19411 Merion Circle
Huntington Beach, CA 92648

Christian Conrad
21006 Dumetz Road
West Hills, CA 91364

Kimbery Conrad
10236 Charing Cross Road
Los Angeles, CA 90077

Paul Conrad
28649 Crestridge Road
Palos Verdes, CA 90274

Dr. Denton Cooley
3014 Del Monte Drive
Houston, TX 77019

Lt. Col. L. Gordon Cooper
5011 Woodley Avenue
Encino, CA 91436

David Copperfield
515 Post Oak Blvd. #300
Houston, TX 77027

Francis Coppola
916 Kearny Street
San Francisco, CA 91433

Roger Corman
2501 La Mesa Drive
Santa Monica, CA 90402

Norman Corwin
1840 Fairburn Avenue #302
Los Angeles, CA 90025

Jenny Craig
445 Marine View Drive #300
Del Mar, CA 92014

Cindy Crawford
132 S. Rodeo Drive, #300
Beverly Hills, CA 90212

Michael Crichton
433 N. Camden Drive #500
Beverly Hills, CA 90210

Judith Crist
180 Riverside Drive
New York, NY 10024

Walter Cronkite
519 E. 84th Street
New York, NY 10028

Norm Crosby
1400 Londonderry Place
Los Angeles, CA 90069

D _____ D

The Dalai Lama
Thekchen Choling
McLeod Gundi, Kangra
Himachal Pradesh, INDIA

Abby Dalton
P.O. Box 100
Mammoth Lakes, CA 93546

Joe Dante
2321 Holly Drive
Los Angeles, CA 90068

Christopher Darden
675 So. Westmoreland Avenue
Los Angeles, CA 90005

Altovise (Mrs. Sammy) Davis
279 S. Beverly Drive #1006
Beverly Hills, CA 90212

Gen. Benjamin O. Davis
1001 Wilson Blvd. #906
Arlington, VA 22209

Jim Davis
3300 Chadam Lame
Muncie, IN 47302

John Dean
9496 Rembert Lane
Beverly Hills, CA 90210

Michael Deaver
4 Chaparrel Lane
Palos Verdes, CA 90274

Hubert De Givenchy
3 Avenue George V
75008, Paris, FRANCE

Oscar De La Renta
Brook Hill Farm
Skiff Mountain Road
Kent, CT 06757

Dino De Laurentiis
Via Poutina Ku 23270
Rome, ITALY

John Z. DeLorean
567 Lamington Road
Bedminster, NJ 07921

Reginald Denny
844 North Vernon Avenue
Azusa, CA 91702

Brian De Palma
270 N. Canon Drive #1195
Beverly Hills, CA 90210

Barry Diller
1365 Enterprise Drive
West Chester, PA 19280

John Derek
3625 Roblar
Santa Ynez, CA 93460

Roy Disney
500 S. Buena Vista
Burbank, CA 91521

Alan Dershowitz
1563 Massachusetts Avenue
Cambridge, MA 02138

Alan Drury
P.O. Box 941
Tiburon, CA 94920

E _____ E

Roger Ebert
P.O. Box 146366
Chicago, IL 60614

Linda Ellerbee
96 Morton Street
New York, NY 10014

Michael Eisner
500 S. Buena Vista
Burbank, CA 91521

Linda Evangelista
2640 Carmen Crest Drive
Los Angeles, CA 90068

F _____ F

Fabio
P.O. Box 4
Inwood, NY 11696

Jules Feiffer
RR #1, Box 440
Vineyard Haven, MA 02568

Rev. Jerry Falwell
P.O. Box 6004
Forest, VA 24551

Cristina Ferrare
1280 Stone Canyon Road
Los Angeles, CA 90077

Min. Louis Farrakhan
4855 South Woodlawn Avenue
Chicago, IL 60615

Bobby Fischer
186 Rt. 9-W
New Windsor, NY 12250

Amy Fisher
3595 State School Road
Albion, NY 14411

Mary Fisher
3075 Hampton Place
Boco Raton, FL 33434

Larry Flynt
9211 Robin Drive
Los Angeles, CA 90069

Ken Follett
P.O. Box 708
London SW10 0DH ENGLAND

Steve Forbes
60 Fifth Avenue
New York, NY 10011

Eileen Otte Ford
344 E. 59th Street
New York, NY 10022

Milos Forman
The Hampshire House
150 Central Park Square
New York, NY 10019

John Fowles
52 Floral Street
London, WC2, ENGLAND

Milton Friedman
Quadrangle Office
Hoover Institute
Stanford University
Palo Alto, CA 94305

Daisy Fuentes
2200 Fletcher Avenue
Ft. Lee, NJ 07024

Mark Fuhrman
P.O. Box 141
Sandpoint, ID 83864

Robert Fulghum
1015 Violta Drive
Alhambra, CA 91801

G _____ G

John Kenneth Galbraith
30 Francis Avenue
Cambridge, MA 02138

Dr. Robert Gale
2501 Roscomare Road
Los Angeles, CA 90077

Dr. George Gallup II
The Great Road
Princeton, NJ 08540

Daryl Gates
756 Portola Terrace
Los Angeles, CA 90042

William "Bill" Gates
1 Microsoft Way
Redmond, WA 98052

Uri Geller
Sonning-on-Thames
Berkshire ENGLAND

Phyllis George
Cave Hill - Box 4308
Lexington, KY 40503

Mrs. J. Paul Getty
1535 N. Beverly Drive
Beverly Hills, CA 90210

Hubert Givency
3 Avenue George V
75008 Paris FRANCE

Bernhard Goetz
55 W. 14th Street
New York, NY 10011

Fred Goldman
P.O. Box 6016
Agoura Hills, CA 91376

William Goldman
50 E. 77th Street #30
New York, NY 10021

Samuel Goldwyn, Jr.
10203 Santa Monica Blvd. #500
Los Angeles, CA 90067

Jane Goodall
P.O. Box 41720
Tucson, AZ 85717

John Gotti #18261-053
Rt. 5, Box 2000
Marion, IL 62959

Lord Lew Grade
8 Queen Street
London, W1X 7PH, ENGLAND

Rev. Billy Graham
1300 Harmon Place
Minneapolis, MN 55403

Katherine Graham
2920 "R" Street N.W.
Washington, DC 20007

Earl G. Graves
130 Fifth Avenue
New York, NY 10011

Ex-Rep. William Gray III
500 East 62nd Street
New York, NY 10021

Graham Greene
121 North San Vicente Blvd.
Beverly Hills, CA 90211

Dick Gregory
P.O. Box 3270
Plymouth, MA 02361

Merv Griffin
9876 Wilshire Blvd.
Beverly Hills, CA 90210

John Grisham
114-A South Lamar Street
Oxford, MS 38655

Bob Guccione
1965 Broadway
New York, NY 10023

Cathy Guisewite
4900 Main Street
Kansas City, MO 64112

H _____ H

Jessica Hahn
6345 Balboa Blvd., #375
Encino, CA 91316

Arthur Hailey
Box N7776, Lyford Cay
Nassau, BAHAMAS

Jack Haley, Jr.
1443 Devlin Drive
Los Angeles, CA 90069

Fawn Hall
1568 Viewsite Drive
Los Angeles, CA 90069

Jerry Hall
304 West 81st Street
New York, NY 10024

Holly Hallstrom
5750 Wilshire Blvd. #475W
Los Angeles, CA 90036

Billy James Hargis
Rose of Sharon Farm
Neosho, MO 64840

Mrs. Jean Harris
c/o General Delivery
Monroe, NH 03771

Paul Harvey
1035 Park Avenue
River Forest, IL 60305

Patricia Hearst
110 - 5th Street
San Francisco, CA 94103

Mrs. Wm. Randolph Hearst
875 Comstock Avenue #16B
Los Angeles, CA 90024

Christie Hefner
680 N. Lake Avenue
Chicago, IL 60611

Hugh Hefner
10236 Charing Cross Road
Los Angeles, CA 90024

Leona Helmsley
36 Central Park South
New York, NY 10019

Don Hewitt
555 W. 57th Street
New York, NY 10019

William Hewlett
1501 Page Mill Road
Palo Alto, CA 94304

Thor Heyerdahl
E-38500 Guimar
(Tenerife) SPAIN

Jack Higgins
Septembertide
Mont DeLa Rocque
Jersey, Channel Islands (U.K.)

Anita Hill
300 Timberdell Road
Norman, OK 73019

Sir Edmund Hillary
278A Remuera Road
Auckland, SE2, NEW ZEALAND

Baron Hilton
28775 Sea Ranch Way
Malibu, CA 90265

John Hinckley, Jr.
St. Elizabeth's Hospital
2700 Martin L. King Avenue
Washington, DC 20005

James Hoffa, Jr.
8325 E. Jefferson Avenue
Detroit, MI 48214

Syd Hoffs
P.O. Box 2463
Miami Beach, FL 33140

Benjamin Hooks
260 Fifth Avenue
New York, NY 10001

Mrs. Dolores Hope
10346 Moorpark North
North Hollywood, CA 91602

Arianna Huffington
3005-45th Street NW
Washington, DC 20016

Howard E. Hunt
1149 NE 101st Street
Miami Shores, FL 33138

Lamar Hunt
1601 Elm Street #2800
Dallas, TX 75021

Rachel Hunter
23 Beverly Park
Beverly Hills, CA 90210

Elizabeth Hurley
3 Cromwell Place
London SW 2JE ENGLAND

Joe Hyams
10375 Wilshire Blvd. #4D
Los Angeles, CA 90024

I _____ I

Lee Iacocca
30 Scenic Oaks
Bloomfield Hills, MI 48013

Iman
111 East 22nd Street #200
New York, NY 10010

Kathy Ireland
P.O. Box 5353
Santa Barbara, CA 93150

Judge Lance Ito
825 So. Madison Avenue
Pasadena, CA 91106

J _____ J

LaToya Jackson
30 Daniel Low Terrace #3-R
Staten Island, NY 10301

Bianca Jagger
530 Park Avenue #18D
New York, NY 10021

Norman Jewison
3000 W. Olympic Blvd. #1314
Santa Monica, CA 90404

Joyce Jillson
64 E. Concord Street
Orlando, FL 32801

Steve Jobs
900 Chesapeake Drive
Redwood City, CA 94063

Paula Jones
1 Third Place
Long Beach, CA 90802

K _____ K

Brian "Kato" Kaelin
8383 Wilshire Blvd. #954
Beverly Hills, CA 90211

Donna Karan
550-7th Avenue #1500
New York, NY 10018

Yousuf Karsh
1 Rideau Street
Ottawa Ontario
K1N 9S7 CANADA

Lawrence Kasdan
10345 W. Olympic Blvd.
Los Angeles, CA 90064

Kitty Kelly
3037 Dunbarton Avenue N.W,
Washington, DC 20007

Caroline Kennedy-Schlossberg
641 - 6th Avenue
New York, NY 10011

John Kennedy, Jr.
20 N. Moore Street
New York, NY 10013

Leon Isaac Kennedy
9427 Via Monique
Burbank, CA 91504

Michael Kennedy
530 Atlantic Avenue #500
Boston, MA 02210

Kirk Kerkorian
4045 South Spencer Street #A57
Las Vegas, NV 89119

Dr. Jack Kevorkian
4870 Lockhart Street
West Bloomfield, MI 48323

Ted Key
1694 Glenhardie Road
Wayne, PA 19087

Victor K. Kiam II
60 Main Street
Bridgeport, CT 06602

Rodney King
9100 Wilshire Blvd. #250-W
Beverly Hills, CA 90212

Stephen King
47 West Broadway
Bangor, ME 04401

Gelsey Kirkland
191 Silver Moss Drive
Vero Beach, FL 32963

Calvin Klein
205 W. 39th Street
New York, NY 10018

Dr. C. Everett Koop
5924 Maplewood Park Place
Bethesda, MD 20814

Stanley Kramer
2530 Shira Drive
Valley Village, CA 91607

Kreskin
P.O. Box 1383
West Caldwell, NJ 07006

William Kristol
6625 Jill Court
McLean, VA 22101

Mrs. Joan Kroc
8939 Villa La Jolla Drive
La Jolla, CA 92037

L   L

Alan Ladd, Jr.
312 North Faring Road
Los Angeles, CA 90077

Dr. Arthur Laffer
5375 Executive Square #330
La Jolla, CA 92037

Melvin Laird
1730 Rhode Island Avenue NW
Washington, DC 20036

Sir Freddie Laker
138 Cheapside
London EC2V 6BL ENGLAND

Ann Landers
435 N. Michigan Avenue
Chicago, IL 60611

John Landis
9369 Lloydcrest Drive
Beverly Hills, CA 90210

Sherry Lansing
1363 Angelo Drive
Beverly Hills, CA 90210

Ring Lardner, Jr.
55 Central Park West
New York, NY 10023

Gary Larson
4900 Main Street #900
Kansas City, MO 62114

Fred Lasswell
1111 N. Westshore Blvd. #604
Tampa, FL 33607

Estee Lauder
767 Fifth Avenue
New York, NY 10153

Ralph Lauren
1107 - 5th Avenue
New York, NY 10128

Arthur Laurents
P.O. Box 582
Quoque, NY 11959

Norman Lear
1999 Avenue of the Stars, #500
Los Angeles, CA 90067

John Le Carre
9 Gainsborough Gardens
London NW3 1BJ ENGLAND

Spike Lee
40 Acres & A Mule Film Works
124 De Kalb Avenue #2
Brooklyn, NY 11217

Elmore Leonard
2192 Yarmouth Road
Bloomfield Village, MI 48301

Ira Levin
40 E. 49th Street
New York, NY 10017

Shari Lewis
603 N. Alta Drive
Beverly Hills, CA 90210

G. Gordon Liddy
9112 Riverside Drive
Ft. Washington, MD 20744

Arthur L. Liman
1285 Avenue of the Americas
New York, NY 10019

Rush Limbaugh
366 Madison Avenue #700
New York, NY 10177

Ann Morrow Lindbergh
P.O. Box 98
St. Johnsbury, VT 05819

Jack R. Lousma
2722 Roseland Street
Ann Arbor, MI 48103

James A. Lovell
5725 E. River Road
Chicago, IL 60611

George Lucas
P.O. Box 2009
San Rafael, CA 94912

Robert Ludlum
P.O. Box 235
Bedford Hills, NY 10507

Sidney Lumet
1 West 81st Street
New York, NY 10024

M   M

Elle MacPherson
107 Greene Street
New York, NY 10112

Garry Marshall
10459 Sarah Street
Toluca Lake, CA 91602

Norman Mailer
142 Columbia Heights
Brooklyn, NY 11201

Mary Matalin
111 Massachusetts Avenue NE
Washington, DC 20001

John Malone
4643 South Ulster
Denver, CO 80237

Sarah McClendon
3133 Connecticut Avenue NW #215
Washington, DC 20008

Leonard Maltin
10424 Whipple Street
Touca Lake, CA 91602

Julie McCullough
8033 Sunset Blvd. #353
Los Angeles, CA 90046

David Mamet
P.O. Box 381589
Cambridge, MA 02238

James McDivitt
9146 Cherry Avenue
Rapid City, MI 49676

William Manchester
Westleyan Station
P.O. Box 329
Middleton, CT 06457

Rod McKuen
1155 Angelo Drive
Beverly Hills, CA 90210

Charles Manson #B33920
Corcoran Prison
House A4R-17L, Box 3471
Corcoran, CA 93212

Terrence McNally
218 W. 10th Street
New York, NY 10014

Forrest Mars
6885 Elm Street
McLean, VA 22101

Robert McNamara
2412 Tracy Place NW
Washington, DC 20008

Timothy McVeigh, #12076-064
9595 W. Quincy Avenue
Littleton, CO 80123

Edwin Meese III
1075 Springhill Road
McLean, VA 22102

Eric Menendez #1878449
CSP-Sac., Box 290066
Represa, CA 95671

Lyle Menendez #1887106
California Correctional Institute
CCI-Box 1031
Tehachapi, CA 93581

Russ Meyer
3121 Arrowhead Drive
Los Angeles, CA 90068

Lorne Michaels
88 Central Park West
New York, NY 10023

James Michener
2706 Mountain Laurel Lane
Austin, TX 78703

Michael Milken
4543 Tara Drive
Encino, CA 91436

Arthur Miller
RR 1, Box 320 - Tophet Road
Roxbury, CT 06783

Charles Mingus
484 W. 43rd Street #43-S
New York, NY 10036

Marvin Mitchelson
2500 Apollo Driv
Los Angeles, CA 90046

Thomas L. Monaghan
3001 Earhart
Ann Arbor, MI 48106

Rev. Sun Myung Moon
4 W. 43rd Street
New York, NY 10010

Dick Morris
20 Beeholm Road
West Redding, CT 06896

Toni Morrison
185 Nassau Street
Princeton, NJ 08544

Mother Delores (Debra Hart)
Regina Laudis Convent
Bethlehem, CT 06751

Stewart Mott
515 Madison Avenue
New York, NY 10022

The Muppets
P.O. Box 20750
New York, NY 10023

Rupert Murdoch
1211 - 6th Avenue
New York, NY 10036

Dee Dee Myers
2200 Fletcher Avenue
Fort Lee, NJ 07024

N _____ N

Ralph Nader
1600-20th Street NW
Washington, DC 20009

Hal Needham
2220 Avenue of the Stars #302
Los Angeles, CA 90067

LeRoy Neiman
One W. 67th Street
New York, NY 10023

Samuel I. Newhouse, Jr.
950 Fingerboard Road
Staten Island, NY 10305

Lynn Nofziger
2000 Pennsylvania Ave. NW #365
Washington, DC 20037

Dr. Thomas Noguchi
1110 Avoca Avenue
Pasadena, CA 91105

Oliver North
P.O. Box 9771
McLean, VA 22102

Robert Novak
1750 Pennsylvania Ave. NW #1312
Washington, DC 20006

O _____ O

Hazel O'Connor
Moneystown
South Roundwood
County Wicklow IRELAND

Patrick Oliphant
4900 Main Street, 9th Floor
Kansas City, MO 64112

Sydner Omarr
201 Ocean Avenue #1706B
Santa Monica, CA 90402

Marcel Ophuls
10 rue Ernst-Deloison
92200 Neuilly FRANCE

Yuri Orlov
Cornell University
Newman Laboratory
Ithaca, NY 14853

Nagisa Osima
4-11-5 Kugenuma-Matsugaoka
Fujisawa-Shi 251 JAPAN

Michael Ovitz
457 Rockingham
Los Angeles, CA 90049

Frank Oz
P.O. Box 20750
New York, NY 10023

P _____ P

Rosa Parks
9336 Wildemere Street
Detroit, MI 48206

I.M. Pei
600 Madison Avenue
New York, NY 10022

H. Ross Perot
1700 Lakeside Square
Dallas, TX 75251

Roman Polanski
43 Avenue Montaigne
75008, Paris, FRANCE

Sidney Pollack
13525 Lucca Drive
Pacific Palisades, CA 90272

Jonathan Pollard
Federal Reformatory
Marion, IL 62959

Pope John Paul II
Palazzo Apostolico Vaticano
Vatican City, ITALY

Paula Poundstone
1223 Broadway #162
Santa Monica, CA 90404

Gen. Colin L. Powell
909 N. Washington Street #767
Alexandria, VA 22314

Lisa-Marie Presley
1167 Summit Drive
Beverly Hills, CA 90210

Wolfgang Puck
805 N. Sierra Drive
Beverly Hills, CA 90210

Mario Puzo
866 Manor Lane
Bay Shore, NY 11706

R _____ R

Ralph Read
P.O. Box 1990
Chesapeake, VA 23327

Ron Reagan, Jr.
2612-28th Avenue West
Seattle, WA 98199

Charles "Bebe" Rebozo
524 Fernwood Drive
Key Biscayne, FL 33149

Sumner Redstone
200 Elm Street
Dedham, MA 02026

Rex Reed
1 W. 72nd Street #86
New York, NY 10023

Faye Resnick
301 North Canon Drive #203
Beverly Hills, CA 90210

Matty Rich
9560 Wilshire Blvd. #500
Beverly Hills, CA 90212

Dr. Sally Ride
9500 Gillman Drive
MS 0221
La Jolla, CA 92093

Harold Robbins
601 West Camino Sur
Palm Springs, CA 92262

Cokie Roberts
1717 DeSales Street
Washington, DC 20036

Oral Roberts
7777 Lewis Street
Tulsa, OK 74130

Pat Robertson
Christian Broadcasting
1000 Centerville Turnpike
Virgina Beach, VA 23463

David Rockefeller, Jr.
30 Rockefeller Plaza #5600
New York, NY 10112

Mrs. Nelson Rockefeller
812 Fifth Avenue
New York, NY 10021

Ed Rollins
510 King Street, #302
Alexandria, VA 22314

Carl T. Rowan
3116 Fessenden Street VW
Washington, DC 20008

Salman Rushdie
c/o Gillon Aitken
29 Fernshaw Road
London SW10 OTG ENGLAND

Mark Russell
2800 Wisconsin Avenue #810
Washington, DC 20007

S
S

William Safire
6200 Elmwood Road
Chevy Chase, MD 20815

J.D. Salinger
R.R. #3, Box 176
Cornish Flat, NH 03746

Vincent Sardi, Jr.
234 W. 44th Street
New York, NY 10036

Vidal Sassoon
1163 Calle Vista
Beverly Hills, CA 90210

Francesco Scavullo
216 E. 63rd Street
New York, NY 10021

Claudia Schiffer
5 Union Square #500
New York, NY 10003

Walter M. Schirra, Jr.
16834 Via de Santa Fe
Rancho Santa Fe, CA 92067

Arthur Schlesinger, Jr.
33 W. 42nd Street
New York, NY 10036

John Schlesinger
1210 N. Kings Road #102
Los Angeles, CA 90069

Daniel Schorr
3113 Woodley Road
Washington, DC 20008

Gen. Norman Schwarzkopf
400 North Ashley Drive #3050
Tampa, FL 33609

Martin Scorsese
445 Park Avenue #700
New York, NY 10022

Erich Segal
53 the Pryors
East Heath Road
London, NW3 1BP, ENGLAND

Stephanie Seymour
12626 High Bluff Drive, #200
San Diego, CA 92130

Robert Shapiro
2590 Walingford Drive
Beverly Hills, CA 90210

Rev. Al Sharpton
1113 Bedford Avenue
Brooklyn, NY 11216

Sidney Sheldon
10250 Sunset Blvd.
Los Angeles, CA 90077

Adm. Alan Shepard, Jr.
6225 Vectorspace Blvd.
Titusville, FL 32780

Fred Silverman
12400 Wilshire Blvd. #920
Los Angeles, CA 90025

Richard Simmons
P.O. Box 5403
Beverly Hills, CA 90209

Neil Simon
10745 Chalon Road
Los Angeles, CA 90077

John Singleton
4223 Don Carlos Drive
Los Angeles, CA 90008

Sirhan Sirhan
#B21014
Corcoran State Prison
P.O. Box 8800
Corcoran, CA 93212

Gene Siskel
1301 North Astor
Chicago, IL 60610

Yakov Smirnoff
1990 South Bundy Drive #200
Los Angeles, CA 90025

Liz Smith
160 E. 38th Street
New York, NY 10016

Susan Smith
#94g-4901-1104
Women's Correctional Facility
4450 Broad River Road
Columbia, SC 29210

Dr. William Kennedy Smith
100 E. 42nd Street #1850
New York, NY 10017

Lord Snowdon
22 Lauceston Place
London W1 ENGLAND

Alexander Solzhenitsyn
Plyushchikha Street
Moscow RUSSIA

Aaron Spelling
594 N. Mapleton Drive
Los Angeles, CA 90077

Gerry Spence
15 South Jackson
Jackson, WY 83001

Steven Spielberg
P.O. Box 8520
Universal City, CA 91608

Dr. Benjamin Spock
P.O. Box 1268
Camden, ME 04843

Kenneth Starr
6455 Madison Court
McLean, VA 22101

Danielle Steel
330 Bob Hope Drive
Burbank, CA 91523

Gloria Steinem
118 E. 73rd Street
New York, NY 10021

Howard Stern
10 East 44th Street #500
New York, NY 10017

Martha Stewart
Lily Pond Lane
East Hampton, NY 11937

Oliver Stone
520 Broadway #600
Santa Monica, CA 90401

Tom Stoppard
Iver Grove
Iver Bucks., ENGLAND

William Styron
RFD
Roxbury, CT 06783

Kathleen Sullivan
1025 N. Kings Road #202
West Hollywood, CA 90069

Jimmy Swaggert
P.O. Box 70821
Baton Rouge, LA 70821

T

T

Gay Talese
154 E. Atlantic Blvd.
Ocean City, NJ 08226

Amy Tan
3315 Sacramento Street #127
San Francisco, CA 94118

Brandon Tartikoff
1479 Lindacrest Drive
Beverly Hills, CA 90210

Niki Taylor
8362 Pines Blvd., #334
Hollywood, FL 33024

Mother Teresa
54A Acharya J. Chandara
Bose Road
Calcutta, 70010, INDIA

Studs Terkel
850 W. Castlewood
Chicago, IL 60640

Dave Thomas
4288 W. Dublin Granville Road
Dublin, OH 53017

Cheryl Tiegs
2 Greenwich Plaza #100
Greenwich, CT 06830

Robert Townsend
2934 1/2 N Beverly Glen Circle #407
Los Angeles, CA 90077

Gary Trudeau
459 Columbus Avenue #113
New York, NY 10024

Donald Trump
721 Fifth Avenue
New York, NY 10022

Ivana Trump
500 Park Avenue #500
New York, NY 10022

Ted Turner
1050 Techwood Drive N.W.
Atlanta, GA 30318

Scott Turow
Sears Tower #8000
Chicago, IL 60606

U

U

Peter Ueberroth
184 Emerald Bay
Laguna Beach, CA 92651

Leon Uris
P.O. Box 1559
Aspen, CO 81611

V   V

Abigail Van Buren
P.O. Box 69440
Los Angeles, CA 90069

Mario Van Peebles
9560 Wilshire Blvd. #516
Beverly Hills, CA 90212

Gore Vidal
1201 Alta Loma Road
Los Angeles, CA 90069

Richard Viguerie
7777 Leesburg Pike
Falls Church, VA 22043

Bob Vila
10877 Wilshire Blvd. #900
Los Angeles, CA 90024

Paul A. Volcker
Prof. International Economics
Princeton University
Princeton, NJ 08544

Diane Von Furstenberg
745 Fifth Avenue
New York, NY 10151

Kurt Vonnegut, Jr.
P.O. Box 27
Sagaponack, NY 11962

W   W

Mort Walker
61 Studio Court
Stamford, CT 06903

The Great Wallendas
138 Frog Hollow Road
Churchville, PA 18966

Lew Wasserman
911 N. Foothill Road
Beverly Hills, CA 90210

John Waters
8942 Wilshire Blvd.
Beverly Hills, CA 90211

Andrew Lloyd Webber
Trump Tower
725 Fifth Avenue
New York, NY 10022

Casper W. Weinberger
700 New Hampshire Avenue NW
Washington, DC 20037

Dr. Ruth Westheimer
900 W. 190th Street
New York, NY 10040

Heather Whitestone
1325 Boardwalk
Atlantic City, NJ 08401

Thomas Wicker
c/o New York Times
229 W. 43rd Street
New York, NY 10036

Elie Wiesel
745 Commonwealth Avenue
Boston, MA 02115

Simon Wiesenthal
Salvtorgasse 6
1010, Vienna, 1, AUSTRIA

George Will
9 Grafton Street
Chevy Chase, MD 20815

Bruce Williams
P.O. Box 547
Elfers, FL 34680

Bob Woodward
2907 "Q" Street NW
Washington, DC 20007

Herman Wouk
303 Crestview
Palm Springs, CA 92264

Steve Wozniak
475 Alberto Way
Los Gatos, CA 95030

Y   Y

Mollie Yard
1000 - 16th Street N.W.
Washington, DC 20036

Gen. Charles E. Yeager
P.O. Box 128
Cedar Ridge, CA 95924

Z   Z

Richard Zanuck
202 N. Canon Drive
Beverly Hills, CA 90210

Franco Zefferelli
91 Regent Street
London W1R 7TB ENGLAND

Bob Zemeckis
1880 Century Park E., #900
Los Angeles, CA 90067

Ron Ziegler
2008 Fort Drive
Alexandria, VA 22307

Index

They're Not A Star Until
They're A Star In Star Guide™

A

Aaron, Henry "Hank" 108
Abbott, Dihanne 4
Abdul, Paula 74
Abdul-Jabbar, Kareem 108
Abdul-Olajuwon, Akeem 108
Abercrombie, Ian 4
Abraham, F. Murray 4
Abramson, Leslie 160
Abril, Victoria 4
Abruzzo, Ray 4
Abzug, Bella 138
AC/DC 74
Ackerman, Leslie 4
Acovone, Jay 4
Adair, Red 160
Adams, Brooke 4
Adams, Bryan 74
Adams, Cindy 4
Adams, Gerry 138
Adams, Mason 4
Adams, Maud 4
Adams, Richard 160
ADC Band 74
Adjani, Isabelle 4
Adler, Louis 160
Adulyadey, King of Thailand 138
Aerosmith 74
Agar, John 4
Agassi, Andre 108
Agutter, Jenny 4
Aiello, Danny 4
Aikman, Troy 108
Ailes, Roger 160
Aimee, Anouk 4
Ainge, Danny 108
Air Supply 74
Akaka, Sen. Daniel K. 138
Akihoto, Emperor 138
Al-Assad, Pres. Hafez 138
Alabama 74
Alan, Brick 74
Albee, Edward 160
Albert, Eddie 4
Albert, Edward 4
Albert, Marv 108
Albert, Prince 138
Albin, Dolores 5
Albright, Medeleine 138
Alcott, Amy 160
Alda, Alan 5
Alden, Ginger 160
Aldrin, Dr. Edwin 160
Aletter, Frank 5
Alexander, Denise 5
Alexander, Jason 5
Alexander, Lamar 138
Alexis, Kim 160
Alfonso, Kristian 5
Ali, Muhammad 108
Ail, Tatyana 5

Alice in Chains 74
Allan, Jed 5
Allen, Chad 5
Allen, Elizabeth 5
Allen, Jonelle 5
Allen, Marcus 108
Allen, Sean Barbara 5
Allen, Steve 5
Allen, Tim 5
Allen, Woody 5
Alley, Kirstie 5
Allison, Mose 74
Allman, Greg 74
Allport, Christopher 5
Allred, Gloria 160
Allyson, June 5
Alomar, Roberto 108
Alonso, Maria Conchita 6
Alpert, Herb 74
Alpert, Hollis 160
Alt, Carol 5
Altman, Jeff 6
Altman, Robert 160
Alvarado, Trini 6
Amanpour, Christiane 160
Amateau, Rodney 160
America 74
Ames, Aldrich 160
Ames, Rachel 160
Amick, Madchen 6
Amin, Idi 138
Amis, Suzy 6
Amory, Cleveland 160
Amos, Tori 74
Ana-Alicia 6
Anderson, Barbara 6
Anderson, Brad 161
Anderson, George "Sparky .... "108
Anderson, Gillian 6
Anderson, Jack 161
Anderson, Loni 6
Anderson, Lynn 74
Anderson, Melissa Sue 6
Anderson, Melody 6
Anderson, Michael J. 6
Anderson Lee, Pamela 6
Anderson, Richard Dean 6
Anderson, Richard 6
Anderson, Terry 161
Andersson, Bibi 6
Andress, Ursula 6
Andretti, Mario 108
Andretti, Michael 108
Andrew, Prince 138
Andrews, Anthony 6
Andrews, Julie 74
Andrews, Patti 74
Andrews, Tige 6
Angelo, Maya 161
Angels, Vanessa 6

Anka, Paul 74
Annan, Kafi 138
Anne, Princess 138
Annenberg, Wallis 161
Ansara, Michael 6
Anspach, Susan 7
Ant, Adam 75
Anthony, Lysette 7
Anthony, Ray 75
Anton, Susan 7
Anwar, Gabrielle 7
Aoki, Rocky 108
Aparicio, Luis 108
Applegate, Christina 7
Arafat, Yassir 138
Arcaro, Eddie 108
Archer, Rep. Bill 138
Archer, Dennis 138
Archerd, Army 161
Arens, Moshe 138
Argenziano, Carmen 7
Arison, Ted 161
Aristide, Jean-Bertrand 138
Arkin, Adam 7
Arkoff, Samuel Z. 161
Arledge, Roone 161
Armani, Giorgio 161
Armstrong, Curtis 7
Armstrong, Garner Ted 161
Armstrong, Neil 161
Arnaz, Jr., Desi 7
Arnaz, Lucie 7
Arness, James 7
Arnold, Tom 7
Arquette, Patricia 7
Arquette, Rosanna 7
Arrested Development 75
Arthur, Beatrice 7
Ash, Mary Kay 161
Asher, Jane 7
Ashford & Simpson 75
Ashkenazv, Valdimir 75
Ashley, Elizabeth 7
Ashley, Jennifer 7
Asleep at the Wheel 75
Asner, Ed 7
Assante, Armand 7
Astin, John 8
Astin, Sean 8
Astley, Rick 75
Atkins, Christopher 8
Auberjonois, Rene 8
Auermann, Nadja 8
Auger, Claudine 8
Aurerbach, Red 108
Austin, Karen 8
Avalon, Frankie 75
Avedon, Richard 161
Axton, Hoyt 75
Aykroyd, Dan 8
Azaria, Hank 8

Azinger, Paul 108
Aznavour, Charles 75
Azzara, Candice 8

B

B-52's 75
Babbitt, Bruce 139
Babilonia, Tai 109
Babyface 75
Bacall, Lauren 8
Bacharach, Burt 75
Bachardy, Don 161
Bachman, Wally 109
Baer, Jr., Max 161
Baez, Joan 75
Bailey, Donovan 109
Bailey, F. Lee 161
Bain, Barbara 8
Bainbridge, Beryl 161
Baio, Scott 8
Bairstow, Scott 8
Baker, Anita 75
Baker, Ex-Sen. Howard 139
Baker, Joe Don 8
Baker, Tyler 8
Bakke, Brenda 8
Bakker, Rev. Jim 162
Bakker, Tammy Faye 162
Baldwin, Alec 8
Baldwin, William 9
Ballard, Hank 75
Ballard, Kaye 75
Banks, Ernie 109
Banner, Bob 162
Bannister, Sir Roger 109
Barbera, Joseph 162
Barbieri, Paula 9
Bardot, Brigitte 9
Barker, Bob 9
Barkin, Ellen 9
Barkley, Charles 109
Barnes, Priscilla 9
Barney 162
Barrett, Majel 9
Barry, Marion 139
Barrymore, Drew 9
Baryshnikov, Mikhail 162
Basinger, Kim 9
Bassette, Angela 9
Bassey, Shirley 75
Batchelor, Amelia 9
Bateman, Jason 9
Bateman, Justine 9
Bates, Alan 9
Bates, Kathy 9
Battle, Kathleeen 76
Bauer, Steven 9
Bay City Rollers 76
Bayh, Birch 139
Baylor, Don 109
Beach Boys 76
Beach, Michael 9

Beals, Jennifer 9
Beame, Abraham 139
Bean, Alan 162
Beasley, Allyce 9
Beastie Boys 76
Beatrix of Holland, Queen 139
Beatty, Ned 9
Beatty, Warren 10
Beavis & Butt-Head 76
Beck 76
Beck, Kimberly 10
Beck, Marilyn 162
Becker, Boris 109
Bee-Gee's 76
Belafonte, Harry 76
Belafonte-Harper, Shari 10
Bell, Albert 109
Bell, Archie 76
Bell, George 109
Bell, Griffin 139
Bellamy Brothers 76
Bell Biv Devoe 76
Beller, Kathleen 10
Bello, Saul 162
Belmondo, Jean-Paul 10
Belushi, James 10
Benatar, Pat 76
Bench, Johnny 109
Bencheley, Peter 162
Benedict, Dirk 10
Bening, Annette 10
Benjamin, Richard 10
Bennet, Sen. Robert F. 139
Bennett, Tony 76
Bennett, William 162
Benson, George 76
Benzali, Daniel 10
Berenger, Tom 10
Bergen, Candice 10
Bergman, Ingmar 162
Bergman, Peter 10
Bergman, Sandahl 10
Berkowitz, David 162
Berle, Milton 10
Bernsen, Corbin 10
Bernstein, Jay 162
Berra, Yogi 109
Berry, Chuck 76
Berry, Halle 10
Berry, Ken 10
Bertil, HRH Prince 139
Bertinelli, Valerie 10
Bettenhausen, Gary 109
Bettenhausen, Tony 109
Bettis, Jerome 109
Bhutto, P.M. Benazir 139
Bialik, Mayim 10
Biden, Jr., Sen. Joseph 139
Biehn, Michael 11
Biggio, Craig 109
Billingsley, Barbara 11

Bingaman, Sen. Jeff 139
Bingham, Traci 11
Biondi, Matt 109
Birch, Thora 11
Bird, Larry 109
Birney, David 11
Bishop, Joey 11
Bisset, Jacqueline 11
Bisson, Yannick 11
Black Oak Arkansas 76
Black, Clint 76
Blackman, Honor 11
Blackwell, Mr. 162
Blair, Bonnie 110
Blair, Linda 11
Blair, Tony 139
Blake, Robert 11
Blakely, Susan 11
Blanchard, Nina 162
Blanda, George 110
Blass, Bill 162
Blauser, Jeff 110
Bledsoe, Drew 110
Bleier, Rocky 110
Blood, Sweat, & Tears 76
Bloodworth-Thompson, Linda 162
Bloom, Lindsay 11
Bloomingdale, Betsy 162
Blue, Vida 110
Blume, Judy 162
Blur 76
Boatman, Michael 11
Bobbitt, John Wayne 163
Bobbitt, Lorena 163
Bogdanovich, Peter 163
Bogguss, Suzy 76
Bohay, Heidi 11
Boitano, Brian 110
Bolton, Michael 77
Bon Jovi, Jon 77
Bond, Julian 139
Bonds, Barry 110
Bonds, Gary "US" 77
Bonet, Lisa 11
Bonilla, Bobby 110
Bonior, Rep. David 139
Bonner, Yelena 163
Bono, Sonny 139
Boone, Debbie 77
Boone, Pat 77
Boorman, Charley 163
Borg, Bjorn 110
Borge, Victor 77
Borgnine, Ernest 11
Bork, Robert 163
Bosley, Tom 11
Bostwick, Barry 11
Bowe, Riddick 110
Bowie, David 77
Bowman, Christopher 110
Boxcar Willie 77

Boxer, Sen. Barbara 139
Boxleitner, Bruce 11
Boy George 84
Boyle, Lara Flynn 12
Boys, The 77
Boyz II Men 77
Bradlee, Benjamin 163
Bradley, Bill 139
Bradley, Ed 12
Bradley, Ex-Mayor Tom 140
Bradshaw, Terry 110
Brady, James & Sarah 140
Branagh, Kenneth 12
Brando, Marlon 12
Braxton, Toni 77
Breaux, Sen. John 140
Brennan, Eileen 12
Brenner, David 12
Brett, George 110
Breyer, Steven 140
Bridges, Beau 12
Bridges, Jeff 12
Bridges, Lloyd 12
Brimley, Wilford 12
Brinkley, Christie 163
Brinkley, David 12
Brittany, Morgan 12
Brock, Lou 110
Broderick, Matthew 12
Brokaw, Tom 12
Brolin, James 12
Bronfman, Edgar 163
Bronson, Charles 12
Brooks, Albert 12
Brooks, Garth 77
Brooks, Mel 12
Brosnan, Pierce 12
Brothers, Dr. Joyce 163
Broussard, Rebecca 12
Brown, Blair 13
Brown, Georg Stanford 13
Brown, Rep. George E. 140
Brown, Sen. Hank 140
Brown, Helen Gurley 163
Brown, James 77
Brown, Ex-Gov. Jerry 140
Brown, Sec. Jesse 140
Brown, Jim 110
Brown, Les 77
Brown, T. Graham 77
Brown Jr., Willie L. 140
Browne, Jackson 77
Browne, Roscoe Lee 13
Brubeck, Dave 77
Bruni, Carla 163
Bryan, Sen. Richard 140
Bryant, Anita 163
Brzezinski, Zbigniew 140
Buchanan, Patrick J. 140
Buchwald, Art 163
Buckingham, Lindsey 77

Buckley, Jr., William F. 163
Buckner, Bill 110
Budd, Zola 110
Buffett, Jimmy 77
Buffett, Warren 163
Bugliosi, Vincent T. 163
Bujold, Genevieve 13
Bullock, Sandra 13
Bumpers, Sen. Dale 140
Bunning, Rep. Jim 140
Burgi, Richard 13
Burnett, Carol 13
Burns, Sen. Conrad 140
Burns, Ken 163
Burrell, Leroy 110
Burstyn, Ellen 13
Busey, Gary 13
Busfield, Timothy 13
Bush 77
Bush, Barbara 140
Bush, Ex-Pres. George 140
Bush, Jr. Gov. George 140
Buss, Dr. Jerry 110
Buthelezi, Gatsha 140
Butler, Brett 13
Butler, Yancy 13
Buttafuoco, Joey 163
Button, Dick 163
Byrd, Sen. Robert 140

C

Caan, James 13
Caesar, Sid 13
Cage, Nicholas 13
Cain, Dean 13
Caine, Michael 13
Calley, Lt. William 164
Camacho, Hector 111
Cameron, James 164
Cameron, Kirk 13
Camp, Colleen 14
Campaneris, Burt 111
Campbell, Sen. Ben 141
Campbell, Bill 14
Campbell, Earl 111
Campbell, Glen 78
Campbell, Kim 141
Campbell, Luther 78
Campbell, Neve 14
Campbell, Tisha 14
Cannell, Stephen 164
Cannon, Dyan 14
Cannon, Freddie 78
Canseco, Jose 111
Cappelletti, John 111
Capriati, Jennifer 111
Capshaw, Kate 14
Cara, Irene 78
Cardin, Pierre 164
Carew, Rod 111
Carey, Mariah 78
Carlin, George 14

Carlisle, Belinda 78
Carlos, King Juan 141
Carlson, Gov. Arne 141
Carlton, Steve 111
Carnes, Kim 78
Carney, Art 14
Caroline, Princess 141
Carothers, A.J. 164
Carpenter, Mary-Chapin 78
Carpenter, Richard 78
Carpenter, Lt. Cmdr. Scott 164
Carr, Allan 164
Carr, Vikki 78
Carradine, David 14
Carradine, Keith 14
Carradine, Robert 14
Carrer, Tia 14
Carreras, Jose 78
Carrey, Jim 14
Carroll, Diahann 14
Carruthers, Kitty 111
Carruthers, Peter........................... 111
Carson, Johnny 14
Carter, Betty 78
Carter, Carlene 78
Carter, Deana 78
Carter, Dixie 14
Carter, Helena Bonham 14
Carter III, Hodding 164
Carter, Ex-Pres. Jimmy 141
Carter, Lynda 14
Carter, Nell 14
Carter, Rosalynn 141
Carteris, Gabrielle 14
Cartland, Barbara 164
Cartwright, Angela 15
Cartwright, Veronica 15
Caruso, David 15
Casals, Rosie 111
Cash, Johnny 78
Cash, Pat 111
Casper, Billy 111
Cassidy, David 78
Cassidy, Joanna 15
Cassidy, Patrick 15
Cassidy, Shaun 78
Cassini, Oleg 164
Castro, Dr. Fidel 141
Cateris, Gabrielle 15
Cates, Phoebe 15
Caufield, Max 15
Caulkins, Tracy 111
Cauthen, Steve 111
Cavett, Dick 15
Cazenove, Christopher 15
Cepeda, Orlando 111
Cernan, Eugene 164
Cerone, Rick 111
Cetera, Peter 78
Cey, Ron 111
Chafee, Sen. John H. 141

Chakiris, George 15
Chamarrol, Violeta 141
Chamberlain, Richard 15
Chambers, Marilyn 15
Champion, Marge 15
Champlin, Charles 164
Chan, Jackie 15
Chang, Michael 111
Channing, Carol 15
Channing, Stockard 15
Chao, Rosalind 15
Chapman, Mark David 164
Charisse, Cyd 15
Charles, HRH Prince 141
Charles, Ray 79
Charles, Suzette 164
Chase, Chevy 15
Chavez, Julio Ceasar 112
Chavis, Benjamin 164
Cheadle, Don 16
Checker, Chubby 79
Cheny, Dick 141
Cher 79
Chestnut, Mark 79
Child, Julia 164
Chiles, Gov. Lawton 141
Chirac, Jacques 141
Chisholm, Shirley 141
Chitwood, Joey 112
Chlumsky, Anna 16
Chong, Rae Dawn 16
Chow, Amy 112
Chretien, Jean 141
Christie, Julie 16
Christopher, Warren 141
Christopher, William 16
Chung, Connie 16
Church, Thomas Haden 16
Cimino, Michael 164
Cisneros, Sec. Henry 141
Claiborne, Liz 164
Clapton, Eric 79
Clark, Dick 79
Clark, Marcia 165
Clark, Mary Higgins 165
Clark, Ramsey 142
Clark, Roy 79
Clarke, Arthur C. 165
Clay, Andrew Dice 16
Clayburgh, Jill 16
Cleaver, Eldridge 165
Cleese, John 16
Clemens, Roger 112
Cliburn, Van 79
Clifford, Clark 142
Clinton, Pres. Bill 142
Clinton, Chelsea 142
Clinton, Hillary Rodham 142
Clohessy, Robert 16
Clooney, Rosemary 79
Close, Glenn 16

Coats, Sen. Dan 142
Coasters, The 79
Coburn, James 16
Cochran, Jr., Johnnie 165
Cochran, Sen. Thad 142
Cody, Iron Eyes 79
Coe, Sebastian 112
Coffey, Paul 112
Cohen, Sen. William S. 142
Cole, Michael 16
Cole, Natalie 79
Coleman, Dabney 16
Coleman, Gary 16
Coleman, Lisa 16
Collie, Mark 79
Collins, Gary 16
Collins, Jackie 165
Collins, Joan 16
Collins, Judy 165
Collins, Marva 165
Collins, Phil 79
Collins, Rep. Cardiss 142
Colson, Charles 165
Colter, Jessie 79
Comaneci, Nadia 112
Combs, Jeffrey 16
Como, Perry 79
Conaway, Jeff 17
Connery, Sean 17
Connick, Jr., Harry 79
Connors, Carol 17
Connors, Jimmy 112
Connors, Mike 17
Conrad, Jr., Capt Charles 165
Conrad, Christian 142
Conrad, Sen. Kent 142
Conrad, Kimberly 165
Conrad, Paul 165
Conrad, Robert 17
Conrad, Shane 165
Constantine, Ex-King 142
Constantine, Michael 17
Conway, Gary 17
Conway, Kevin 17
Conway, Tim 17
Conyers, Rep. John 142
Cooley, Dr. Denton 165
Coolidge, Rita 79
Cooper, Alice 79
Cooper, Jackie 17
Cooper, Lt. Col. Gordon 165
Copley, Teri 17
Copperfield, David 165
Coppola, Francis 165
Corby, Ellen 17
Corman, Roger. 165
Cornelius, Don 17
Corea, Chick 80
Cort, Bud 17
Corwin, Norman 165
Cosby, Bill 17

Costas, Bob 112
Costello, Elvis 80
Costner, Kevin 17
Couples, Fred 112
Couric, Katie 17
Courier, Jim 112
Cousins, Robin 112
Cousy, Bob 112
Coverdell, Sen. Paul 142
Cox, Archibald 142
Coyote, Peter 17
Craddock, Billy Crash 80
Craig, Jenny 165
Craig, Sen. Larry 142
Craig, Yvonne 17
Crane, Rep. Phillip 142
Cranston, Ex-Sen. Alan 142
Crawford, Cindy 165
Crenna, Richard 18
Crenshaw, Ben 112
Cretien, Jean 142
Crichton, Michael 166
Crist, Judith 166
Cronkite, Walter 166
Cronyn, Hume 18
Crosby, Cathy Lee 18
Crosby, David 80
Crosby, Norm 166
Crosby, Stills, & Nash 80
Cross, Christopher 80
Crow, Sheryl 80
Crowell, Rodney 80
Cruise, Tom 18
Crum, Denny 112
Crystal, Billy 18
Culkin, Macaulay 18
Culp, Robert 18
Cunningham, Randall 112
Cuomo, Sec. Andrew 142
Cuomo, Ex-Gov. Mario 142
Currie, Cherie 80
Curry, Mark 18
Curry, Tim 18
Curtin, Jane 18
Curtin, Valerie 18
Curtis, Jamie Lee 18
Curtis, Tony 18
Cutter, Lise 18
Cyrus, Billy Ray 80

D

d'Abo, Maryam 18
d'Abo, Olivia 18
D'amato, Sen. Alfonse M 143
D'Angelo, Beverly 19
D'Arbanville, Patti 19
D'Arby, Terence Trent 80
Dafoe, Willem 18
Daggett, Tim 112
Dalai Lama, The 166
Daley, Mayor Richard 143
Daley, Sec. William 143

Dalton, Abby 166
Dalton, Timothy 18
Daltry, Roger 80
Daly, John 112
Daly, Tyne 19
Damone, Vic.................................. 80
Dangerfield, Rodney 19
Daniels Band, Charlie 80
Daniels, Jeff 19
Danson, Ted 19
Dante, Joe 166
Danza, Tony 19
Darden, Christopher..................... 166
Darling, Ron 113
Daschle, Sen. Thomas 143
Davenport, Lindsay 113
Davi, Robert 19
Davidson, John 80
Davis, Al 113
Davis, Altovise (Mrs. Sammy 166
Davis, Gen. Benjamin 166
Davis, Clifton 19
Davis, Jim..................................... 166
Davis, Ossie 19
Dawber, Pam 19
Dawes, Dominique 113
Day, Doris 19
De La Hoya, Oscar 113
De La Renta, Oscar 166
De Laurentiis, Dino 166
De Palma, Brian 167
Dean, Jimmy 80
Dean, John 166
Deaver, Michael 166
Decker-Slaney, Mary 113
Deconcini, Dennis 143
Dee, Ruby 19
Dee, Sandra 19
Deep Purple 80
Dees, Rick 80
Def Leppard 81
DeGeneres, Ellen.......................... 19
DeGivenchy, Hubert 166
DeHavilland, Olivia 19
deKlerk, Pres. WF 143
Delany, Dana 19
Dellums, Rep. Ronald V. 143
DeLorean, John Z. 166
DeLorenzo, Michael 19
DeMornay, Rebecca...................... 19
Dempsey, Patrick 19
Deneuve, Catherine 19
Denier, Lydie 20
DeNiro, Robert 20
Dennehy, Brian 20
Denny, Reginald 166
Dent, Bucky 113
Denver, Bob 20
Denver, John 81
Depeche Mode 81
Depp, Johnny 20

Derek, Bo 20
Derek, John 167
Dern, Bruce 20
Dern, Laura 20
Dershowitz, Alan 167
Deukmejian, George 143
Devane, William 20
Devers, Gail 113
Devine, Loretta 20
Devito, Danny 20
DeWine, Sen. Mike 143
Dewitt, Joyce 20
Dey, Susan 20
Diamond Rio 81
Diamond, Neil 81
Dibble, Rob 113
Dickinson, Angie 20
Diddley, Bo 81
Dierdorf, Dan 113
Diffie, Joe 81
Diller, Barry 167
Diller, Phyliss 20
Dillon, Matt 20
Dimaggio, Joe 113
Dingell, Rep. John 143
Dinkins, David 143
Dion, Celine 81
Dire Straits 81
Disney, Roy 167
Ditka, Mike 113
Dixon, Donna 20
Dobson, Kevin 20
Dobson, Peter 20
Dodd, Sen. Christopher 143
Doherty, Shannen 20
Dolan, Tom 113
Dole, Elizabeth 143
Dole, Sen. Robert 143
Dolenz, Mickey 81
Domenici, Sen. Pete 143
Domingo, Placido 81
Domino, Fats 81
Donahue, Elinor 21
Donahue, Phil 21
Donahue, Troy 21
Donohue, Terry............................. 113
Donaldson, Sam 21
Doobie Brothers 81
Doohan, James 21
Doors, The 81
Dorff, Stephen 21
Dornan, Ex-Rep. Robert 143
Dorsett, Tony 113
Douglas, James "Buster" 113
Douglas, Kirk 21
Douglas, Michael 21
Douglas, Mike 21
Down, Leslie Ann 21
Downey, Jr., Robert 21
Downs, Hugh 21
Drago, Billy 21

Drexler, Clyde............................... 113
Dreyfuss, Richard......................... 21
Drifters, The 81
Drury, Alan 167
Drury, James 21
Duchin, Peter 81
Duffy, Julia 21
Duffy, Patrick 21
Dukakis, Ex-Gov. Michael 143
Dukakis, Olympia 21
Duke, Patty 21
Dukes, David 21
Dumars, Joe 113
Dunaway, Faye 22
Duncan, Sandy 81
Dundee, Angelo 113
Dunn, Holly 81
dupont, Ex-Gov. Pierre 143
Duran Duran 81
Durning, Charles 22
Dusay, Marj 22
Dutton, Charles 22
Duvall, Robert 22
Duvall, Shelly 22
Dykstra, Lenny 113
Dylan, Bob.................................... 81

E

Eagleburger, Lawrence 144
Eagleton, Ex-Sen. Thomas 144
Earnhardt, Dale 114
Eastwood, Clint 22
Ebert, Roger 167
Ebsen, Buddy 22
Eckersley, Dennis......................... 114
Edberg, Stefan 114
Eddy, Duane 82
Eden, Barbara 22
Edgar, Gov. Jim 144
Edlund, Richard 22
Edward, Prince 144
Edwards, Anthony 22
Eggar, Samantha 22
Eggert, Nicole 22
Eikenberry, Jill 22
Eisner, Michael............................. 167
Elder, Lee 114
Elders, Joycelyn 144
Elgart, Larry 82
Electric Light Orchestra 82
Elizabeth (Queen Mother) 144
Elizabeth II, HRH Queen 144
Ellerbee, Linda 167
Elliot, Gordon 22
Elliott, Sam 22
Elliott, Sean 114
Ellis, Jimmy 114
Elway, John 114
Emir of Bahrain 144
Emir of Kuwait 144
En Vogue 82

Enberg, Dick 114
Engler, Gov. John 144
Englund, Robert 22
Entwhistle, John 82
Engvall, Bill 23
Erving, Julius 114
Eshoo, Rep. Anna 144
Estefan, Gloria 82
Estevez, Emilio 23
Estrada, Erik 23
Etheridge, Melissa 82
Eubanks, Kevin 82
Evan-Roger, Dale 23
Evangelista, Linda 167
Evans, Janet 114
Evans, Linda 23
Everet, Chris 114
Everly Brothers 82
Evers, Charles 144
Evers-Williams, Myrilie 144
Evigan, Greg 23
Ewing, Patrick 114
Exon, Sen. James 144
Extreme 82

F

Fabares, Shelley 23
Fabio 167
Fahd, HRH King 144
Fahey, Jeff 23
Fairbairn, Bruce 23
Fairchild, Morgan 23
Faith No More 82
Faithful, Marianne 82
Falana, Lola 82
Falk, Peter 23
Falwell, Rev. Jerry 167
Farentino, Deborah 23
Farentino, Linda 23
Fargo, Donna 82
Farina, Dennis 23
Farley, Chris 23
Farnon, Shannon 23
Farnsworth, Richard 23
Farr, Felicia 23
Farr, Jamie 24
Farrakhan, Min. Louis 167
Farrell, Mike 24
Farrell, Shea 24
Farrell, Terry 24
Farrow, Mia 24
Fascell, Dante 144
Fat Boys 82
Favre, Brett 114
Fawcett, Farrah 24
Faye, Alice 24
Dr. Feelgood 82
Feiffer, Jules 167
Feingold, Sen. Russell 145
Feinstein, Alan 24
Feinstein, Sen. Dianne 145
Feldman, Corey 24

Feldon, Barbara 24
Feliciano, Jose 83
Fell, Norman 24
Feller, Bob 114
Fellows, Edith 24
Fender, Freddie 83
Fenneman, George 24
Ferguson, Maynard 83
Fernandez, Mary Jo 114
Ferrante & Teicher 83
Ferrare, Cristina 167
Ferraro, Geraldine 145
Ferrell, Conchata 24
Ferrigno, Lou 24
Fidrych, Mark 114
Field, Chelsea 24
Field, Sally 24
Fielder, Cecil 115
Fields, Kim 24
Fingers, Rollie 115
Finkle, Fyvush 24
Fiorentino, Linda 24
Firm, The 83
Fischer, Bobby 167
Fishburne, Laurence 25
Fisher, Amy 168
Fisher, Carrie 25
Fisher, Eddie 83
Fisher, Frances 25
Fisher, Joely 25
Fisher, Mary 168
Fisk, Carlton 115
Fittipaldi, Christian 115
Fittipaldi, Emerson 115
Fitzwater, Marlin 145
Flack, Roberta 83
Flanagan, Fionnula 25
Flannery, Susan 25
Mick Fleetwood 83
Fleming, Peggy 115
Fleming, Rhonda 25
Fletcher, Louise 25
Floren, Myron 83
Floyd, Raymond 115
Flynt, Larry 168
Foch, Nina 25
Fogelberg, Dan 83
Foley, Rep. Thomas 145
Follett, Ken 168
Follows, Megan 25
Fonda, Bridget 25
Fonda, Jane 25
Fonda, Peter 25
Fontaine, Joan 25
Forbers, Steve 168
Ford, Betty 145
Ford, Eileen Otte 168
Ford, Faith 25
Ford, Ex-Pres. Gerald R 145
Ford, Glenn 25

Ford, Harrison 25
Ford, Sen. Wendell 145
Ford, Whitey 115
Foreigner 83
Foreman, George 115
Forester Sisters 83
Forman, Milos 168
Forrest, Frederic 25
Forster, Brian 25
Forster, Robert 25
Forsythe, John 26
Forsythe, William 26
Forte, Fabian 26
Foster, Jodie 26
Foster, Meg 26
Fountain, Pete 83
Four Season, The 83
Fowles, John 168
Fox, Michael J. 26
Foxworth, Robert 26
Foyt, A.J. 115
Frakes, Jonathan 26
Frampton, Peter 83
Franciosa, Tony 26
Francis, Anne 26
Francis, Connie 83
Francis, Genie 26
Frank, Joanna 26
Frank, Rep. Barney 145
Franklin, Aretha 83
Franklin, Bonnie 26
Frann, Mary 26
Franz, Dennis 26
Fraser, Brendan 26
Frazier, Joe 115
Frazier, Walt 115
Freeh, William 145
Freeman, Mona 26
Freeman, Morgan 26
Frelich, Phyllis 26
French, Susan 26
Frewer, Matt 27
Frey, Glen 83
Fricke, Janie 83
Friedman, Milton 168
Frost, David 27
Frye, Soleil Moon 27
Fuentes, Daisy 168
Fuhrman, Mark 168
Fulghum, Robert 168
Funicello, Annette 27
Furlong, Edward 27
Furst, Stephen 27

G

G, Kenny 84
Gabor, Zsa Zsa 27
Gabriel, Roman 115
Gaddafi, Col. Mu' ammar 145
Gains, Courtney 27
Galbraith, John Kenneth 168
Gale, Dr. Robert 168

Galligan, Zack 27
Gallup II, Dr. George 168
Ganzel, Teresa 27
Garagiola, Joe 115
Garcia, Andy 27
Gardner, Randy 115
Garfunkel, Art 84
Garner, James 27
Garofalo, Janeane 27
Garr, Teri 27
Garrison, Zina 115
Garvey, Steve 115
Gastineau, Mark 115
Gaston, Cito 116
Gates, Daryl 168
Gates, William "Bill" 168
Gatlin, Larry 84
Gault, Willie 116
Gayheart, Rebecca 27
Gayle, Crystal 84
Gaynor, Gloria 84
Geffen, David 84
Geldof, Bob 84
Gellar, Sarah Michelle 27
Geller, Uri 168
Genesis 84
Gentry, Bobby 84
George, Jeff 116
George, Lynda Day 27
George, Phyllis 169
George, Susan 27
Gephart, Rep. Richard 145
Gere, Richard 28
Gershon, Gina 28
Getty, Estelle 28
Getty, Mrs. J. Paul 169
Gibb, Barry 84
Gibbons, Leeza 28
Gibbs, Marla 28
Gibson, Charles 28
Gibson, Debbie 84
Gibson, Kirk 116
Gibson, Mel 28
Gibson-Darbeu, Althea 116
Gifford, Frank 116
Gilbert, Melissa 28
Gilbert, Sara 28
Gill, Johnny 84
Gilley, Mickey 84
Gimpe, Erica 28
Gingrich, Rep. Newt 145
Ginsburg, Ruth Bader 145
Giuliani, Rudolph 145
Givency, Hubert 169
Givens, Robin 28
Glaser, Paul Michael 28
Glass, Philip 84
Glavine, Tom 116
Glenn, Sen. John 145
Gless, Sharon 28
Glover, Danny 28
Goetz, Bernhard 169

Gold, Tracey 28
Goldberg, Whoopi 28
Goldblum, Jeff 28
Goldin, Ricky Paul 28
Goldman, Fred 169
Goldman, William 169
Goldsboro, Bobby 84
Goldwater, Ex-Sen. Barry 145
Goldwyn, Jr., Samuel 169
Golino, Valeria 28
Goodall, Jane 169
Gooden, Dwight 116
Goorjian, Michael 28
Gorbachev, Chmn Mikhail 145
Gordeeva, Ekaterina 116
Gordon, Jeff 116
Gordy, Berry 84
Gore, Jr., V.P. Albert 146
Gore, Lesley 84
Gore, Tipper 146
Gorme, Eydie 85
Gorton, Sen. Slade 146
Gosselaar, Mark Paul 29
Gossett, Jr., Louis 29
Gotti, John 169
Gould, Elliott 29
Goulet, Robert 85
Gowdy, Curt 116
Grace, Mark 116
Grade, Lord Lew 169
Graff, Steffi 116
Graham, Rev. Billy 169
Graham, Katherine 169
Graham, Otto 116
Graham, Sen. Bob 146
Gramm, Sen. Phil 146
Grammer, Kelsey 29
Grandy, Rep. Fred 146
Grant, Amy 85
Grant, Horace 116
Grant, Hugh 29
Grassley, Sen. Charles E. 146
Grateful Dead 85
Graves, Earl G. 169
Graves, Peter 29
Gray III, William H. 169
Gray, Erin 29
Gray, Linda 29
Grayson, Kathryn 29
Green, Rev. Al 85
Green, Brian Austin 29
Green, Dennis 116
Greene, Graham 169
Greene, Michele 29
Greenspan, Alan 146
Greenwood, Lee 85
Gregory, Dick 169
Greise, Bob 116
Gretzky, Wayne 116
Grey, Jennifer 29
Grieco, Richard 29
Grier, Rosie 116

Griffey, Jr., Ken 116
Griffey, Sr., Ken 117
Griffin, Merv 169
Griffin, Archie 117
Griffith, Andy 29
Griffith, Melanie 29
Griffith, Thomas Ian 29
Griffith-Joyner, Florence 117
Grisham, John 169
Grissom, Marquis 117
Groom, Sam 29
Groza, Lou 117
Guccione, Bob 169
Guidry, Ron 117
Guillaume, Robert 29
Guisewite, Cathy 169
Gumbel, Bryant 29
Gumbel, Greg 117
Gunn, Janet 29
Guns & Roses 85
Guthrie, Arlo 85
Guttenberg, Steve 30
Guy, Jasmine 30
Gwynn, Tony 117

H

Hack, Shelly 30
Hackman, Gene 30
Hagar, Sammy 85
Hager, Sen. Chuck 146
Haggard, Merle 85
Hagler, Marvin 117
Hagman, Larry 30
Hahn, Jessica 170
Haig, Jr., Gen. Alexander 146
Hailey, Authur 170
Haim, Corey 30
Haje, Khrystyne 30
Haley, Jr., Jack 170
Hall & Oates 85
Hall, Anthony Michael 30
Hall, Arsenio 30
Hall, Fawn 170
Hall, Gus 146
Hall, Jerry 170
Hall, Tom T. 85
Hallstrom, Holly 170
Hamel, Veronica 30
Hamill, Dorothy 117
Hamill, Mark 30
Hamilton, George 30
Hamilton, Linda 30
Hamilton, Rep. Lee 146
Hamilton, Scott 117
Hamlisch, Marvin 85
Hampton, Lionel 85
Hancock, Herbie 85
Hanks, Tom 30
Hannah, Daryl 30
Harbaugh, Jim 117
Hardaway, Anfernee 117
Hardaway, Tim 117
Harding, Tonya 117

Hardison, Kadeem 30
Harewood, Dorian 30
Hargis, Billy James 170
Hargitay, Mariska 30
Harkin, Sen. Tom 146
Harlem Globetrotters 117
Harmon, Mark 31
Harper, Tess 31
Harper, Valerie 31
Harrelson, Woody 31
Harris, EmmyLou 85
Harris, Franco 117
Harris, Mel 31
Harris, Mrs. Jean 170
Harris, Neil Patrick 31
Harris, Richard 31
Harrison, George 85
Harrison, Jenilee 31
Harrold, Kathryn 31
Harry, Deborah 85
Hart, Bert "Hit Man" 118
Hart, Corey 86
Hart, Ex-Sen. Gary 146
Hart, Mary 31
Hart, Melissa Joan 31
Hartley, Mariette 31
Hartman, Lisa 31
Harvey, Paul 170
Hassan II, King 146
Hasselhoff, David 31
Hastings, Rep. Alcee 146
Hatch, Sen. Orrin G. 146
Hatcher, Teri 31
Hauer, Rutger 31
Hauser, Wings 31
Havel, Pres. Vaclav 146
Havens, Richie 86
Havlicek, John 118
Hawke, Ethan 31
Hawkin, Edwin 86
Hawn, Goldie 31
Hayden, Tom 147
Hayes, Bob 118
Hayes, Isaac 86
Heard, John 31
Hearns,Tommy 118
Hearst, Patricia 170
Hearst, Mrs. Wm. Randolph 170
Heart 86
Heavener, David 32
Hecht, Jessica 32
Heflin, Sen. Howell 147
Hefner, Christie 170
Hefner, Hugh 170
Heiden, Beth 118
Heiden, Eric................................. 118
Helmond, Katherine 32
Helms, Sen. Jesse 147
Helmsley, Leona 170
Hemingway, Mariel 32
Hemsley, Sherman 32
Henderson, Rickey 118

Henderson, Thomas 118
Henley, Don 86
Henner, Marilu 32
Hensley, Pamela 32
Herger, Rep. Wally 147
Herman, Sec. Alexis 147
Herman, Pee Wee 32
Hernandez, Keith 118
Hershiser, Orel 118
Hesseman, Howard 32
Heston, Charlton 32
Hewitt, Christopher 32
Hewitt, Don 170
Hewlett, William........................... 170
Heyerdahl, Tor 170
Hickman, Dwayne 32
Hicks, Catherine 32
Higgins, Jack 170
Hill, Anita 171
Hill, Faith 86
Hillary, Sir Edmund 171
Hilton, Baron 171
Hinckley, Jr., John 171
Hines, Gregory 32
Hingis, Martina 118
Hirsch, Judd 32
Hirt, Al 86
Hoffa, Jr., James 171
Hoffman, Dustin 32
Hoffs, Syd 171
Hogan, Ben 118
Hogan, Hulk 118
Hogan, Paul 32
Holbrook, Hal 32
Hole 86
Holliday, Polly 32
Hollings, Sen. Ernest 147
Holly, Lauren 32
Holmes, Larry 118
Holtz, Lou 118
Holyfield, Evander 118
Hooks, Benjamin 171
Hooks, Robert 33
Hootie & the Blowfish 86
Hoover III, Herbert 147
Hope, Bob 33
Hope, Dolores 171
Hopkins, Anthony 33
Hopkins, Linda 86
Horne, Lena 86
Horning, Paul 118
Hornsby, Bruce 86
Horsley, Lee 33
Hosteller, Jeff 118
Houk, Ralph 118
Houston, Thelma 86
Houston, Whitney 86
Howard, Arliss 33
Howard, Ken 33
Howard, Ron 33
Howe, Gordie 118
Hubley, Season 33

Hubley, Whip 33
Huffington, Arianna 171
Huffington, Michael 147
Hughes, Finola 33
Hughes, Miko 33
Hull, Bobby 118
Humperdinck, Englebert 86
Humphrey III, Hubert 147
Humphrey, Renee 33
Hunt, Helen 33
Hunt, Howard 171
Hunt, Lamar 171
Hunt, Linda 33
Hunt, Marsh 33
Hunter, Holly 33
Hunter, Jim "Catfish" 118
Hunter, Rachel 171
Hunter, Tab 33
Hurd, Douglas 147
Hurley, Elizabeth 171
Hurt, William 33
Hussein I, King 147
Hussein, Saddam 147
Huston, Anjelica 33
Hutchins, Will 33
Hutchison, Sen. Kay Bailey 147
Hutton, Betty 34
Hutton, Lauren 34
Hyams, Joe 171
Hyde, Rep. Henry J. 147

I

Iacocca, Lee 171
Ice Cube 86
Ice-Tea 86
Idol, Billy 87
Iman 171
Indigo Girls 87
Inglesias, Julio 87
Ireland, Kathy 171
Irons, Jeremy 34
Ironside, Michael 34
Irvin, Michael 119
Irving, Amy 34
Irwin, Hale 119
Isaak, Chris 34
Isley Brothers 87
Ito, Lance 171
Ivey, Judith 34
Ivory, James 34

J

Jackee 34
Jackson, Alan 87
Jackson, Anne 34
Jackson, Bo 119
Jackson, Freddie 87
Jackson, Glenda 34
Jackson, Janet 87
Jackson, Jermaine 87
Jackson, Rev. Jesse 147
Jackson, Jr., Rep. Jesse 147
Jackson, Joe 87

Jackson, Kate 34
Jackson, Keith 119
Jackson, LaToya 172
Jackson, Marlon 87
Jackson, Mary Ann 34
Jackson, Maynard 147
Jackson, Melody 34
Jackson, Michael 87
Jackson, Jr., Paul 34
Jackson, Phil 119
Jackson, Reggie 119
Jackson, Samuel L. 34
Jackson, Sherry 35
Jackson, Stoney 35
Jackson, Tito 87
Jackson, Victoria 35
Jacobi, Lou 35
Jacobs, Lawrence-Hilton 35
Jacoby, Billy 35
Jagger, Bianca 172
Jagger, Mick 87
Jaglom, Henry 35
James, Etta 87
James, John 35
Jane's Addiction 87
Janis, Conrad 35
Jansen, Dan 119
Janssen, Famke 35
January, Lois 35
Jarman, Jr., Claude 35
Jarreau, Al 87
Jarvis, Graham 35
Jason, Sybil 35
Jean, Gloria 35
Jean-Baptiste, Marianne 35
Jeffreys, Anne 35
Jenner, Bruce 119
Jennings, Peter 35
Jennings, Waylon 87
Jens, Salome 35
Jethro Tull 87
Jett, Joan 88
Jewel 88
Jewison, Norman 172
Jillian, Ann 35
Jillson, Joyce 172
Jobs, Steve 172
Joel, Billy 88
John, Elton 88
John, Tommy 119
Johncock, Gordon 119
Johns, Glynis 36
Johnson, Anne-Marie 36
Johnson, Arte 36
Johnson, Ben 119
Johnson, Don 36
Johnson, Ervin "Magic" 119
Johnson, Jimmy 119
Johnson, Kevin 119
Johnson, Kristen 36
Johnson, Lady Bird 147

Johnson, Laura 36
Johnson, Lynn-Holly 36
Johnson, Michelle 36
Johnson, Rafer 36
Johnson, Russell 36
Johnson, Sen. Tim 148
Jolie, Angelina 36
Jones, Davey 88
Jones, Dean 36
Jones, Dub 36
Jones, Grace 36
Jones, James Earl 36
Jones, Janet 36
Jones-Simon, Jennifer 36
Jones, Jenny 36
Jones, Jesus 88
Jones, Marcia Mae 36
Jones, Paula 172
Jones, Quincy 88
Jones, Rickie Lee 88
Jones, Sam 36
Jones, Shirley 37
Jones, Tom 88
Jones, Tommy Lee 37
Jordan, James Carroll 37
Jordan, Michael 119
Jordan, Montell 88
Jordan, Jr., Vernon 148
Jordan, William 37
Joseph, Jackie 37
Jourdan, Louis 37
Journey 88
Jovovich, Milla 37
Joyner-Kersee, Jackie 119
Judd, Naomi 88
Jump, Gordon 37

K

K.C. & the Sunshine Band 88
Kaelin, Brian "Kato" 172
Kagen, David 37
Kahn, Madeline 37
Kaline, Al 120
Kallianotes, Helena 37
Kampmann, Steven 37
Kanaly, Steve 37
Kanan, Sean 37
Kane, Carol 37
Kantor, Mickey 148
Kaplan, Gabriel 37
Kaplan, Marvin 37
Kapture, Mitzi 37
Karan, Donna 172
Karolyi, Bela 120
Karpov, Anatoly 120
Karras, Alex 120
Karsh, Yousuf 172
Kasdan, Lawrence 172
Kasem, Casey 88
Katt, William 38
Kavner, Julie 38
Kazan, Lainie 38

Keach, James 38
Keach, Jr., Stacy 38
Keach, Sr., Stacy 38
Kean, Jane 38
Keanan, Staci 38
Keaton, Diane 38
Keaton, Michael 38
Keefer, Don 38
Keel, Howard 38
Keeshan, Bob 38
Keith, David 38
Keith, Penelope 38
Kell, George 120
Keller, Martha 38
Kellerman, Sally 38
Kelley, Sheila 38
Kelly, Kitty 172
Kelly, Moira 38
Kelly, Roz 38
Kemp, Jack 148
Kemp, Shawn 120
Kempthorne, Sen. Dirk 148
Kennedy, Justice Anthony 148
Kennedy, Caroline 172
Kennedy, George 39
Kennedy, Jayne 39
Kennedy, Jr., John 172
Kennedy, Rep. Joseph P. 148
Kennedy, Rep. Patrick 148
Kennedy, Leon Isaac 172
Kennedy, Michael 172
Kennedy, Mimi 39
Kennedy, Sen. Ted 148
Kensit, Patsy 39
Kercheval, Ken 39
Kerkorian, Kirk 172
Kerns, Joanna 39
Kerns, Sandra 39
Kerr, Deborah 39
Kerridge, Linda 39
Kerrigan, Nancy 120
Kerry, Sen. Bob 148
Kerry, Sen. John F. 148
Kerwin, Brian 39
Ketchum, Hal 88
Kevorkian, Dr. Jack 173
Key, Ted 173
Keyes, Dr. Allan 148
Keyes, Evelyn 39
Keyloun, Mark 39
Khan, Chaka 88
Kiam II, Victor K. 173
Kidd, Jason 120
Kidder, Margot 39
Kidman, Nicole 39
Killebrew, Harmon 120
Killey, Jeane-Claude 120
Kilmer, Val 39
Kilpatrick, Lincoln 39
Kind, Richard 39
Kind, Roslyn 39

King, Andrea 39
King, B. B. 88
King, Ben E. 88
King, Billy Jean 120
King, Carol 89
King, Coretta Scott 148
King, Don 120
King, Larry 39
King, Perry 40
King, Rodney 173
King, Stephen 173
Kingsley, Ben 40
Kinmont, Kathleen 40
Kinnear, Greg 40
Kinski, Nastassja 40
Kirk-Bush, Phyllis 40
Kirkland, Gelsey 173
Kirkland, Lane 148
Kirkland, Sally 40
Kiser, Terry 40
Kiss 89
Kissinger, Dr. Henry 148
Kitaen, Tawny 40
Kite, Tom 120
Klammer, Franz 120
Klein, Calvin 173
Klemperer, Werner 40
Kline, Kevin 40
Kline, Richard 40
Klous, Patricia 40
Klugman, Jack 40
Knievel, Evel 120
Knight, Bobby 120
Knight, Christopher 40
Knight, Gladys 89
Knight, Michael E. 40
Knight, Shirley 40
Knopfler, Mark 89
Knotts, Don 40
Knox, Chuck 120
Koch, Ex-Mayor Edward 148
Koenig, Walter 40
Kohl, Chancellor Helmut 148
Kohl, Sen. Herbert 148
Kollek, Mayor Teddy 149
Kool & the Gang 89
Koop, Dr. C. Everett 173
Koppel, Ted 40
Korbut, Olga 120
Korda, Maria 41
Korman, Harvey 41
Kosar, Bernie 121
Kotto, Yaphet 41
Koufax, Sandy 121
Kove, Martin 41
Kozak, Harley Jane 41
Kozlowski, Linda 41
Kramer, Jack 121
Kramer, Stanley 173
Kramer, Stepfanie 41
Krause, Brian 41

Krauss, Alison 89
Kravitz, Lenny 89
Kreskin 173
Kristal, Sylvia 41
Kristofferson, Kris 89
Kristol, William 173
Kroc, Mrs. Joan 173
Krzyzewski, Mike 121
Kubek, Tony 121
Kudrow, Lisa 41
Kukoc, Toni 121
Kupcinet, Kari 41
Kurtz, Swoosie 41
Kyl, Sen. Jon 149

L

LaBelle, Patti 89
Laborteaux, Mathew 41
Laborteaux, Patrick 41
Ladd, Jr., Alan 173
Ladd, Alana 41
Ladd, Cheryl 41
Ladd, Diane 41
Laettner, Christian 121
Laffer, Dr. Arthur 173
Lahti, Christine 41
Laird, Melvin 173
Lake, Ricki 42
Laker, Freddie 173
LaLanne, Jack 121
Lalonde, Donny 121
Lamarr, Hedy 42
Lamas, Lorenzo 42
Lambert, Jack 121
Lamm, Ex-Gov. Richard 149
Lamotta, Jake 121
Lampley, Jim 121
Lance, Bert 149
Landau, Martin 42
Landers, Andrey 42
Landers, Ann 173
Landesberg, Steve 42
Landis, John 173
Landrieu, Sen. Mary 149
Landry, Tom 121
Lane, Nathan 42
Lang, k.d. 89
Langdon, SueAnne 42
Lange, Hope 42
Lange, Jessica 42
Lange, Ted 42
Langella, Frank 42
Langenkamp, Heather 42
Langer, Bernhard 121
Lansbury, Angela 42
Lansing, Sherry 174
Lantos, Rep. Tom 149
Lardner, Jr., Ring 174
Largent, Rep. Steve 149
Larkin, Barry 121
Larroquette, John 42

Larson, Gary 174
LaRue, Eva 42
LaSorda, Tommy 121
Lasswell, Fred 174
Lauder, Estee 174
Laughlin, John 42
Lauper, Cyndi 89
Lauren, Ralph 174
Laurents, Arthur 174
Lautenberg, Sen. Frank 149
Laver, Rod 121
Laxalt, Paul 149
Law, John Phillip 42
Lawrence, Carol 42
Lawrence, Martin 42
Lawrence, Tracy 89
Lawrence, Vicki 43
Lazier, Buddy 121
Leach, Rep. Jim 149
Leach, Robin 43
Leahy, Sen. Patrick 149
Lear, Norman 174
Learned, Michael 43
Leavitt, Gov. Mike 149
LeBlanc, Matt 43
LeBrock, Kelly 43
Le Carre, John 174
Ledoux, Chris 89
Lee, Brenda 89
Lee, Christopher 43
Lee, Hyaptia 43
Lee, Peggy 43
Lee, Spike 174
Leigh, Janet 43
Leigh, Jennifer Jason 43
Lemieux, Mario 122
Lemmon, Chris 43
Lemmon, Jack 43
Lemon, Bob 122
Lemond, Greg 122
Lendl, Ivan 122
Lennon, Julian 89
Lennon, Sean 89
Leno, Jay 43
Lenska, Rula 43
Leo, Melissa 43
Leonard, Elmore 174
Leonard, Sugar Ray 122
Letterman, David 43
LeVert 89
Levin, Ira 174
Levin, Sen. Carl 149
Levy, Marv 122
Lewis, Carl 122
Lewis, Daniel Day 43
Lewis, Dawn 43
Lewis, Huey 89
Lewis, Jerry 43
Lewis, Rep. Jerry 149
Lewis, Jerry Lee 90
Lewis, Rep. John 149

Lewis, Lennox 122
Lewis, Richard 43
Lewis, Shari 174
Li Peng, Premier 149
Liddy, G. Gordon 174
Lieberman, Sen. Joseph I 149
Light, Juidth 44
Lightfoot, Gordon 90
Liman, Arthur L. 174
Limbaugh, Rush 174
Lindbergh, Ann Morrow 174
Lindley, Audra 44
Lindros, Eric 122
Linkletter, Art 44
Linney, Laura 44
Liotta, Ray 44
Lithgow, John 44
Little Richard 96
Little, Rich 44
LL Cool J 90
Lloyd, Christopher 44
Lloyd, Norman 44
Locke, Sondra 44
Lockhart, June 44
Locklear, Heather 44
Loggia, Robert 44
Loggins, Kenny 90
London, Julie 44
Long, Shelly 44
Lopez, Nancy 122
Lords, Traci 44
Loren, Sophia 44
Lost Boyz 90
Lott, Ronnie 122
Lott, Sen. Trent 149
Louganis, Greg 122
Loughlin, Lori 44
Louise, Tina 44
Lousma, Jack R. 174
Love, Courtney 90
Lovelace, Linda 44
Loveless, Patty 90
Lovell, James A. 174
Lovett, Lyle 90
Lovitz, Jon 45
Lowdermilk, Dale 45
Lowe, Chad 45
Lowe, Rob 45
Lowey, Rep. Nita 150
Lucas, George 174
Lucci, Susan 45
Ludlum, Robert 175
Luft, Lorna 45
Lugar, Sen. Richard 150
Lujack, Johnny 122
Lumet, Sidney 175
Lunden, Joan 45
Luzinski, Greg 122
Lynch, Kelly 45
Lynn, Loretta 90
Lynyrd Skynyrd 90

M

MacGraw, Ali 45
Macht, Stephen 45
Mack, Sen. Connie 150
MacLachlan, Kyle 45
MacLaine, Shirley 45
MacNee, Patrick 45
MacPherson, Elle 175
Macy, William H. 45
Madden, John 122
Maddox, Lester 150
Madlock, Bill 122
Madonna 90
Madsen, Michael 45
Madsen, Virgina 45
Maffett, Debra Sue 45
Mahal, Taj 90
Maher, Bill 45
Maheu, Robert 46
Mahre, Phil 122
Mahre, Steve 122
Mailer,Norman 175
Major, P.M . John 150
Majors, Lee 46
Makepeace, Chris 46
Malandro, Kristina 46
Malden, Karl 46
Malone, John 175
Malone, Karl 123
Maltin, Leonard 175
Mamas & the Papas, The 90
Mamet, David 175
Manatt, Charles 150
Manchester, Melissa 90
Manchester, William 175
Mancini, Ray "Boom Boom" 123
Mancuso, Nick 46
Mandela, Nelson 150
Mandela, Winnie 150
Mandrell, Howie 46
Mandrell, Barbara 90
Mandrell, Erline 90
Mandrell, Louise 90
Manilow, Barry 90
Manning, Danny 123
Mansell, Nigel 123
Manson, Charles 175
Maples, Marla 46
Maradona, Diego 123
Marceau, Sophie 46
Marcos, Imelda 150
Margaret, Princess 150
Margret-Smith, Ann 46
Margulies, Julianne 46
Marichal, Juan 123
Marino, Dan 123
Marky Mark 91
Marilyn Manson 91
Marinovich, Todd 46
Marley, Ziggy 91

Mars, Jr., Forrest 175
Marsalis, Branford 91
Marsalis, Wynton 91
Marshall, E. G. 46
Marshall, Garry 175
Marshall, Penny 46
Marshall, Peter 46
Martin, Jared 46
Martin, Pamela Sue 46
Martin, Steve 46
Martindale, Wink 46
Martinez, A 46
Marx, Richard 91
Maryland, Russell 123
Mason, Marsha 47
Mason, Tom 47
Masterson, Mary Stuart 47
Matalin, Mary 175
Mathers, Jerry 47
Matheson, Tim 47
Mathis, Johnny 91
Matlin, Marlee 47
Matthau, Walter 47
Mattingly, Don 123
Mauch, Gene 123
Maule, Brad 47
Mayo, Virgina 47
Mays, Willie 123
McCain, Sen. John 150
McCallum, David 47
McCarthy, Andrew 47
McCarthy, Eugene J. 150
McCarthy, Jenny 47
McCarthy, Kevin 47
McCarthy, Nobu 47
McCartney, Paul 91
McCarver, Tim 123
McClendon, Sarah 175
McCloskey, Paul 150
McCollum, Rep. Bill 150
McConnell, Sen. Mitch 150
McCoo, Marilyn 91
McCormack, Mary 47
McCoy, Matt 47
McCullough, Julie 175
McDaniel, James 47
McDivitt, James 175
McDonald, "Country Joe" 91
McDowell, Roddy 47
McEnroe, John 123
McEntyre, Reba 91
McFerrin, Bobby 91
McGavin, Darren 47
McGee, Vonette 47
McGillis, Kelly 48
McGoohan, Patrick 48
McGovern, Elizabeth 48
McGovern, George 150
McGovern, Maureen 91
McGraw, Tim 91
McGraw, Tug 123

McGregor, Ewan 48
McGuire Sisters, The 91
McGuire, Dorothy 48
McGwire, Mark 123
McKay, Jim 123
McKean, Michael 48
McKeon, Nancy 48
McKeon, Philip 48
McKinney, Rep. Cynthia 150
McKuen, Rod 175
McLain, Denny 123
McLish, Rachel.............................. 48
McMahon, Ed 48
McNair, Steve 123
McNally, Terrence 175
McNamara, Robert 175
McNichol, Kristy 48
McQueen, Chad 48
McVeigh, Timothy 176
Meadows-Allen, Jayne 48
Mears, Rick 123
Meese III, Edwin 176
Mehta, Zubin 91
Mellenchamp, John 91
Menendez, Eric 176
Menendez, Lyle 176
Mendez, Sergio 91
Menudo 91
Menuhin, Yehudi 91
Meredith, Burgess 48
Meredith, Don 123
Meriwether, Lee Ann 48
Metallica 92
Metcalf, Laurie 48
Metheny, Pat 92
Metzenbaum, Howard 150
Meyer, Russ 176
Mfumel, Kweisi 151
Michael, Bob 151
Michael, George 92
Michaels, Al 124
Michaels, Lorne 176
Michelmore, Guy 48
Michener, James 176
Midler, Bette 92
Mifune, Toshiro 48
Mikulski, Sen. Barbara 151
Miles, Joanna 48
Miles, Sarah 48
Milken, Michael 176
Miller, Authur 176
Miller, Cheryl 124
Miller, Dennis................................ 49
Miller, Johnny 124
Miller, Johnny Lee 49
Miller, Mitch 92
Miller, Penelope Ann 49
Miller, Reggie 124
Miller, Shannon 124
Mills, Donna 49
Mills, Hayley 49

Milsap, Ronnie 92
Mimieux, Yvette 49
Mingus, Charles 176
Mink, Rep. Patsy 151
Minnelli, Liza 92
Mirer, Rick 124
Mitchell, Joni 92
Mitchelson, Marvin 176
Miyori, Kim 49
Mize, Larry 124
Mobley, Mary Ann 49
Modine, Matthew 49
Moffett, D. W. 49
Moll, Richard 49
Monaghan, Thomas L. 176
Mondale, Walter 151
Monday, Rick 124
Money, Eddie 92
Montalban, Ricardo 49
Montana, Joe 124
Moon, Rev. Sun Myung 176
Moon, Warren 124
Moore, Archie 124
Moore, Clayton 49
Moore, Demi 49
Moore, Dudley 49
Moore, Mary Tyler 49
Moore, Melba 49
Moore, Roger 49
Morales, Esai 49
Moranis, Rick 49
Moreno, Rita.................................. 50
Morgan, Harry 50
Morgan, Jaye P. 50
Morgan, Lorrie 92
Moriarity, Cathy 50
Moriarty, Michael 50
Morissette, Alanis 92
Morita, Noriyuki Pat 50
Morning, Alonzo 124
Morris, Dick 176
Morrison, Mark 92
Morrison, Toni 176
Morrison, Van 92
Morse, Robert 50
Moseley-Braum, Sen. Carol 151
Moses, Edwin 124
Moss, Kate 50
Mota, Manny 124
Mother Delores............................ 176
Mother Teresa 182
Motley Crue 92
Mott, Stewart 176
Moyers, Bill................................... 50
Moynihan, Sen. Daniel 151
Mubarak, Pres. Hosni 151
Mueller-Stahl, Armin 50
Muldaur, Maria 92
Muldoon, Patrick 50
Muldowney, Shirley 124
Mulkey, Chris................................. 50

Mull, Martin.................................... 50
Mulligan, Richard 50
Mulroney, Dermot 50
Mumy, Billy 50
Muppets, The 176
Murcer, Bobby 124
Murdoch, Rupert 176
Murkowski, Sen. Frank................ 151
Murphy, Ben 50
Murphy, Eddie 50
Murray, Anne 92
Murray, Bill 50
Murray, Don 50
Murray, Sen. Patty 151
Musburger, Brent 124
Musial, Stan 124
Muster, Thomas 124
Mutombo, Dikembe 124
Myers, Dee Dee 176

N

Nader, Ralph 177
Najimy, Kathy 51
Namath, Joe 125
Napier, Hugo 51
Nash, Graham 92
Nastase, Ille 125
Naughty By Nature 92
Navratilova, Martina 125
Neal, Patricia 51
Needham, Hal 177
Needham, Tracey 51
Neeson, Liam 51
Neiman, LeRoy 177
Nelson, Byron 125
Nelson, Craig T............................. 51
Nelson, Judd 51
Nelson, Willie 93
Nero, Peter 93
Nesmith, Michael 93
Netanyahu, Benjamin 151
Neville, Aaron 93
Nevine, Claudette 51
New Edition 93
New Kids on the Block 93
Newhart, Bob 51
Newhouse, Samuel I 177
Newman, Paul 51
Newman, Phyllis............................ 51
Newmar, Julie................................ 51
Newsom, Tommy 93
Newton, Juice 93
Newton, Wayne 93
Newton-John, Olivia 93
Nicholas, Thomas Ian 51
Nichols, Bobby 125
Nichols, Nichelle 51
Nicholson, Jack 51
Nicklaus, Jack 125
Nickles, Sen. Don 151
Nickson, Julia 51
Niekro, Joe 125

Niekro, Phil 125
Nielsen, Brigitte 51
Nielsen, Leslie 51
Nimoy, Leonard 52
Nirvana 93
Nofziger, Lynn 177
Noguchi, Dr. Thomas 177
Noll, Chuck 125
Nolte, Nick 52
Nomo, Hideo 125
Noriega, Gen. Manuel 151
Norman, Greg 125
Norris, Chuck 52
North, Oliver 177
Norton, Edward 52
Norton, Ken 125
Norville, Deborah 52
Nouri, Michael 52
Novak, Robert 177
Nugent, Ted 93
Nunn, Sen. Sam 151

O

O'Brian, Hugh 52
O'Brien, Conan 52
O'Brien, Pat 125
O'Connor, Carrol 52
O'Connor, Donald 52
O'Connor, Justice Sandra 151
O'Connor, Hazel 177
O'Donnell, Chris 52
O'Donnell, Rosie 52
O'Hara, Maureen 52
O'Jays, The 93
O'Keeffe, Miles 52
O'Neal, Ryan 53
O'Neal, Shaquille 125
O'Neil, Jennifer 53
O'Toole, Annette 53
O'Toole, Peter 53
Oak Ridge Boys 93
Obey, Rep. David 151
Ocean, Billy 93
Ogi, Pres. Adolf 152
Oh, Soon-Teck 52
Oldfield, Mike 93
Oldman, Gary 52
Olin, Ken 52
Oliphant, Patrick 177
Olmos, Edward James 52
Omarr, Sydner 177
Ono-Lennon, Yoko 93
Ontkean, Michael 53
Ophuls, Marcel 177
Orlando, Tony 93
Orlov, Yuri 177
Orr, Bobby 125
Ortiz, Rep. Solomon 152
Osbourne, Ozzy 94
Osbourne, Tom 125
Osima, Nagisa 177
Oslin, K. T. 94

Osment, Haley Joel 53
Osmond, Donny 94
Osmond, Marie 94
Osterwald, Bibi 53
Overstreet, Paul 94
Ovitz, Michael 177
Owens, Buck 94
Oxenberg, Catherine 53
Oz, Frank 177

P

Pablo Cruise 94
Pacino, Al 53
Packard, Rep. Ron 152
Packer, Billy 126
Pacula, Joanna 53
Page, Patti 94
Pahlavi, Princess Ashraf 152
Paisley, Rev. Ian 152
Palance, Holly 53
Palance, Jack 53
Palminteri, Chaz 53
Palmer, Arnold 126
Palmer, Jim 126
Palmer, Robert 94
Paltrow, Bruce 53
Paltrow, Gwyneth 53
Papas, Rep. Mike 152
Paquin, Anna 53
Pardee, Jack 126
Paris, Johnny 94
Parker, Dave 126
Parker, Eleanor 53
Parker, Fess 53
Parker, Jamerson 54
Parker, Sarah Jessica 54
Parks, Rosa 178
Parseghian, Ara 126
Parton, Dolly 94
Pataki, Gov. George 152
Paterno, Joe 126
Patinkin, Mandy 54
Patric, Jason 54
Patterson, Floyd 126
Patton, Gov. Paul 152
Paul, Adrian 54
Paul, Les 94
Pauley, Jane 54
Pavarotti, Luciano 94
Paven, Corey 126
Paxson, Rep. Bill 152
Paycheck, Johnny 94
Paymer, David 54
Payton, Walter 126
Peaches & Herb 94
Pearl Jam 94
Peck, Gregory 54
Peete, Rodney 126
Pei, I. M. 178
Pele 126
Pelosi, Rep. Nancy 152
Pena, Sen. Federico 152

Pendergrass, Teddy 94
Penghlis, Thaao 54
Penguins, The 94
Penn, Chris 54
Penn, Sean 54
Penny, Joe 54
Penske, Roger 126
Pepitone, Joe 126
Percy, Charles 152
Peres, Shimon 152
Perez, Rosie 54
Perkins, Carl 95
Perlman, Ron 54
Peron, Mme Isabel 152
Perot, H. Ross 178
Perrine, Valerie 54
Perry, Gaylord 126
Perry, Luke 54
Perry, William 152
Pesci, Joe 54
Pescow, Donna 54
Peter, Paul & Mary 95
Peters, Bernadette 54
Peterson, Oscar 95
Petty, Kyle 126
Petty, Richard 126
Petty, Tom 95
Pfeiffer, Michelle 54
Philbin, Regis 55
Philip, HRH Prince 152
Phillips, Chynna 95
Phillips, Julianne 55
Phillips, Lou Diamond 55
Phillips, Michelle 95
Philips, Sam 95
Pickering, Donald 152
Pickett, Wilson 95
Pierce, Mary 126
Pileggi, Mitch 55
Pillow, Ray 95
Pinchot, Bronson 55
Piniella, Lou 127
Pink Floyd 95
Pinkett, Jada 55
Pinson, Vada 127
Pippen, Scottie 127
Pitt, Brad 55
Place, Mary Kay 55
Platters, The 95
Player, Gary 127
Pleshette, Suzanne 55
Plummer, Amanda 55
Plummer, Christopher 55
Plunkett, Jim 127
Poison 95
Poitier, Sidney 55
Polanski, Roman 178
Police, The 95
Pollack, Sydney 178
Pollard, Jonathan 178
Pombo, Rep. Richard 152

Pop, Iggy 95
Pope John Paul II 178
Post, Markie 55
Potts, Annie 55
Pounder, CCH 55
Poundstone, Paula 178
Povich, Maury 55
Powell, Gen. Colin L. 178
Powell, Jane 55
Powers, Stefanie 55
Prentiss, Paula 55
Presley, Priscilla 55
Presley, Lisa-Marie 178
Preston, Billy 95
Previn, Andre 95
Price, Leontyne 95
Price, Nick 127
Pride, Charlie 95
Priestly, Jason 56
Prince (formely known) 95
Principal, Victoria 56
Prine, Andrew 56
Prinz, Jr., Freddie 56
Pryor, Richard 56
Public Enemy 95
Puck, Wolfgang 178
Pulliam, Keshia Knight- 56
Pullman, Bill 56
Purl, Linda 56
Puzo, Mario 178

Q

Quaid, Dennis 56
Quaid, Randy 56
Quayle, Vice Pres. Dan 153
Quayle, Marilyn 153
Queen 96
Quiet Roit 96
Quinlan, Kathleen 56
Quinn, Aiden 56
Quinn, Anthony 56
Quinn, Francesco 56

R

Rabbitt, Eddie 96
Rahal, Bobby 127
Railback, Steve 56
Raitt, Bonnie 96
Ramos, Fidel 153
Randall, Tony 56
Randle, Theresa 57
Randolph, Willie 127
Rangel, Rep. Charles B. 153
Ranier II, Crown Prince 153
Raphael, Sally Jessy 57
Rashad, Ahmad 127
Rashad, Phylicia 57
Rather, Dan 57
Raven, Eddy 96
Rawls, Lou 96
Rea, Stephen 57
Read, Ralph 178

Reagan, Nancy 153
Reagan, Jr., Ron 178
Reagan, Ex-Pres. Ronald 153
Rebozo, Charles 178
Reckell, Peter 57
Red Hot Chili Peppers 96
Reddy, Helen 96
Redford, Robert 57
Redgrave, Lynn 57
Redgrave, Vanessa 57
Redstone, Sumner 178
Reed, Rex 179
Reese, Pee Wee 127
Reeve, Christopher 57
Reeves, Keanu 57
Reeves, Martha 96
Regehr, Duncan 57
Rehnquist, Justice Wm. 153
Reid, Tim 57
Reinhold, Judge 57
Reiser, Paul 57
REM 96
Reno, Janet 153
Resnick, Faye 179
Retton, Mary Lou 127
Revere & the Raiders, Paul 96
Reynolds, Burt 57
Reynolds, Debbie 57
Rhames, Ving 57
Rhodes, Dusty 127
Ribicoff, Abraham 153
Ricci, Christina 57
Rice, Jerry 127
Rice, Jim 127
Rich, Matty 179
Richard, Cliff 96
Richards, Gov. Ann 153
Richards, Keith 96
Richardson, Bill 153
Richardson, Bobby 127
Richardson, Dot 127
Richie, Lionel 96
Richmond, Branscombe 57
Richter, Jason James 58
Rickles, Don 58
Ride, Dr. Sally 179
Rigby-McCoy, Cathy 127
Riggleman, Jim 127
Righteous Brothers 96
Riley, Jeannie C. 97
Riley, Pat 128
Riley, Sec. Richard 153
Rimes, Leann 97
Ringwald, Molly 58
Riordan, Mayor Richard 153
Ripken, Jr. Cal 128
Ripken, Sr., Cal 128
Ritter, John 58
Rivera, Geraldo 58
Rivera, Mariano 128
Rivers, Joan 58

Rivers, Mickey 128
Rizzuto, Phil 128
Robards, Jason 58
Robb, Sen. Charles 153
Robbins, Harold 179
Robelot, Jane 58
Roberts, Cokie 179
Roberts, Eric 58
Roberts, Julia 58
Roberts, Oral 179
Roberts, Pernell 58
Roberts, Tanya 58
Robertson, Cliff 58
Robertson, Oscar 128
Robertson, Pat 179
Robinson, Brooks 128
Robinson, David 128
Robinson, Eddie 128
Robinson, Frank 128
Robinson, Glen 128
Robinson, Holly 58
Robinson, Smokey 97
Rochon, Debbie 58
Rochon, Lela 58
Rockefeller, David 179
Rockefeller, Mrs. Nelson 179
Rockefeller, Sen. John D. 153
Rodman, Dennis 128
Rodriguez, Alex 128
Rodriguez, Chi Chi 128
Rodriquez, Ivan 128
Rodriquez, Johnny 97
Rogers, Bill 128
Rogers, Kenny 97
Rogers, Mimi 58
Rogers, Mr. (Fred) 58
Rogers, Roy 58
Rogers, Tristan 58
Rogers, Wayne 59
Rolando (Watts) 59
Rolling Stones 97
Rollins, Ed 179
Rollins, Sonny 97
Ronstadt, Linda 97
Rooker, Michael 59
Rooney, Andy 59
Rooney, Mickey 59
Rose, Axl 97
Rose, Pete 128
Roseanne 59
Rosemarie 97
Rosewall, Ken 128
Ross, Diana 97
Ross, Katharine 59
Rossellini, Isabella 59
Rostenkowski, Dan 154
Rote, Kyle 128
Roth, David Lee 97
Roundtree, Richard 59
Rourke, Mickey 59
Rowan, Carl T. 179

Rowe, Misty 59
Rowlands, Gena 59
Royal, Billy Joe 97
Rozelle, Pete 129
Rubin, Jennifer 59
Rubin, Sec. Robert 154
Rubinstein, Zelda 59
Ruehl, Mercedes 59
Run-DMC 97
Runyon, Jennifer 59
Rupaul 97
Rushdie, Salman 179
Russell, Bill 129
Russell, Jane 59
Russell, Kurt 59
Russell, Mark 179
Rutherford, Johnny 129
Ryan, Meg 59
Ryan, Nolan 129
Rydell, Bobby 97
Ryder, Winona 59

S

Sabatini, Gabriela 129
Saberhagen, Bert 129
Sadat, Mme Jehan El- 154
Sade 97
Safer, Morely 60
Safire, William 179
Sagal, Katey 60
Sager, Carol Bayer 97
Saget, Bob 60
Saint, Eva Marie 60
Saint-Marie, Buffy 98
Sajak, Pat 60
Sales, Soupy 60
Salinger, J. D. 179
Salt & Pepper 98
Saltan of Brunei 154
Samms, Emma 60
Sampras, Pete 129
Sanchez-Gijon, Aitana 60
Sand, Paul 60
Sanders, Barry 129
Sanders, Deion 129
Sanders, Summer 129
Sandler, Adam 60
Sands, Julian 60
Santana, Carlos 98
Santo, Ron 129
Sarah, Duchess of York 154
Sarandon, Chris 60
Sarandon, Susan 60
Sardi, Jr., Vincent 179
Sassoon, Vidal 179
Satterfield, Paul 60
Savant, Doug 60
Sawyer, Diane 60
Sayers, Gale 129
Sbarge, Raphael 60
Scaggs, Boz 98
Scalia, Justice Antonin 154

Scavullo, Francesco 180
Scheider, Roy 60
Schiffer, Claudia 180
Schifrin, Lalo 98
Schirra, Jr., Walter M. 180
Schlafly, Phyllis 154
Schlesinger, Jr., Arthur 180
Schlessinger, John 180
Schmidt, Mike 129
Schmoke, Mayor Kurt 154
Schorr, Daniel 180
Schott, Mrs. Marge 129
Schramm, Tex 129
Schroder, Rick 61
Schroeder, Rep. Patricia 154
Schumer, Rep. Charles 154
Schwarzenegger, Arnold 61
Schwarzkopf, Gen. Norman 180
Schweig, Eric 61
Schwimmer, David 61
Sciorra, Annabella 61
Scoggins, Tracy 61
Scorsese, Martin 180
Scott, George C. 61
Scott, Lizabeth 61
Scott, Willard 61
Scowcroft, Gen. Brent 154
Scruggs, Earl 98
Scully, Vin 129
Seagal, Steven 61
Seau, Junior 129
Seaver, Tom 129
Sebastian, John 98
Secada, Jon 98
Sedaka, Neil 98
Seeger, Pete 98
Segal, Erich 180
Segal, George 61
Seger, Bob 98
Seinfeld, Jerry 61
Seles, Monica 130
Selig, Bud 130
Selleca, Connie 61
Selleck, Tom 61
Severinsen, Doc 98
Seymour, Jane 61
Seymour, Stephanie 180
Shackleford, Ted 61
Shaffer, Paul 98
Shalala, Sen. Donna 154
Shalikashvili, Gen. John 154
Sha Na Na 98
Shandling, Garry 61
Shanice 98
Shapiro, Robert 180
Sharif, Omar 61
Sharpton, Rev. Al 180
Shatner, William 61
Shaver, Helen 61
Shaw, Artie 98
Shaw, Tommy 98
Sheedy, Ally 62

Sheen, Charlie 62
Sheen, Martin 62
Sheffield, Gary 130
Shelby, Sen. Richard 154
Sheldon, Sidney 180
Shenandoah 98
Shepard, Jr., Adm Alan 180
Shepherd, Cybill 62
Sheppard, T.G. 98
Sheridan, Nicholette 62
Sherman, Bobby 98
Shevardnadze, Eduard 154
Shields, Brooke 62
Shimada, Yoko 62
Shoemaker, Bill 130
Shore, Pauly 62
Short, Martin 62
Shower, Kathy 62
Shriner, Kin 62
Shriner, Wil 62
Shriver, Maria 62
Shriver, Pam 130
Shue, Elizabeth 62
Shula, Don 130
Sills, Beverly 99
Silva, Henry 62
Silver, Ron 62
Silverman, Fred 180
Silverstone, Alicia 62
Simmons, Gene 99
Simmons, Jean 62
Simmons, Richard 180
Simms, Phil 130
Simon, Neil 180
Simon, Paul 99
Simon, Sen. Paul 154
Simone, Nina 99
Simpson, O. J. 130
Sinatra, Frank 99
Sinatra, Jr., Frank 99
Sinatra, Nancy 99
Sinatra, Tina 99
Sinbad 62
Singer, Marc 62
Singleton, John 180
Sinise, Gary 63
Sirhan, Sirhan 180
Siskel, Gene 180
Skaggs, Ricky 99
Skelton, Red 63
Skerritt, Tom 63
Slater, Christian 63
Slater, Sec. Rodney 154
Slick, Grace 99
Smashing Pumpkins 99
Smirnoff, Yakov 181
Smith, Allison 63
Smith, Bruce 130
Smith, Buffalo Bob 63
Smith, Dean 130
Smith, Emmitt 130
Smith, Jaclyn 63

Smith, Keely 63
Smith, Liz 181
Smith, Susan 181
Smith, Vince 99
Smith, Wil 63
Smith, William Kennedy 181
Smits, Jimmy 63
Smothers, Dick 63
Smothers, Tom 63
Snead, J. C. 130
Snead, Sam 130
Sneva, Tom 130
Snipes, Wesley 63
Snodgress, Carrie 63
Snoop Doggy Dog 99
Snow, Hank 99
Lord Snowden 181
Snowe, Sen. Olympia 154
Snyder, Tom 63
Solti, Sir George 99
Solzhenitsyn, Alexander 181
Somers, Suzanne 63
Sommer, Elke 63
Sorenson, Ted 155
Sorenstam, Annika 130
Soul, David 63
Soundgarden 99
Souter, Justice David 155
Spacek, Sissy 63
Spacey, Kevin 63
Spade, David 64
Spader, James 64
Spahn, Warren 130
Specter, Sen. Arlen 155
Spector, Phil 99
Spector, Ronnie 99
Spelling, Aaron 181
Spence, Gerry 181
Spielberg, Steven 181
Spinal Tap 99
Spinks, Leon 130
Spinks, Michael 130
Spitz, Mark 130
Springfield, Rick 99
Springsteen, Bruce 100
Spock, Dr. Benjamin 181
Spurrier, Steve 130
Spyro Gyro 100
Squier, Billy 100
Stable, Ken 131
Stack, Robert 64
Stahl, Leslie 64
Stallone, Frank 64
Stallone, Sylvester 64
Stamos, John 64
Stanky, Eddie 131
Stanley, Florence 64
Stansfield, Lisa 100
Stanton, Harry Dean 64
Stapleton, Jean 64
Stargell, Willie 131
Starr, Bart 131

Starr, Kenneth 181
Starr, Ringo 100
Statler Brothers 100
Staubach, Roger 131
Steele, Danielle 181
Steenburgen, Mary 64
Steinbrenner, George 131
Steinem, Gloria 181
Stephanie, Princess 155
Stephanopoulos, George 155
Stephenson, Jan 131
Stern, David 131
Stern, Howard 181
Stern, Isaac 100
Stevens, Andrew 64
Stevens, Connie 100
Stevens, Justice John Paul 155
Stevens, Ray 100
Stevens, Sen. Ted 155
Stevens, Shadoe 100
Stevens, Stella 64
Stevenson III, Adlai 155
Stevenson, Parker 64
Stewart, Jackie 131
Stewart, Martha 181
Stewart, Payne 131
Stewart, Rod 100
Stiller, Ben 64
Stich, Michael 131
Sting 100
Stockdale, James 155
Stockton, John 131
Stockwell, Dean 64
Stockwell, Guy 64
Stockwell John 64
Stokes, Rep. Louis 155
Stone, Oliver 181
Stone, Sly 100
Stoppard, Tom 181
Stowe, Madeleine 64
Strait, George 100
Stram, Hank 131
Strassman, Marcia 64
Strauss, Robert 155
Strawberry, Darryl 131
Streep, Meryl 65
Streisand, Barbra 100
Struthers, Sally 65
Stuart, Marty 100
Styron, William 181
Sullivan, Danny 131
Sullivan, Kathleen 181
Summer, Donna 100
Summerall, Pat 131
Sununu, John 155
Sutherland, Donald 65
Sutherland, Joan 100
Sutherland, Kiefer 65
Sutton, Don 131
Svenson, Bo 65
Swaggart, Jimmy 181
Swan, Michael 65

Swann, Lynn 131
Swayze, Don 65
Swayze, Patrick 65
Sweat, Keith 100
Sweeney, D.B. 65
Swit, Loretta 65
Switzer, Barry 131
Swoopes, Sheryl 131
SWV 100

T

T, Mr. 65
Tagliabue, Paul 132
Takei, George 65
Talese, Gay 182
Tan, Amy 182
Tanner, Roscoe 132
Tarkington, Fran 132
Tartikoff, Brandon 182
Taupin, Bernie 101
Taylor, Elizabeth 65
Taylor, James 101
Taylor, Lawrence 132
Taylor-Young, Leigh 65
Taylor, Meshach 65
Taylor, Niki 182
Taylor, Noah 65
Temple-Black, Shirley 155
Temptations, The 101
Teng-Hui, Pres. Lee 155
Tennille, Toni 101
Terkel, Studs 182
Terrell, Ernie 132
Terry, Clark 101
Tesh, John 65
Testaverde, Vinny 132
Tewes, Lauren 65
Thatcher, Hon. Margaret 155
Theisman, Joe 132
Thicke, Alan 66
Thiessen, Tiffani-Amber 66
Thinnes, Roy 66
Thomas, B. J. 101
Thomas, Justice Clarence 155
Thomas, Dave 182
Thomas, Debi 132
Thomas, Frank 132
Thomas, Heather 66
Thomas, Henry 66
Thomas, Isaiah 132
Thomas, Marlo 66
Thomas-Scott, Melody 66
Thomas, Philip Michael 66
Thomas, Richard 66
Thomas, Thurman 132
Thompson Twins 101
Thompson, Emma 66
Thompson, Hank 101
Thompson, John 132
Thompson, Lea 66
Thompson, Linda 66
Thompson, Gov. Tommy 155

Thomson, Gordon 66
Three Degrees, The 101
Thurman, Uma 66
Thurmond, Sen. Strom 155
Tiegs, Cheryl 182
Tiffany 101
Tillis, Mel 101
Tillis, Pam 101
Tilly, Meg 66
Tilton, Charlene 66
Tippin, Aaron 101
Tittle, Y.A. 132
TLC 101
Tomba, Alberto 132
Tomczak, Mike 132
Tomlin, Lily 66
Tompkins, Angel 66
Toney, James 132
Tony! Tony! Tony! 101
Torme, Mel 101
Torn, Rip 66
Torre, Joe 132
Torrence, Gwen 132
Torres, Liz 101
Torville & Dean 133
Toto 101
Townsend, Kathleen Kennedy 156
Townsend, Robert 182
Travalena, Fred 66
Travanti, Daniel J. 67
Travis, Nancy 67
Travis, Randy 102
Travolta, Joey 102
Travolta, John 67
Trebek, Alex 67
Trevino, Lee 133
Tritt, Travis 102
Trudeau, Gary 182
Trump, Donald 182
Trump, Ivana 182
Tucker Band, Marshall 102
Tucker, Tanya 102
Tuinei, Mike 133
Turlington, Christy 67
Turner, Kathleen 67
Turner, Ted 182
Turner, Tina 102
Turow, Scott 182
Turturo, Nicholas 67
Tutu, Bishop Desmond 156
Tweed, Shannon 67
2 Live Crew 102
Tyler, Bonnie 102
Tyson, Cicely 67
Tyson, Mike 133
Tyson, Richard 67

U

UFO 102
U2 102
Udall, Ex-Rep. Morris K. 156
Ueberroth, Peter 182

Uecker, Bob 133
Uggams, Leslie 102
Uhlig, Anneliese 67
Ulene, Dr. Art 67
Ullman, Liv 67
Ullman, Tracey 102
Underwood, Blair 67
Underwood, Jay 67
Unitas, Johnny 133
Unser, Al 133
Unser, Jr. Al 133
Unser, Bobby 133
Upshaw, Gene 133
Upton, Rep. Fred 156
Urich, Robert 67
Uris, Leon 182
Urseth, Bonnie 67
Ustinov, Peter 67

V

Vale, Jerry 102
Valentine, Karen 68
Valenzuela, Fernando 133
Valli, Frankie 102
Van Allen, Richard 102
Van Ark, Joan 68
Van Buren, Abigail 183
Van Damme, Jean-Claude 68
Van Doren, Mamie 68
Van Dyke, Dick 68
Van Dyke, Jerry 68
Van Halen, Eddie 102
Van Patten, Dick 68
Van Patten, Vincent 68
Van Peebles, Mario 183
Van Zandt, Steve 103
Vance, Cyrus 156
Vandross, Luther 103
Vanilla Ice 103
Vanity 103
Vaugn, Mo 133
Vaughn, Robert 68
Vee, Bobby 103
Vega, Suzanne 103
Velazquez, Rep. Nydia 156
Vento, Rep. Bruce 156
Venturi, Ken 133
Vermeil, Dick 133
Vidal, Gore 183
Vigoda, Abe 68
Viguerie, Richard 183
Vila, Bob 183
Vilas, Guillermo 133
Village People, The 103
Vincent, Jan-Michael 68
Vinton, Bobby 103
Viola, Frank 133
Voight, Jon 68
Voinovich, Gov. George 156
Volcker, Paul A. 183
Von Furstenberg, Diane 183

Von Sydow, Max 68
Vonnegut, Jr., Kurt 183
Voorhies, Lark 68

W

Wade, Virginia 134
Wadkins, Lanny 134
Wagner, Lindsay 68
Wagner, Robert 68
Wagoner, Porter 103
Wahl, Ken 69
Waits, Tom 103
Waitz, Greta 134
Waldheim, Pres. Kurt 156
Walesa, Lech 156
Walken, Christopher 69
Walker, Clay 103
Walker, Doak 134
Walker, Junior 103
Walker, Mort 183
Wallace, Ex-Gov. George 156
Wallace, Mike 69
Wallendas, The Great 183
Walsh, Bill 134
Walters, Barbara 69
Walters, Jamie 69
Walton, Bill 134
Waltrip, Darrell 134
Wapner, Judge Joseph 69
Ward, Fred 69
Ward, Megan 69
Ward, Sela 69
Warfield, Marsha 69
Wariner, Steve 103
Warner, Sen. John 156
Warner, Julia 69
Warner, Malcolm-Jamal 69
Warren, Lesley Ann 69
Warwick, Dionne 103
Washington, Denzel 69
Washington, Malival 134
Wasserman, Lew 183
Waters, John 183
Waters, Rep. Maxine 156
Watley, Jody 103
Watson, Tom 134
Watt, James G. 156
Watters, Ricky 134
Watts, Andre 103
Watts, Jr., Rep. J.C. 157
Waxman, Rep. Henry 157
Wayans, Keenan Ivory 69
Weatherly, Shawn 69
Weathers, Carl 69
Weaver, Dennis 69
Weaver Earl 134
Weaver, Sigourney 69
Webber, Andrew Lloyd 183
Webber, Chris 134
Webster, William H. 157
Weinberger, Casper 183
Weiskopf, Tom 134

Weitz, Bruce 69
Welch, Raquel 70
Welch, Tahnee 70
Weld, Gov. William 157
Weld, Tuesday 70
Wells, Kitty 103
Wellstone, Sen. Paul 157
Wendt, George 70
West, Jerry 134
Westheimer, Dr. Ruth 183
Westmoreland, Gen. Wm 157
Wettig, Patricia 70
Wheaton, Wil 70
Whelchel, Lisa 70
Whitaker, Forest 70
White, Barry 103
White, Ex-Justice Byron 157
White, Jaleel 70
White, Karyn 104
White, Reggie 134
White, Vanna 70
Whitestone, Heather 183
Whitman, Slim 104
Whitman, Stuart 70
Whitmore, James 70
Whittaker, Roger 104
Wicker, Thomas 184
Wiesel, Elie 184
Wiesenthal, Simon 184
Wilander, Mats 134
Wilder, Gene 70
Wilhelm, Hoyt 134
Wilkens, Lenny 134
Wilkes, Jamaal 135
Will, George 184
Prince William 157
Williams, Andy 104
Williams, Billy 135
Willaims, Billy Dee........................ 70
Williams, Bruce 184
Williams, Cindy 70
Williams, Deniece......................... 104
Williams, Jr., Hank........................ 104
Williams, Jobeth 70
Williams, Joe 104
Williams, John 104
Williams, Matt 135
Williams, Kimberly 70
Williams, Montel 70
Williams, Paul................................ 104
Williams, Robin 70
Williams, Ted 135
Williams, Vanessa 104
Willis, Bruce 70
Wilson Phillips 104
Wilson, Brian 104
Wilson, Carnie 104
Wilson, Flip.................................... 71
Wilson, Gov. Pete 157
Wilson, Mara 71
Wilson, Mary 104
Wilson, Nancy 104

Wilson, Rita 71
Winans, The 104
Winfield, Dave 135
Winfield, Paul 71
Winfrey, Oprah 71
Winger, Debra 71
Winkler, Henry 71
Winslet, Kate 71
Winters, Jonathan 71
Winters, Shelly 71
Winwood, Steve 104
Wirth, Billy 71
Witt, Katarina 135
Wohlers, Mark 135
Womack, Bobby 104
Wonder, Stevie 104
Wood, Elijah 71
Woodbridge, Todd 135
Wooden, John 135
Woods, James 71
Woods, Tiger 135
Woodward, Bob 184
Woodward, Edward 71
Woodward, Joanne 71
Wouk, Herman 184
Wozniak, Steve 184
Wright, Jr., Ex-Rep. James 157
Wyman, Jane 71
Wynette, Tammy 104

Y

Yamaguchi, Kristi 135
Yankovic, "Weird" Al 105
Yanni 105
Yarborough, Caleb 135
Yarborough, Glen 105
Yard, Mollie 184
Yasbeck, Amy............................... 71
Yastrzemski, Carl 135
Yeager, Gen. Chuck 184
Yearwood, Trisha 105
Yeltsin, Boris 157
Yoakum, Dwight 105
Yorty, Ex-Mayor Sam 157
Young, Ex-Mayor Andrew 157
Young, Mayor Coleman................ 157
Young, Jesse Colin 105
Young, Neil 105
Young, Robert 71
Young, Sean 72
Young, Steve 135
Youngman, Henny......................... 72

Z

Zabriskie, Grace 72
Zadora, Pia.................................... 72
Zahn, Paula 72
Zahn, Steve 72
Zal, Roxana 72
Zane, Billy 72
Zanuch, Richard 184
Zapata, Carmen 72

Zappa, Dweezil 105
Zappa, Moon 105
Zefferelli, Franco 184
Zeman, Jacklyn 72
Zemeckis, Bob 184
Ziegler, Ron.................................. 184
Ziering, Ian 72
Zimbalist, Jr., Efrem 72
Zimbalist, Stephanie 72
Zimmer, Kim 72
Zmed, Adrian................................. 72
Zmeskal, Kim 135
Zoeller, Fuzzy 135
Zuckerman, Pinchas 105
Zuniga, Daphne 72
ZZ Top 105